THE CAMBRIDGE COMPANION TO
AMERICAN SCIENCE FICTION

The Cambridge Companion to American Science Fiction explores the relationship between the ideas and themes of American science fiction and their roots in the American cultural experience. Science fiction in America has long served to reflect the country's hopes, desires, ambitions, and fears. The ideas and conventions associated with science fiction are pervasive throughout American film and television, comics and visual arts, games and gaming, and fandom, as well as across the culture writ large. Through essays that address not only the history of science fiction in America but also the influence and significance of American science fiction throughout media and fan culture, this *Companion* serves as a key resource for scholars, teachers, students, and fans of science fiction.

Eric Carl Link is a professor of American literature and an associate dean of the College of Arts and Sciences at the University of Memphis. He is the author of several books, including *Crosscurrents: Readings in the Disciplines, Understanding Philip K. Dick, The Vast and Terrible Drama: American Literary Naturalism in the Late Nineteenth Century,* and *Neutral Ground: New Traditionalism and the American Romance Controversy.* He has also published numerous articles in the field of American literature.

Gerry Canavan is an assistant professor of twentieth- and twenty-first-century literature at Marquette University. He is the coeditor, with Kim Stanley Robinson, of *Green Planets: Ecology and Science Fiction.* He has published frequently on myriad topics related to science fiction in such journals as *Extrapolation, Science Fiction Film and Television, Science Fiction Studies,* and *Paradoxa.*

A complete list of books in the series is at the back of this book.

THE CAMBRIDGE
COMPANION TO
AMERICAN SCIENCE FICTION

THE CAMBRIDGE
COMPANION TO
AMERICAN
SCIENCE FICTION

EDITED BY

ERIC CARL LINK
University of Memphis

GERRY CANAVAN
Marquette University

CAMBRIDGE
UNIVERSITY PRESS

CAMBRIDGE
UNIVERSITY PRESS

32 Avenue of the Americas, New York NY 10013-2473, USA

Cambridge University Press is part of the University of Cambridge.

It furthers the University's mission by disseminating knowledge in the pursuit of education, learning and research at the highest international levels of excellence.

www.cambridge.org
Information on this title: www.cambridge.org/9781107694279

First published 2015

A catalogue record for this publication is available from the British Library

Library of Congress Cataloguing in Publication data
The Cambridge companion to American science fiction / [edited by] Eric Carl Link, University of Memphis, Gerry Canavan, Marquette University.
pages   cm. – (Cambridge companions to literature)
Includes bibliographical references and index.
ISBN 978-1-107-05246-8 (hardback) – ISBN 978-1-107-69427-9 (paperback)
1. Science fiction, American – History and criticism.   I. Canavan, Gerry, editor.
II. Link, Eric Carl, editor.
PS374.S35C36   2015
813'.0876209–dc23   2014032788

ISBN 978-1-107-69427-9 Paperback

Eric Carl Link would like to dedicate this volume to Bradley Link.

*Gerry Canavan would like to dedicate this volume to
Jaimee Hills and Zoey and Connor Canavan.*

CONTENTS

CONTENTS

CONTRIBUTORS

MARK BOULD is a reader in film and literature at the University of the West of England and coeditor of *Science Fiction Film and Television*. His most recent books are *Solaris* (2014), *Africa SF* (2013), and *Science Fiction: The Routledge Film Handbook* (2012).

GERRY CANAVAN is an assistant professor of twentieth- and twenty-first-century literature in the Department of English at Marquette University. With Kim Stanley Robinson, he is the coeditor of *Green Planets: Ecology and Science Fiction* (2014); current projects include a critical monograph on science fiction and totality, and another on the work of African-American science fiction author Octavia Butler.

MATTHEW J. COSTELLO is a professor of political science at Saint Xavier University in Chicago. For the past several years, his research has focused on Cold War culture in film and comic books. He has edited symposia, including "Appropriating and Transforming Comic Books," in *Transformative Works and Cultures* (Volume 13, 2013), and, most recently (with Kent Worcester), "The Politics of the Superhero," in *PS: Political Science and Politics* (Volume 47.1, 2014). He has also written several articles, book chapters, and the book *Secret Identity Crisis: Comic Books and the Unmasking of the American Cold Warrior* (2009).

DARREN HARRIS-FAIN is chair of the Department of English and Philosophy at Auburn University in Montgomery, Alabama, where he teaches British and American literature from the nineteenth century to the present. He is the author of *Understanding Contemporary American Science Fiction: The Age of Maturity, 1970–2000* (2005); the editor of three volumes of the *Dictionary of Literary Biography* on British fantasy and science fiction writers; and the author of more than twenty articles, introductions, and book chapters on science fiction, fantasy, horror, comics, and graphic novels.

KAREN HELLEKSON has published in the fields of science fiction and fan studies. She is the founding coeditor of the journal *Transformative Works and Cultures*. Her most recent book, coedited with Kristina Busse, is *The Fan Fiction Studies Reader* anthology (2014).

DAVID M. HIGGINS's research explores transformations in imperial fantasy that occur during the Cold War era and beyond. His article "Toward a Cosmopolitan Science Fiction" (published in the June 2011 issue of *American Literature*) won the 2012 SFRA Pioneer Award for excellence in scholarship, and he recently coedited a special issue of *Science Fiction Studies* on "Science Fiction and Globalization." He teaches literature and composition in the English department at Inver Hills College in Minnesota, where he is the codirector of the Learning Communities program and serves as the campus coordinator for the Minnesota Undergraduate Scholars program.

PATRICK JAGODA is an assistant professor of English and an affiliate of cinema and media studies at the University of Chicago. Jagoda specializes in new media studies, twentieth- and twenty-first-century American literature, and digital game theory and design. His current book project, *Network Aesthetics*, examines how late twentieth- and twenty-first-century American fiction, film, television, and digital media aestheticize and animate network form. A coeditor of *Critical Inquiry*, he has coedited two special issues: "Comics and Media" (with Hillary Chute for *Critical Inquiry*) and "New Media and American Literature" (with Wendy Chun and Tara McPherson for *American Literature*). Jagoda has also worked on several projects related to digital storytelling, transmedia game design, and new media learning. He is the cofounder of the Game Changer Chicago Design Lab (http://gamechanger.uchicago.edu), where he has led the design of projects, including card games, interactive narratives, and alternate reality games related to various social justice topics.

ROB LATHAM is a professor of English at the University of California, Riverside, where he codirects the Science Fiction and Technoculture Studies program. A senior editor of the journal *Science Fiction Studies* since 1997, he is the author of *Consuming Youth: Vampires, Cyborgs, and the Culture of Consumption* (2002) and editor of *The Oxford Handbook of Science Fiction* (2014).

ERIC CARL LINK is a professor of American literature and associate dean of the College of Arts and Sciences at the University of Memphis. He is the author of several books, including *Crosscurrents: Reading in the Disciplines* (2012), *Understanding Philip K. Dick* (2010), *The Vast and Terrible Drama: American Literary Naturalism in the Late Nineteenth Century* (2004), and *Neutral Ground: New Traditionalism and the American Romance Controversy* (coauthored with G. R. Thompson 1999).

ALEXIS LOTHIAN is an assistant professor of women's studies at University of Maryland, College Park, where she researches and teaches at the intersections of gender studies, digital media, speculative fiction, and queer theory. Her research focuses on speculative fiction's engagements with race, gender, and sexuality from the late nineteenth century to the present, and she also works on digital artistic forms that are emerging from science fiction fan communities, especially as these forms engage in social justice activism. Her work has been published by *International Journal of Cultural Studies, Cinema Journal, Camera Obscura, Social Text Periscope, Journal of Digital Humanities,* and the feminist science fiction publisher Aqueduct Press; in 2013, she edited a special issue of *Ada: A Journal of Gender, New Media, and Technology* on feminist science fiction. Her Web site is http://queergeektheory.org.

ROGER LUCKHURST is a professor of modern literature at Birkbeck College, University of London. His research focuses on Gothic and science fiction literature and film. He is the author most recently of *Alien* (2014) and a cultural history of zombies (2015), as well as *Science Fiction* (2005) and *The Mummy's Curse* (2012), and he has edited Bram Stoker, Robert Louis Stevenson, and H. P. Lovecraft for Oxford World's Classics.

JOHN RIEDER, a professor of English at the University of Hawai'i at Mānoa, is the author of *Colonialism and the Emergence of Science Fiction* (2008) and winner of the 2011 Science Fiction Research Association's Pioneer Award for his essay "On Defining SF, or Not: Genre Theory, SF, and History" (2010). Topics of his most recently published essays include science fiction and postcolonial theory; jazz musician Sun Ra; fairy tales and commercial television (in collaboration with Cristina Bacchilega); and the influence of Mary Shelley's *Frankenstein* and Olaf Stapledon's *Sirius* on SF conventions. His current book project is on science fiction and the mass cultural genre system. He currently serves on the editorial board of *Extrapolation.*

REBEKAH C. SHELDON is an assistant professor in the English department at Indiana University. She is completing her first book project on the figure of the child in contemporary American catastrophe and apocalypse narratives for the University of Minnesota Press. She also writes on feminist new materialisms, occult postmodernisms, and queer theories of childhood.

SHERRYL VINT is a professor of science fiction media studies at the University of California, Riverside, where she codirects the Science Fiction and Technoculture Studies program. The author or editor of a number of books on science fiction, she also edits the journals *Science Fiction Studies* and *Science Fiction Film and Television.*

PRISCILLA WALD is a professor of English at Duke University. She is the author of *Contagious: Cultures, Carriers, and the Outbreak Narrative* (2008) and *Constituting Americans: Cultural Anxiety and Narrative Form* (1995). She also serves as the editor of the journal *American Literature*. She is currently working on a book-length study entitled *Human Being after Genocide.*

GARY WESTFAHL, who serves as an adjunct professor in the University of La Verne's writing programs, is the author, editor, or coeditor of twenty-four books about science fiction and fantasy, including the Hugo Award–nominated *Science Fiction Quotations: From the Inner Mind to the Outer Limits* (2005) and the three-volume *Greenwood Encyclopedia of Science Fiction and Fantasy* (2005). He has also published hundreds of articles, reviews, and contributions to reference books. His most recent works are two books on science fiction films, *The Spacesuit Film: A History, 1918–1969* (2012) and *A Sense-of-Wonderful Century: Explorations of Science Fiction and Fantasy Films* (2012); a contribution to the University of Illinois Press's Modern Masters of Science Fiction series, *William Gibson* (2013); and a three-volume survey of past and present professions, *A Day in a Working Life: 300 Trades and Professions through History* (2014). In 2003, he received the Science Fiction Research Association's Pilgrim Award for his lifetime contributions to science fiction and fantasy scholarship.

LISA YASZEK is a professor in the School of Literature, Media, and Communication at Georgia Tech and past president of the Science Fiction Research Association. Her research interests include science fiction, cultural history, critical race and gender studies, and science and technology studies. Her essays on science fiction as a global language appear in journals including *Extrapolation, NWSA Journal,* and *Rethinking History.* She is the author of books including *Galactic Suburbia: Recovering Women's Science Fiction* (2008) and coeditor of collections including the *Configurations* special double issue on science fiction author Kim Stanley Robinson (Winter–Spring 2012). She is currently completing an edited anthology on women's work in the early science fiction community for Wesleyan Press and serving as an associate producer for the independent science fiction film *Rite of Passage.*

PREFACE AND ACKNOWLEDGMENTS

The science fictional imagination is fundamental to the arc of history across the so-called American century. *The Cambridge Companion to American Science Fiction* explores the relationship between the ideas, themes, and conventions of American science fiction and their roots in the American cultural experience, as well as to distinctly American visions of what the future might be like. Science fiction in America serves as an index to twentieth- and twenty-first-century U.S. culture, reflecting America's hopes, desires, ambitions, and fears. The very term "science fiction," after all, was coined in the United States in 1929 by Hugo Gernsback, founding editor of *Amazing Stories* – and it was in American pulp magazines of the 1920s and 1930s that science fiction first coalesced as a distinct and recognizable literary genre. Nor is the cultural impact of science fiction in the United States contained solely within literary production: the ideas and conventions associated with science fiction are pervasive throughout U.S. film and television, comics and visual arts, games and gaming, and fandom, as well as across the culture writ large. With essays that address not only the history of science fiction in America but also the influence and significance of American science fiction throughout media and fan culture, as well as essays addressing several key themes in science fiction central to the U.S. cultural experience, *The Cambridge Companion to American Science Fiction* serves as a key resource for scholars, teachers, students, and fans of science fiction.

One of the great pleasures of being able to edit a volume like *The Cambridge Companion to American Science Fiction* is the chance to work with so many excellent scholars and writers, and to learn from them. Thus the editors would like to thank all of the writers in this volume for their many fine contributions. We would also like to extend our thanks to Ray Ryan and the rest of the staff at Cambridge University Press for their advocacy and guidance. In addition, we would like to thank Jenny Bryant at the

University of Memphis and Justice Hagan at Marquette University for their research and editorial assistance, as well as John Bealle, to whom we are extremely grateful for help preparing the index to this volume. Finally, we would like to thank Farah Mendelsohn and Edward James for providing us with such a wonderful model for this book.

CHRONOLOGY

1900   Frank L. Baum, *The Wonderful Wizard of Oz*

1903   Pauline Hopkins, *Of One Blood*

1904   Edward A. Johnson, *Light Ahead for the Negro*

1908   Jack London, *The Iron Heel*

1910   Jack London, "The Unparalleled Invasion"

1911   Hugo Gernsback, *Ralph 124C 41+* (book 1925)

1912   Edgar Rice Burroughs, "Under the Moons of Mars" (book 1914)
         Jack London, *The Scarlet Plague*

1915   George Allan England, *The Air Trust*
         Charlotte Perkins Gilman, *Herland* (sequel *With Her in Ourland* [1916])
         Roger Sherman Tracy, *The White Man's Burden: A Satirical Forecast*

1920   W. E. B. Du Bois, "The Comet"

1923   *Weird Tales* launches

1926   G. Peyton Wertenbaker, "The Coming of the Ice"
         Hugo Gernsback starts *Amazing Stories*

1927   H. P. Lovecraft, "The Colour Out of Space"

1928   H. P. Lovecraft, "The Call of Cthulhu"
         E. E. Smith, *The Skylark of Space*
         Buck Rogers debuts in "Armageddon 2419 A.D." (comic 1929)

1929   David H. Keller, "The Conquerors"
         Leslie F. Stone, "Letter of the Twenty-Fourth Century"

1930   Lilith Lorraine, "Into the 28th Century"
         Philip Wylie, *Gladiator*
         Astounding Stories launched
         The Comet appears, the first science fiction fanzine

1931   Edmond Hamilton, "The Man Who Evolved"
         H. P. Lovecraft, "The Whisperer in Darkness"
         George S. Schuyler, *Black No More*
         Frankenstein (dir. James Whale)

1932   Amelia Long Reynolds, "Omega"

1933   John W. Campbell, "Twilight"
Laurence Manning, *The Man Who Awoke*
Philip Wylie and Edwin Balmer, *When Worlds Collide* (sequel
After Worlds Collide [1934])

1934   E. E. Smith, "Lensman" series (multiple sequels)
Donald Wandrei, "Colossus"
Stanley G. Weinbaum, "A Martian Odyssey"
Jack Williamson, *The Legion of Space* (novel 1947)
Flash Gordon debuts
D.C. Comics founded (as National Allied Publications)

1935   John W. Campbell, "Night"
Sinclair Lewis, *It Can't Happen Here*
Nat Schachner (as Chan Corbett), "When the Sun Dies"

1936   H. P. Lovecraft, "At the Mountains of Madness"
George S. Schuyler, *Black Empire*

1938   John W. Campbell Jr., "Who Goes There?"
John W. Campbell becomes editor of *Astounding Science-Fiction*
Superman debuts in *Action Comics* #1
Orson Welles, *War of the Worlds* radio hoax

1939   L. Sprague De Camp, "Lest Darkness Fall" (novel 1941)
Dalton Trumbo, *Johnny Got His Gun*
Marvel Comics founded (as Timely Comics)
New York World's Fair
The first WorldCon is held in New York City

1940   *Superman* radio serial premieres

1941   Isaac Asimov, "Nightfall"
Robert Heinlein, "By His Bootstraps"
Theodore Sturgeon, "Microcosmic God"
A. E. van Vogt, *Slan*

1942   Isaac Asimov, "Foundation" (book 1951 and multiple sequels)

1943   Ayn Rand, *The Fountainhead*

1944   C. L. Moore, "No Woman Born"

1947   Robert Heinlein, *Rocket Ship Galileo*

1948   Shirley Jackson, "The Lottery"
Judith Merril, "That Only a Mother"
B. F. Skinner, *Walden Two*

1949   George R. Stewart, *Earth Abides*
Magazine of Fantasy and Science Fiction launched

1950   Isaac Asimov, *I, Robot* (linked collection)
Ray Bradbury, *The Martian Chronicles* (linked collection)
Jack Vance, *The Dying Earth*
Galaxy Science Fiction (dir. Irving Pichel)

1951   *The Day the Earth Stood Still* (dir. Robert Wise)

1952   Ray Bradbury, "A Sound of Thunder"
Vladimir Nabokov, "Lance"
Clifford D. Simak, *City* (linked collection)

1953   Alfred Bester, *The Demolished Man,* winner of the first Hugo
Award for Best Novel
Ray Bradbury, *Fahrenheit 451*
Ward Moore, *Bring the Jubilee* and "Lot" (sequel, "Lot's
Daughter," 1954)
Frederik Pohl and C. M. Kornbluth, *The Space Merchants*
Theodore Sturgeon, *More Than Human*
War of the Worlds (dir. Byron Haskin)

1954   Isaac Asimov, *The Caves of Steel* (multiple sequels)
Tom Godwin, "The Cold Equations"
Richard Matheson, *I Am Legend*
Frederik Pohl, "The Tunnel under the World"
This Island Earth (dirs. Joseph M. Newman and Jack
Arnold)

1955   Isaac Asimov, *The End of Eternity*
Fredric Brown, *Martians, Go Home*
Jack Finney, *The Body Snatchers*
Tomorrowland opens at Disneyland

1956   Alfred Bester, *Tiger! Tiger!* (United States: *The Stars My
Destination,* 1957)
Philip K. Dick, "Minority Report"
Forbidden Planet (dir. Fred M. Wilcox)
Invasion of the Body Snatchers (dir. Don Siegel)

1957   Ayn Rand, *Atlas Shrugged*

1958   James Blish, *A Case of Conscience*
        Robert Heinlein, "All You Zombies"

1959   Alfred Bester, "The Men Who Murdered Mohammed"
        William S. Burroughs, *Naked Lunch*
        Philip K. Dick, *Time Out of Joint*
        Pat Frank, *Alas, Babylon*
        Robert A. Heinlein, *Starship Troopers*
        Daniel Keyes, "Flowers for Algernon" (book 1966)
        Kurt Vonnegut, *The Sirens of Titan*
        Richard Condon, *The Manchurian Candidate*
        The Twilight Zone premieres
        Extrapolation founded

1960   Rachel Carson, *Silent Spring*
        Walter M. Miller Jr., *A Canticle for Leibowitz*
        The Time Machine (dir. George Pal)

1961   Harry Harrison, *The Stainless Steel Rat*
        Robert Heinlein, *Stranger in a Strange Land*
        Leó Szilárd, "The Voice of the Dolphins"
        Fantastic Four debut in *Fantastic Four* #1

1962   Philip K. Dick, *Man in the High Castle*
        Madeline L'Engle, *A Wrinkle in Time*
        The Manchurian Candidate (dir. John Frankenheimer)
        The Jetsons premieres
        Spacewar! (first computer game)

1963   Kurt Vonnegut, *Cat's Cradle*
        The Outer Limits premieres

1964   Philip K. Dick, *Martian Time-Slip*
        Robert Heinlein, *Farnham's Freehold*
        Dr. Strangelove (dir. Stanley Kubrick)
        New York World's Fair

1965   Philip K. Dick, *Dr. Bloodmoney*
        Harlan Ellison, "'Repent, Harlequin!' Said the Ticktockman"
        Frank Herbert, *Dune* (multiple sequels)
        Jack Vance, *Space Opera*
        Lost in Space premieres

1966 Samuel R. Delany, *Babel-17*
Philip K. Dick, "We Can Remember It For You Wholesale"
Harry Harrison, *Make Room! Make Room!*
Robert A. Heinlein, *The Moon Is a Harsh Mistress*
Frederik Pohl, "Day Million"
Thomas Pynchon, *The Crying of Lot 49*
Star Trek premieres

1967 Samuel R. Delany, *The Einstein Intersection*
Philip Jose Farmer, *Riders of the Purple Wage*
Pamela Zoline, "The Heat Death of the Universe"
Harlan Ellison (ed.), *Dangerous Visions* (anthology)

1968 Philip K. Dick, *Do Androids Dream of Electric Sheep?*
Thomas M. Disch, *Camp Concentration*
Anne McCafferty, *Dragonflight*
2001: A Space Odyssey (dir. Stanley Kubrick)
Planet of the Apes (dir. Franklin J. Schaffner)

1969 Michael Crichton, *The Andromeda Strain*
Philip K. Dick, *Ubik*
Harlan Ellison, "A Boy and His Dog"
Ursula K. Le Guin, *The Left Hand of Darkness*
Anne McCafferty, *The Ship Who Sang*
Vladimir Nabokov, *Ada, or Ardor*
Alice Sheldon (as James Tiptree, Jr.), "The Last Flight of Dr. Ain"
Kurt Vonnegut, *Slaughterhouse-Five*

1970 Larry Niven, *Ringworld*
The first ComicCon is held in San Diego
Science Fiction Research Association founded

1971 Samuel R. Delany, *Driftglass*
Larry Niven, "All the Myriad Ways"
Ursula K. Le Guin, *The Lathe of Heaven*

1972 Isaac Asimov, *The Gods Themselves*
Thomas Disch, *334*
David Gerrold, *The Man Who Folded Himself*
Ursula K. Le Guin, "The Word for World Is Forest"
 (book 1976)
Ishmael Reed, *Mumbo Jumbo*
Joanna Russ, "When It Changed"

Gene Wolfe, *The Fifth Head of Cerebus*
Harlan Ellison (ed.), *Again, Dangerous Visions* (anthology)
A Clockwork Orange (dir. Stanley Kubrick)
Darko Suvin, "On the Poetics of the Science Fiction Genre"
  (book *Metamorphoses of Science Fiction* [1979])
Science Fiction Foundation begins the journal *Foundation*
The first *Star Trek* convention is held in New York

1973   Ursula K. Le Guin, "The Ones Who Walk Away from Omelas"
Thomas Pynchon, *Gravity's Rainbow*
Mack Reynolds, *Looking Backward, from the Year 2000*
Alice Sheldon (as James Tiptree, Jr.), *Ten Thousand Light Years from Home* and "The Women Men Don't See"
Sleeper (dir. Woody Allen)
Soylent Green (dir. Richard Fleischer)
Science-Fiction Studies begins publication

1974   Suzy McKee Charnas, *Walk to the End of the World*
Joe Haldeman, *The Forever War*
Ursula K. Le Guin, *The Dispossessed*
Larry Niven and Jerry Pournelle, *The Mote in God's Eye*
  (sequel *The Gripping Hand* [1993])
Land of the Lost premieres

1975   Ernest Callenbach, *Ecotopia*
Samuel R. Delany, *Dhalgren*
Joseph Haldeman, *The Forever War*
Joanna Russ, *The Female Man*
Robert Shea and Robert Anton Wilson, *Illuminatus!*
Space Is the Place (dir. John Coney, featuring jazz musician Sun Ra)

1976   Octavia E. Butler, *Patternmaster*
Samuel R. Delany, *Triton*
Marge Piercy, *Woman on the Edge of Time*
Alice Sheldon (as James Tiptree, Jr.), "Houston, Houston, Do You Read?"
Logan's Run (dir. Michael Anderson)

1977   Mack Reynolds, *After Utopia*
Joanna Russ, *We Who Are About To . . .*

Alice Sheldon (as James Tiptree, Jr.), "The Screwfly Solution"
Close Encounters of the Third Kind (dir. Steven Spielberg)
Star Wars (dir. George Lucas, sequels *The Empire Strikes Back* [1979] and *The Return of the Jedi* [1983])

1978   Stephen King, *The Stand*
Vonda MacIntyre, *Dreamsnake*
Dawn of the Dead (dir. George Romero)
Invasion of the Body Snatchers (dir. Philip Kaufman)
Battlestar Galactica (original series) premieres
Space Invaders (Taito Corporation)

1979   Octavia E. Butler, *Kindred*
Sally Miller Gearhart, *The Wanderground*
Frederik Pohl, *Gateway* (multiple sequels)
Mack Reynolds, *Lagrange 5*
Alien (dir. Ridley Scott, sequel *Aliens* [1986])
Star Trek: The Motion Picture (dir. Robert Wise)
Superman (dir. Richard Donner)

1980   Gregory Benford, *Timescape*
Suzy McKee Charnas, *The Vampire Tapestry*
Gene Wolfe, *The Shadow of the Torturer* (first volume of *The Book of the New Sun*)
Missile Command (Atari)

1981   Philip K. Dick, *VALIS*
William Gibson, "The Gernsback Continuum"
Vernor Vinge, "True Names"

1982   *Blade Runner* (dir. Ridley Scott)
E.T. the Extra-Terrestrial (dir. Steven Spielberg)
The Thing (dir. John Carpenter)
TRON (dir. Joseph Kosinski)
EPCOT Center opens
International Association for the Fantastic in the Arts founded

1983   David Brin, *Startide Rising*
Born in Flames (dir. Lizzie Borden)
WarGames (dir. John Badham)
V and *The Day After* premiere

1984 Octavia E. Butler, "Bloodchild"
   Samuel R. Delany, *Stars in My Pocket Like Grains of Sand*
   Suzette Haden Elgin, *Native Tongue*
   William Gibson, *Neuromancer*
   Kim Stanley Robinson, "The Lucky Strike" and *The Wild Shore*
   The Brother from Another Planet (dir. John Sayles)
   Terminator (dir. James Cameron, multiple sequels)

1985 Margaret Atwood (Canadian), *The Handmaid's Tale*
   Greg Bear, *Blood Music*
   Orson Scott Card, *Ender's Game* (multiple sequels)
   Don DeLillo, *White Noise*
   Ursula K. Le Guin, *Always Coming Home*
   Alan Moore and Dave Gibbons, *Watchmen*
   James Morrow, *This Is the Way the World Ends*
   Carl Sagan, *Contact*
   Kurt Vonnegut, *Galápagos*
   Back to the Future (dir. Robert Zemeckis, sequels 1989 and 1990)
   Brazil (dir. Terry Gilliam)

1986 Lois McMaster Bujold, *Ethan of Athos*
   Orson Scott Card, *Speaker for the Dead*
   Ken Grimwood, *Replay*
   Frank Miller and Klaus Jansen, *The Dark Knight Returns*
   Pamela Sargent, *The Shore of Women*
   Joan Slonczewski, *A Door into Ocean*
   Bruce Sterling (ed.), *Mirrorshades* (anthology)
   Metroid (Nintendo)

1987 Octavia E. Butler, *Dawn* (sequels *Adulthood Rites* [1988] and *Imago* [1989])
   Pat Cadigan, *Mindplayers*
   Robocop (dir. Paul Verhoeven)
   Star Trek: The Next Generation and *Max Headroom* premiere
   Mega-Man (Capcom)

1988 Terry Bisson, *Fire on the Mountain*
   David Markson, *Wittgenstein's Mistress*
   Sheri S. Tepper, *The Gate to Women's Country*

They Live! (dir. John Carpenter)
Mystery Science Theater 3000 premieres

1989   Dan Simmons, *Hyperion*
         Batman (dir. Tim Burton)
         Alien Nation and *Quantum Leap* premiere

1990   David Brin, *Earth*
         Kim Stanley Robinson, *Pacific Edge*
         Dan Simmons, *Hyperion*

1991   Pat Cadigan, *Synners*
         Ted Chiang, "Understand"
         Michael Crichton, *Jurassic Park*
         Karen Joy Fowler, *Sarah Canary*
         Nancy Kress, "Beggars in Spain" (novel 1993)
         Marge Piercy, *He, She, It*

1992   Derrick Bell, "The Space Traders"
         Greg Egan, *Quarantine*
         Maureen McHugh, *China Mountain Zhang*
         Kim Stanley Robinson, *Red Mars* (sequels *Green Mars* [1994]
            and *Blue Mars* [1996])
         Starhawk, *The Fifth Sacred Thing*
         Neal Stephenson, *Snow Crash*
         Vernor Vinge, *A Fire Upon the Deep*
         Connie Willis, *Doomsday Book*
         The X-Files premieres

1993   Octavia E. Butler, *Parable of the Sower* (sequel *Parable of the
            Talents* [1998])
         Niccola Griffith, *Ammonite*
         Lois Lowry, *The Giver* (film 2014)
         Star Trek: Deep Space Nine premieres
         Doom (id Software, multiple sequels) and *X-Wing* (LucasArts,
            multiple sequels)

1994   Greg Egan, *Permutation City*
         Jonathan Lethem, *Gun, with Occasional Music*
         Babylon Five premieres

1995   Neal Stephenson, *The Diamond Age*
         Tim LaHaye and Jerry Jenkins, *Left Behind*
         Daniel Quinn, *Ishmael*

1996   Orson Scott Card, *Pastwatch: The Redemption of Christopher Columbus*
        Mary Doria Russell, *The Sparrow* (sequel *Children of God* [1998])
        David Foster Wallace, *Infinite Jest*
        Independence Day (dir. Roland Emmerich)
        Twelve Monkeys (dir. Terry Gilliam)

1997   *Contact* (dir. Robert Zemeckis)
        Cube (dir. Vincenzo Natali)
        Gattaca (dir. Andrew Niccol)
        Men in Black (dir. Barry Sonnenfeld)
        Starship Troopers (dir. Paul Verhoeven)
        Buffy, the Vampire Slayer and *Stargate SG-1* premiere
        Fallout (Interplay Entertainment) (multiple sequels)

1998   Lois McMaster Bujold, *Komarr*
        Ted Chiang, "Story of Your Life"
        Nalo Hopkinson, *Brown Girl in the Ring*
        Dark City (dir. Alex Proyas)
        The Truman Show (dir. Peter Weir)
        Starcraft (Blizzard Entertainment) and *Half-Life* (Valve Entertainment)

1999   Greg Bear, *Darwin's Radio*
        Neal Stephenson, *Cryptonomicon*
        Vernor Vinge, *A Deepness in the Sky*
        Connie Willis, *To Say Nothing of the Dog*
        Star Wars: The Phantom Menace (dir. George Lucas, sequels 2002 and 2005)
        The Matrix (dirs. Andy and Lana Wachowski, sequels 2003 and 2003)
        Galaxy Quest (dir. Dean Parisot)
        Futurama premieres

2000   Michael Chabon, *The Amazing Adventures of Kavalier and Clay*
        Mark Z. Danielewski, *House of Leaves*
        Ursula K. Le Guin, *The Telling*
        Sheree Renée Thomas (ed.), *Dark Matter: A Century of Speculative Fiction from the African Diaspora* (anthology)
        X-Men (dir. Bryan Singer)

2001   Kelly Link, *Stranger Things Happen*
        Walter Mosley, *Futureland*
        Donnie Darko (dir. Richard Kelly)
        Halo (Bungie)

2002   M. T. Anderson, *Feed*
        Ted Chiang, *Stories of Your Life and Others*
        Kim Stanley Robinson, *The Years of Rice and Salt*
        Brian K. Vaughn, *Y: The Last Man*
        Minority Report (dir. Steven Spielberg)
        Spider-Man (dir. Sam Raimi)
        Firefly premieres

2003   Margaret Atwood (Canadian), *Oryx and Crake* (sequels *The Year of the Flood* [2009] and *MaddAddam* [2013])
        Steve Barnes, *Charisma*
        William Gibson, *Pattern Recognition*
        Nalo Hopkinson (ed.), *Mojo: Conjure Stories*
        Jonathan Lethem, *Fortress of Solitude*
        Audrey Niffenegger, *The Time Traveler's Wife*
        Robert Kirkman, *The Walking Dead* (television series 2010, video game 2012)
        Star Wars: Knights of the Old Republic (LucasArts) and *EVE Online* (CCP)

2004   Bill Campbell, *Sunshine Patriots*
        Kim Stanley Robinson, *Forty Signs of Rain* (sequels *Fifty Degrees Below* [2005] and *Sixty Days and Counting* [2006])
        Philip Roth, *The Plot Against America*
        Eternal Sunshine of the Spotless Mind (dir. Michel Gondry)
        Primer (dir. Shane Carruth)
        Battlestar Galactica (2000s series) premieres
        Lost premieres

2005   Ray Kurzweil, *The Singularity Is Near*
        Kelly Link, *Magic for Beginners*
        George Saunders, *The Brief and Frightening Reign of Phil*
        John Scalzi, *Old Man's War*
        Robert Charles Wilson, *Spin*
        Batman Begins (dir. Christopher Nolan, sequels 2008 and 2012)
        Serenity (dir. Joss Whedon)

2006 Max Brooks, *World War Z*
Andrea Hairston, *Mindscape*
Cormac McCarthy, *The Road* (film 2009)

2007 Michael Chabon, *The Yiddish Policeman's Union*
Junot Díaz, *The Brief Wondrous Life of Oscar Wao*
Portal (Valve, sequel *Portal 2* [2011]), *Bioshock* (2K Boston, multiple sequels), and *Mass Effect* (Bioware, multiple sequels)

2008 Paul Auster, *Man in the Dark*
Paolo Bacigalupi, *Pump Six*
Ted Chiang, "Exhalation"
Suzanne Collins, *The Hunger Games* (multiple sequels, film 2012)
John Rieder, *Colonialism and the Emergence of Science Fiction*
Nisi Shawl, *Filter House*
Sleep Dealer (dir. Alex Rivera)
WALL-E (dir. Andrew Stanton)
Fringe and *Star Wars: The Clone Wars* premiere
Braid (Number None, Inc.) and *Spore* (Maxis Corporation)

2009 Paolo Bacigalupi, *The Wind-Up Girl*
Stephen King, *Under the Dome*
Avatar (dir. James Cameron)
Star Trek (dir. J. J. Abrams)
Dollhouse premieres
Andrew Hussie, *Homestuck*
Minecraft (Mojang)

2010 Andrea Hairston, *Redwood and Wildfire*
Nnedi Okorafor, *Who Fears Death*
Charles Yu, *How to Live Safely in a Science Fictional Universe*
Eliezer Yudkowsky, *Harry Potter and the Methods of Rationality*
Inception (dir. Christopher Nolan)

2011 Stephen King, *11/22/63*
Nnedi Okorafor, "Hello Moto"
Colson Whitehead, *Zone One*
Rise of the Planet of the Apes (dir. Rupert Wyatt, sequel 2014)

2012   Samuel R. Delany, *Through the Valley of the Nest of Spiders*
Junot Díaz, "Monstro"
Kim Stanley Robinson, *2312*
John Scalzi, *Redshirts*
Andy Weir, *The Martian*
Brian K. Vaughan and Fiona Staples, *Saga*
The Avengers (dir. Joss Whedon)
Looper (dir. Rian Johnson)
Star Wars Episodes VII–IX announced

2013   Karen Joy Fowler, *We Are All Completely Beside Ourselves*
Balogun Ojetdae (ed.), *Steamfunk!*
Elysium (dir. Neill Blomkamp)
Her (dir. Spike Jonze)
Pacific Rim (dir. Guillermo del Toro)
Rick and Morty premieres (created by Dan Harmon and Justin Roiland)
Injustice: Gods Among Us (D.C. Entertainment)

2014   Octavia E. Butler, *Unexpected Stories*
Nnedi Okorafor, *Lagoon*
Jeff VanderMeer, *Annihilation*
Captain America: The Winter Soldier (dir. Anthony Russo and Joe Russo)
The Guardians of the Galaxy (dir. James Gunn)
Interstellar (dir. Christopher Nolan)

GERRY CANAVAN AND ERIC CARL LINK

Introduction

This volume owes an obvious intellectual debt to Farah Mendlesohn and Edward James's earlier *Cambridge Companion to Science Fiction*, to which it serves as a kind of unofficial sequel. Indeed, the general excellence of that volume when set against the newly narrowed specificity of our title poses a certain inevitable question: Why develop a project devoted to *American* science fiction – interpreted in this volume primarily to mean U.S. fiction – in the first place? Why limit ourselves to SF from just one nation?

All literary forms are cross-cultural and transnational at some level, a fact that has never been truer than in the increasingly globalized literary world of the twentieth and now twenty-first centuries – the centuries during which SF developed, thrived, and ultimately came to dominate much of the cultural landscape of both the United States and the world. Indeed, the global interconnectedness of literary forms is, if anything, even more emblematic of SF than it is of other genres; SF – as a foundation for popular fandom, as an object of critical inquiry, as an interactive framework through which individuals engage their worlds and envision their collective futures – has never been easily bordered. Even on the level of SF's own favored themes, limiting our investigation to only American SF seems somehow distasteful, even perverse; SF's attitude toward the form of the nation-state has characteristically been quite hostile. No genre has offered more powerful examinations of the problems with cultural blindness and unchecked aggression toward the Other; no genre has more vividly impressed upon us the threats posed by non-global thinking, nationalism, and provincialism. From H. G. Wells's *War of the Worlds* and its many successors to Gene Roddenberry's cosmopolitan Federation to the rousing speech at the end of Roland Emmerich's *Independence Day* (1996), the very idea of the extraterrestrial seems to produce, in opposition, the vision of a single human race united together under a common flag. No less patriotic a soul than Ronald Reagan was frequently carried away by such fantasies, as in his Address to the 42nd Session of the United Nations General Assembly:

> Cannot swords be turned to plowshares? Can we and all nations not live in peace? In our obsession with antagonisms of the moment, we often forget how much unites all the members of humanity. Perhaps we need some outside, universal threat to make us recognize this common bond. I occasionally think how quickly our differences worldwide would vanish if we were facing an alien threat from outside this world.[1]

Even in the absence of the fantasy of an alien threat, SF frequently produces expressly anti-nationalistic sentiments as a matter of course; in Ursula K. Le Guin's celebration of Soviet writer Yevgeny Zamyatin in the pages of *Science Fiction Studies* she even suggests this as the genre's highest distinction: "The intellectual crime for which Zamyatin was reviled and silenced was that of being an 'internal *émigré*.' (The American equivalent would be 'un-Americanism.') This smear-word is a precise and noble description of the finest writers of SF, in all countries."[2] The sublime tableau of the Earth as viewed from space – first imagined in such SF texts as Jules Verne's *Around the Moon* (1870), about American tinkerer-astronauts, a century before real-world technology caught up – demands that we see ourselves not as so many squabbling nations but as one species living together on this "pale blue dot." New technologies for communication and transportation uniformly serve to shrink the globe, disrupt artificial political boundaries, and make every news story simultaneously local and universal. As our increasingly immersive online experiences foretell – to say nothing of the transnational power of social media technologies, media piracy, and classified document leaks – our intellectual and cultural lives are already becoming globalized, even as the concept of the nation-state persists, at least for now. And when the apocalypse comes, as it does in so many SF texts, it is almost certain to be a worldwide phenomenon; neither nuclear fallout nor ecological disasters nor robot killers nor lurching zombies respect our carefully drawn political borders.

Despite all this, it remains overwhelmingly common both in and outside the academy to rely on the nation-state as a principle of inclusion and exclusion – to speak of the realist novel in its particular French manifestations in the early nineteenth century, in its Victorian British tradition, in its post-1865 American phase, and so on. Custom has made such divisions natural, and with language barriers and unique historical and cultural contexts to justify the divisions, this manner of categorization based in geopolitical realities and regional nationalism has become embedded in curriculums and hiring committees across the United States and beyond. One may critique the philosophy of the nation-state and illuminate in sophisticated ways the hollowness and provincialism associated with nationalism, but the linguistic, historical, social, and aesthetic contexts in which Balzac wrote *La Comédie humaine* in France in the 1830s are notably different from the contexts in which Jane Austen wrote *Pride and Prejudice* in 1813 or William Dean Howells wrote *The Rise of Silas Lapham* in 1885. Thus national borders continue to frame both national literatures and the history of criticism that has sprung up around them. Even in a world made new by decolonization, the paradoxical result has been *more* reliance on the nation as a principle for mapping and understanding the world, not less.

This tension is alive in SF scholarship as well. Given the genre's origins and favored themes it is not surprising that none of the major scholarly journals devoted to SF criticism are nation-specific in their orientation. Classes devoted to introducing students to the critical analysis of SF hop from the England of H. G. Wells to the America of Octavia E. Butler to the Poland of Stanislaw Lem to the Russia of Arkady and Boris Strugatsky to the South Africa of Lauren Beukes with ease. Hollywood SF blockbusters match – and frequently surpass – their American receipts with their world-wide earnings, with international cooperation and coproduction not only increasingly common but also increasingly important in scripting, casting, and development. Shared interest in new developments in games, animation, and graphic novels with science fiction and fantasy themes has probably done more to bridge the cultural divide between Asia and the West among rising generations than decades of diplomacy ever did; the neon megacity of the post-1980s, post-cyberpunk future looks as much like Tokyo as it does New York or LA.

And yet the ongoing importance of the nation-state even within SF cannot be in dispute either. Wells's Martians attack where else but England, while Roddenberry's Federation is both overwhelmingly modeled on the postwar American state and commanded by a white male from Iowa; the *Enterprise* even retains the "U.S.S." prefix of the U.S. Navy. In Emmerich's alien inva-sion fantasy, Earth's "Independence Day" becomes (of course) July 4 – as grand an imperial takeover as one can fathom in that rousing speech made by a fictional American president who declares himself the representative of the entire globe. Nowhere is the ongoing relevance of the nation within SF clearer than in the renewed centrality of American superpower and the American military-industrial complex – its wars, its surveillance practices, its newly obvious fragility – as an object of both fantasy and terror in the post-9/11 cultural imaginary (the subject of Chapter 3 of this volume, "American Science Fiction after 9/11"). Superheroes sprung from the pages of mid-century American comics have new life fighting not communists but terrorists (the subject of Chapter 9, "U.S. Superpower and Superpowered

Americans in Science Fiction and Comic Books"), and have topped both the domestic and the global box office for most of the past decade. Not only in terms of its continued dominance of the global cultural industry, but also in terms of its outsized position as the world's largest economy, its largest military, and its largest polluter, the sheer gravitational mass of the United States continues to drive both utopian and dystopian speculation about the shape of the present and the prospects for the future.

The simple premise of the present volume, then, despite all of these caveats, is that the science fictional imagination is so fundamental to the arc of history across the so-called American Century that we might productively talk about a specifically *American* SF. Many of the ideas, themes, and conventions of contemporary science fiction take their roots in a distinctly American cultural experience, and so SF in America serves as a provocative index to twentieth- and twenty-first-century American culture, reflecting America's hopes, desires, ambitions, and fears. As Gary Westfahl has written previously, and elaborates on in Chapter 1 of this volume, "The Mightiest Machine":

> When [British and European science fiction critics] look at their native literatures in the period from 1890 to 1920, they find more than enough examples of works classifiable as science fiction that are far superior to anything produced in America at that time; but as they extend their chronological surveys past 1920, they watch their own traditions fade and fall apart, while American science fiction expands and grows stronger to the point that, by 1950, American writers and ideas dominated the world, and British and European authors were forced to imitate or respond to the American tradition.

Westfahl even finds Sweden's Sam J. Lundwall bemoaning that science fiction was "stolen" from Europe by the Americans![3] From film and television to music, genre fiction, comics, games, and canonical literature, the United States of the twentieth- and twenty-first centuries has embraced science fiction with open arms, less as a fantasy than as an electric anticipation of the world it was about to create. The American twentieth century was born in Edison's laboratories and Ford's factories, came into maturity with television, the atomic bomb, and the advent of digital computing, and finds us now, in the first quarter of the twenty-first century, talking about Ray Kurzweil's prognostications about a coming technological "Singularity" not as a playful metaphor but as a concrete prediction about what the future will be like. SF and U.S. culture in the past hundred years have been mutually informative spheres of influence, in which the predictive powers of SF have shaped real-world science and technology, which then spur further speculation. Perhaps nowhere is this clearer than in the military, where the nuclear bomb, rockets, satellites, and drone warfare are all science fictional devices that have been made real. "Science fiction is now a research and development department within a futures industry that dreams of the prediction and control of tomorrow," warns Afrofuturist scholar Kodwo Eshun,[4] in the same cultural moment that Homeland Security has begun bringing in science fiction writers to speculate on and anticipate possible threats to the nation. Likewise, the social impact of SF narratives can be felt across twentieth-century and twenty-first-century American history, from the triumph of the Apollo program to once unthinkable civil rights advances to the now ubiquitous usefulness of the Internet to genomic medicine to the apocalyptic anxieties that now drive contemporary environmentalist jeremiads. As much as, if not more than, any other literary genre in the United States since WWI and WWII, SF has mirrored – in both celebratory and critical ways – the evolution of postwar America itself. This volume is constructed around this proposition, providing a companion to Mendlesohn and James that charts the complex and intense relationship between science fiction, the American state, and American life.

At the same time, we hope the *Cambridge Companion to American Science Fiction* will intervene in science fiction studies by taking seriously Gary Westfahl's suggestion that mainline contemporary science fiction across the globe in fact bears a specifically American stamp. The very term "science fiction," after all, was coined in the United States in 1929 by Hugo Gernsback, founding editor of *Amazing Stories* – and it was in American pulp magazines of the 1920s and 1930s that science fiction first coalesced as a distinct and recognizable literary genre. Indeed, our chosen focus on American science fiction directs us to question even the force of that qualifying "literary," as books are rarely the most popular delivery system for these ideas; the middle section of this volume is correspondingly dedicated to media (as opposed to strictly literary) criticism, with essays dedicated to the importance of Hollywood film and television, comic books, game culture, and science fiction fan culture alongside the prose novel. This expanded focus is fitting for a companion dedicated to American SF, as America's mass culture industry (above and beyond its book publishing arm) has been and remains by far the largest distributor and popularizer of science fictional speculations in the world. The vast canon to which all contemporary creators of SF (in all media, forms, and genres) respond is thus (for better and for worse) tightly linked to American ideas, experiences, cultural assumptions, and entertainment markets, as well as to distinctly American visions of what the future might be like.

The story of SF in the United States does not begin with the pulps of the 1920s, but all the same the United States does not boast any SF authors in the nineteenth century who can match in popularity and influence Mary Shelley, H. G. Wells, or Jules Verne. Having said that, the American nineteenth century was not devoid of SF – even if it was not thought of as SF at the time, and perhaps still isn't – and, more importantly, nineteenth-century American literature exhibits the kind of keen and sustained interest in cutting-edge developments in science and technology that is reflected in American SF from the Golden Age forward.

As with any literary type, identifying the first example of a new thing is an exercise in futility. Long narrative prose fiction in the United States did not take root until the early national period, and to the extent that the European (principally English) Gothic novel paved the way for the emergence of SF in Shelley's *Frankenstein* (1818) and beyond, one can make a similar claim for the influence of the Gothic on U.S. literature. As important as the Gothic tradition was to the emergence of SF, so, too, were the fantastic voyage narratives of Francis Godwin, Cyrano de Bergerac, and Jacques Guttin, the long tradition of utopian speculation launched by Thomas More's *Utopia* (1516), the satiric narratives of Daniel Defoe and Jonathan Swift, the *contes philosophiques* of Voltaire and others, and the Enlightenment itself, which turned the attention of the academy toward scientific methodologies and experimentation.

In the first half of the nineteenth century in American letters, one finds a variety of texts that prefigure SF and wear their literary influences on their sleeves. In 1820, *Symzonia; Voyage of Discovery* by "Captain Adam Seaborn" (perhaps either John Cleves Symmes or Nathaniel Ames) took the Hollow Earth theory trumpeted by Symmes on the lecture circuit and extrapolated a fantastic voyage into the crust of the Earth, and into a utopian community where a wondrous society and strange technologies abound. In 1827, George Tucker published *A Voyage to the Moon*, arguably the first U.S. novel to feature extraplanetary travel, which builds on the satiric traditions of Jonathan Swift and borrows some narrative framework from Francis Godwin and other writers in the moon-centric fantastic voyage tradition. Meanwhile, the Gothic influence predominates in the SF tales of Edgar Allan Poe and Nathaniel Hawthorne. Of these two, Poe's influence on later SF is much more pronounced. Several of his Gothic tales prefigure major developments in SF, with the tale of "Mellonta Tauta" (1849) set in the year 2848; his own peculiar and elusive take on the Hollow Earth theory of John Cleves Symmes and *Symzonia* in *The Narrative of Arthur Gordon Pym of Nantucket* (1838); his weird tales of mesmerism such as "Facts in the Case of M. Valdemar" (1845); his own satiric take on the "fantastic voyage to the moon" tradition, "The Unparalleled Adventure of One Hans Pfaall" (1835); and his cosmic and philosophical speculations in *Eureka* (1848). At the same time, although not as influential in the history of SF as the works of Poe, Hawthorne's stories "The Artist of the Beautiful" (1844), "The Birthmark" (1843), and "Rappaccini's Daughter" (1844), among others, are all centrally concerned in one way or another with scientific extrapolation and a reexamination of the human condition as a result of the impact of scientific developments on culture, society, and individual human relationships.

In more ways than one, the publication of Charles Darwin's *On the Origin of Species* (1859) proved a turning point in the emergence of SF in U.S. letters. Indeed, viewing Darwin's *Origin* as a kind of pivot point, one can observe three major developments in the late nineteenth century that set the stage for SF in the twentieth century. The first of these developments – considered in more detail in Mark Bould's contribution to this volume – was the rise of a strong and influential tradition in utopian thinking in the late nineteenth century, spearheaded by Edward Bellamy's paradigm-defining *Looking Backward* (1888) and including such a wide-ranging group of texts as William Dean Howell's *A Traveler from Altruria* (1894) and Charlotte Perkins Gilman's *Herland* (1915), as well as John McCoy's *A Prophetic Romance* (1896) and Alice Jones and Ella Merchant's *Unveiling a Parallel: A Romance* (1893), both of which feature either receiving a visitor from Mars (McCoy) or a traveler to Mars (Jones and Merchant). Bellamy's book also ignited a fierce anti-utopian backlash in such works as Richard C. Michaelis's pro-capitalist *Looking Further Forward* (1890), J. W. Roberts's anti-utopian *Looking Within* (1893), and Arthur Dudley Vinton's racist Yellow Peril narrative *Looking Further Backward* (1890).

The second development was the emergence – particularly evidenced in young adult fiction – of what has since been dubbed the Edisonade: tales of remarkable applied science in which inventors (often boy geniuses) use their technological facility to save the day and win acclaim. The pattern was established, in many ways, by Edward S. Ellis's *The Steam Man of the Prairies* (1868), and continued through the several Frank Reade stories by Harold Cohen and continued as the adventures of Frank Reade Jr. in a long series of stories by Luis Senarens, who also penned the long series of "boy inventor" tales starring Jack Wright in the 1890s. Frank Baum would make his own contribution – of a sort – to the "boy hero" tradition of young adult fiction with his *The Master Key* (1901). Such stories characteristically linked invention to war machines; this connection may be no clearer than in Garrett P. Serviss's quasi-sequel to Wells's *War of the Worlds, Edison's Conquest of Mars*, in which *Thomas Edison himself* leads Earth's successful counterattack against the Martians.

The third development was the rise of literary naturalism in the late nineteenth century. Although rarely discussed in literary histories as a precursor to twentieth-century SF, literary naturalism was a remarkably important step along the road to the Golden Age. Strongly influenced by post-Darwinian developments in the biological sciences and intrigued by emergent theories of human nature in the late nineteenth century, the literary naturalists were central figures in the merging of scientific thought and fictional narrative. Among this group (which includes Frank Norris, Theodore Dreiser, and Stephen Crane), Jack London stands out, for among his vast canon are a number of works that are unmistakably SF and point toward twentieth-century SF more directly than the satiric fantasies, utopian dreams, and weirdly Gothic tales that preceded them in the nineteenth century. From the dystopian visions of *The Iron Heel* (1907) to an array of tales such as "The Unparalleled Invasion" (1910), "War" (1911), "The Red One" (1918), "Goliah" (1908), "The Scarlet Plague" (1912), and a dozen more, London helped pave the way in American letters for idea-rich SF throughout the twentieth century.

Participating in and around these three principal developments in late nineteenth-century American literary history are a handful of other SF texts that helped set the stage for what was to emerge after WWI. These include Fitz-James O'Brien's "The Diamond Lens" (1858) and "The Wonder Smith" (1859), various efforts by Ambrose Bierce, Edward Everett Hale's "The Brick Moon" (1869) and "Hands Off!" (1881), John A. Mitchell's *The Last American* (1889), as well as Frank Stockton's "The Water Devil" (1871) and "A Tale of Negative Gravity" (1884). Mark Twain's *A Connecticut Yankee in King Arthur's Court* (1889) is a brilliant time-travel fantasy that satirizes utopian idealism and the "inventor saves the day" trope that would soon become the ur-plot of dozens of Edisonades. The Hollow Earth fantasy comes back into vogue with John Uri Lloyd's *Etidorpha* (1895) and Willis George Emerson's *The Smokey God* (1908), and the fantastic-voyage-meets-interplanetary-romance tradition remains alive and well in Gustavus Pope's *Journey to Mars* (1894) and *Journey to Venus* (1895). Capitalizing on the fame of H. G. Wells and Thomas Edison, Garrett P. Serviss published *Edison's Conquest of Mars* in 1898, and followed that up with another SF novel, *The Sky Pirate*, in 1909. By the second decade of the twentieth century, Hugo Gernsback himself had entered the scene with his *Ralph 124C 41+* (1911), and Edgar Rice Burroughs had launched his Barsoom series with *A Princess of Mars* (1917). In 1926 Hugo Gernsback founded *Amazing Stories*, and the age of the SF pulps in the United States had begun.

In one sense, the boom in American SF in the first half of the twentieth century (which in turn would structure so much of the form of SF in the second half of the century) had a certain inevitability to it. The convergence in the second half of the nineteenth century of several aspects of U.S. culture – the real and imagined idea of the great American frontier, the techno-centric entrepreneurial drive of Edison and others, the fascination the literary naturalists and utopian writers had with the leading edge of scientific exploration – seemed to call for a modernist literature that would push these interests to their logical conclusions. Of all of the distinctive themes that one might call *American*, none stands out more prominently as a calling card of U.S. identity than the myth of the frontier. With the official closing of the American frontier with the census of 1890, the stage was set for Frederick Jackson Turner's celebrated frontier thesis in 1893 – and the quest to reclaim lost frontiers through re-imaginings quickly followed. The opening words of every original-run *Star Trek* episode – the unmistakable "Space – the Final Frontier" – strike a distinctively American chord. "So powerful was the myth of the West as a place where the future was to be found and made, however," notes Brian Stableford in the *Cambridge Companion to Science Fiction*, "that American Vernian fiction soon began to outstrip the ambitions of European Vernians. Writers like Frank R. Stockton, in *The Great War Syndicate* (1889) and *The Great Stone of Sardis* (1898), and Garrett P. Serviss, in *The Moon Metal* (1900) and *A Columbus of Space* (1909), helped pave the way for the development of popular SF of a distinctively American kind."[5]

The paradigmatically American space of the frontier unites the two strategies of critique that have tended to dominate SF scholarship in the academy. The utopian valence of the frontier calls to mind the critical interventions of such theorists of SF as Fredric Jameson (*Archaeologies of the Future: The Desire Called Utopia and Other Science Fictions* [2005]) and Darko Suvin ("On the Poetics of the Science Fiction Genre" [1972], expanded into *Metamorphoses of Science Fiction* [1979]), whose work sought to legitimize science fiction and science fiction studies through association with forward-looking socialist politics. In the hands of such thinkers, SF is essentially about utopian speculation, either through the positive construction of utopian blueprints or, more commonly in the American tradition, the negative depiction of the wretched dystopias that will arise "if this goes on." The frontier (now relocated to outer space) becomes an archetypal space of hope where humanity might start over with a clean slate, with examples from Isaac Asimov, Frank Herbert, Gene Roddenberry, and Robert Heinlein to Ursula K. Le Guin, Octavia Butler, Philip K. Dick, Kim Stanley Robinson, and others far too numerous to enumerate here.

The other major strain of contemporary SF scholarship, exemplified by such thinkers as John Rieder (*Colonialism and the Emergence of Science Fiction*), Istvan Csicsery-Ronay ("Science Fiction and Empire"), and Patricia

Kerslake (*Science Fiction and Empire*), finds SF more concerned with the production of death than with utopia. But the space of the frontier is no less critically vital for this shift in perspective; here the frontier is less a space of hope than a proof of the inevitability of war, as seen in the perpetual popularity of military SF and "space empire" fantasies. Csicsery-Ronay calls particular attention to those "fantasies of physical mastery and engineering know-how" that continue to drive so much science fiction as part and parcel of the way imperialism "facilitated the subjugation of less developed cultures, wove converging networks of technical administration, and established standards of 'objective measurement' that led inevitably to myths of racial and national supremacy."[6] Rieder, too, who writes the chapter on the frontier for the third section of this volume, finds in most SF the expression of a "colonial gaze"[7] that distributes power unevenly between the one that looks and the one that is looked at; from this perspective the paradigmatic SF of the frontier might not be the bustling space colony but rather the unblinking eye of the military spy satellite. In our time the myth of the frontier has accordingly turned sour, calling to mind not renewal or rebirth but the hair-trigger violence of postapocalyptic zombie fictions: used up, exhausted, already dead.

The Venn intersection between these two critical perspectives drives much of the analysis in *The Cambridge Companion to American Science Fiction*: utopia versus empire, optimism versus pessimism, progress versus regress, hope versus despair. Since WWI science fiction has been the genre of choice for authors who wanted the narrative freedom to explore new ideas and new philosophies in compelling, challenging, and provocative ways, as well as to talk back against the trends of contemporary culture. During this period – the so-called American century – SF has served as an important pop cultural medium for the exchange of such ideas in the United States and beyond, particularly with respect to the growing influence of science and technology on the way we think about the human condition (as Priscilla Wald discusses at length in Chapter 13). SF has also – as an intellectual and artistic endeavor – been a major source of socioeconomic, political, and cultural critique, providing creative and provocative outlets for ongoing countercultural interventions that have served as a running commentary on the world of the future as we recognize it emerging in the present. This work of the imagination seems only more urgent today. With neural interface devices, strong artificial intelligence, augmented reality, and molecular assemblers all in various stages of research and development in U.S. laboratories, and a shrinking world in which the U.S. military-industrial complex still reflects elements of Manifest Destiny, the Monroe Doctrine, and lingering and evolving Cold War geopolitics, and the cascading series of interrelated ecological catastrophes popularly called "climate change" no longer theoretical but already here, SF and U.S. culture in the past one hundred years become clearly visible as mutually informative spheres of influence. The predictive power of SF has shaped real-world science and technology, calling its own remarkable gadgetry into existence, while American ambitions and anxieties have been mirrored in SF literature and media that speak to a world in flux – from the cosmic, all-conquering optimism of the Golden Age to the countercultural energy of the '60s and '70s New Wave to the cyberpunk machinations of the '80s and '90s through the apocalyptic terrors and zombie futures predominant in our new century.

In pursuit of these ideas, the *Cambridge Companion to American Science Fiction* begins with a "Histories and Contexts" subdivision that traces the development of American science fiction out of the pulps into the mainstream in the context of these parallel developments in American culture. This section begins with three historical essays:

- The Mightiest Machine: The Development of American Science Fiction from the 1920s to the 1960s
- Dangerous Visions: New Wave and Post–New Wave Science Fiction (1960s–1990s)
- American Science Fiction after 9/11 (2000s)

The first essay contextualizes the emergence of science fiction as a recognizable literary genre out of American pulp magazines of the 1920s and 1930s into a thriving Cold War subgenre during the Golden Age of Asimov and Heinlein. The second essay details the political and aesthetic challenges to American science fiction posed by New Wave writers in the 1960s, marked by the publication of Harlan Ellison's counterculture *Dangerous Visions* anthology in 1967, and the ways responses to the New Wave characterize American science fiction across the second half of the twentieth century. The third essay deals specifically with American science fiction of the past fifteen years, looking at the terrorist events of 9/11 as a "hinge point" that has turned science fiction's focus squarely back on questions of national allegory, identity construction, imperial fantasy, total surveillance, violence, and war. Three additional essays round out this section, taking up the interlocking importance of race, gender and sexuality, and class in the production and reception of American science fiction diachronically across all three periods. These essays put the lie to the widespread misapprehension that science fiction is primarily the purview of white middle-class adolescents; in fact, nineteenth- and early twentieth-century Afrofuturist, feminist, and utopian approaches to science fiction significantly predate the genre's naming and organization in the pulps, and remain vitally important contexts across the field today.

In the second major subdivision of the volume, "Media and Form," we focus on the importance of science fiction in major media forms of the twentieth-century U.S. culture industry. The first, "American Slipstream: Science Fiction and Literary Respectability," considers intersections and cross-pollinations between "pulp" science fiction novels and the mainstream literary canon of the United States, exploring, for instance, the near-awarding of Thomas Pynchon's *Gravity's Rainbow* of a Nebula Award in 1973, and the recent "canonization" of Philip K. Dick by the Library of America. "Hollywood Science Fiction" considers the importance of the science fiction genre in visual media since the dawn of film and television, both in terms of raw capital and as a strong driver of technical innovation in cinema. "U.S. Superpower and Superpowered Americans in Science Fiction and Comic Books" explores superhero narrative and the dominance of this science fictional subgenre in comics almost to the exclusion of all other narrative possibilities in the medium, with particular focus on the relationship between the fantasy of the superhero and American "superpower" during and after the Cold War. "Digital Games and Science Fiction" considers the science fictional aspects of play in twentieth-century America, particularly with respect to video games and virtual environments whose technical sophistication has now finally almost "caught up" to cyberpunk fantasies of the 1980s – as well as the increasingly tight relationship between American game culture and the U.S. military-industrial complex. Finally, "Fandom and Fan Culture" considers the importance of fandom (conventions, Internet forums, letters pages, fan fiction, and fan criticism) in the reception and perpetuation of American science fiction, as well as why science fiction has generated such fierce and vibrant fan communities in the United States and around the world.

In the third subdivision, "Themes and Perspectives," the chapters take up a thematic approach to American science fiction, with a focus squarely on the relationship between science fiction and American culture, history, and national identity as manifested across the genre. This section of the volume looks at how science fiction in America has mirrored (in both positive and critical ways) key aspects of twentieth- and twenty-first-century American experience: the frontier imaginary in war and peace; science, technology, and the environment; adjacent genres and subcultures like the Lovecraftian "weird"; and persistent anxieties about the apocalypses, collapses, and other forms of radical change and transformation that always seem to be right around the corner. These chapters reflect science fiction's continuing usefulness as a way of thinking through the vertiginous tumult of an era when, in the words of William Gibson, "the sort of thing we used to think in science fiction has colonized the rest of our reality" – our strange era, when, as Kim Stanley Robinson has it, "science fiction turns out to be the realism of our time."[8]

NOTES

1 Ronald Reagan, "Address to the 42d Session of the United Nations General Assembly in New York, New York" (September 21, 1987), Ronald Reagan Presidential Library, http://www.reagan.utexas.edu.
2 Ursula K. Le Guin, "Surveying the Battlefield," *Science Fiction Studies* 2 (Fall 1973): 88–90, www.depauw.edu/sfs/backissues/2/marx2forum.htm.
3 Gary Westfahl, *The Mechanics of Wonder: The Creation of the Idea of Science Fiction* (Liverpool: Liverpool University Press, 1998), 27.
4 Kodwo Eshun, "Further Considerations on Afrofuturism," *CR: The New Centennial Review* 3.2 (Summer 2003): 287–302 (291).
5 Edward James and Farah Mendlesohn, eds., *The Cambridge Companion to Science Fiction* (Cambridge: Cambridge University Press, 2003), 22.
6 Istvan Csicsery-Ronay Jr., "Science Fiction and Empire," *Science Fiction Studies* 30.2 (July 2003): 231–45 (233–4).
7 John Rieder, *Colonialism and the Emergence of Science Fiction* (Wesleyan, CT: Wesleyan University Press, 2008), 6.
8 Mavis Linnemann, "William Gibson Overdrive," Phawker.com (August 15, 2007), http://www.phawker.com/2007/08/15/coming-atraction-william-gibson-qa/; Alison Flood, "Kim Stanley Robinson: Science Fiction's Realist," TheGuardian. com (11 November 2009), http://www.theguardian.com/books/2009/nov/10/kim-stanley-robinson-science-fiction-realist.

PART I

Histories and Contexts

I

GARY WESTFAHL

The Mightiest Machine: Th Development of American Science Fiction from the 1920s to the 1960s

In 1920, a global survey of the literature now regarded as science fiction would reveal distinctive and substantive bodies of work in several nations, including Great Britain, France, Germany, the Soviet Union, and Japan. The United States had science fiction too, yet it largely consisted of adventure stories written for pulp magazines, and its writers like Garrett P. Serviss and Edgar Rice Burroughs were not particularly impressive in comparison to, say, Britain's H. G. Wells or France's J.-H. Rosny aîné. Forty years later, the situation had entirely changed: American science fiction was widely recognized as the best in the world, and the books and magazines of other countries were largely devoted to translations of American stories and original works following American models.

What caused this dramatic transformation? Needless to say we cannot attribute the triumph of American science fiction to any peculiar virtues in the American character, although I have been falsely accused of making such arguments.[1] A more plausible, though equally wrongheaded, answer would be that after the end of World War II, a victorious United States had the power to impose its culture on other nations ravaged by war, and its science fiction became prominent merely as one minor consequence of its social and ideological conquest of the world. Yet one observes no universal surrender to the superiority of American culture. Foreign filmmakers, rather than slavishly imitating Hollywood products, continued to develop unique national styles that garnered American attention and respect in the 1950s; there is no evidence that the world's composers, painters, choreographers, or architects felt any pressure or desire to emulate American creators; and while baseball became popular in Japan, American sports otherwise had little impact on the world, as foreign nations remained devoted to their soccer and cricket. Only a few aspects of American culture were enthusiastically embraced throughout the world – such as rock 'n' roll, science fiction, and blue jeans – and these particular successes require particular explanations.

Scholars in other fields must address why rock 'n' roll and blue jeans proved so appealing, but I am prepared to explain why American science fiction dramatically improved in the decades after 1920 and came to dominate the world. As I have argued elsewhere,[2] it was largely due to the work of Hugo Gernsback, who provided an inchoate genre with a name, persuasive arguments for its special importance, and a support system of organized fans; he also promulgated, almost against his will, a characteristic narrative that contributed to its remarkable growth. Then, Gernsback's most prominent successor, John W. Campbell Jr., added a final key ingredient – intellectual respectability. It is these singular developments that account for the special strength and ongoing impact of American science fiction.

While it may seem a minor matter, one cannot promote and popularize a form of literature unless it has an appropriate and resonant name, and this is one service to science fiction that Gernsback performed. At first, when he published science fiction stories in his science magazines, he called them "scientific fiction." In 1926, when he launched the world's first science fiction magazine, *Amazing Stories*, he created and copyrighted a portmanteau version of the term, "scientifiction." Finally, in 1929, when he lost control of *Amazing Stories* and his own clunky neologism, he was fortuitously obliged to come up with another name, "science fiction."[3] Soon, everyone else in America was using this term.

"Science fiction" proved effective and popular for several reasons. It firmly linked the genre to science, which was becoming more respected and prominent in the public eye as new technologies kept improving American life and as scientists ranging from Thomas Alva Edison to Albert Einstein became media celebrities. Seemingly similar terms that might have become standard, like "scientific romance" (used most frequently in Great Britain) and "pseudo-scientific stories" (briefly common in American pulp magazines), suggested that the science in the stories might be fanciful; "science fiction," however, solidly promised *accurate* science, an implication that Gernsback heavily stressed in proselytizing for the genre. An additional advantage of "science fiction" was that it was easy to pronounce and easy to spell, unlike the generally unwieldy alternatives.[4]

Still, to attract readers to a form of literature, one needs more than a catchy name; one must explain why these stories are especially important, especially valuable, especially worth reading. Previous defenses of science fiction had been imperfect, hesitant, even flippant, but in numerous editorials, introductions, and responses to readers' letters, Gernsback crafted and tirelessly promoted three effective arguments for his newly christened genre, which corresponded to its three basic elements, as announced in the definition of science fiction given in his first *Amazing Stories* editorial, "A New Sort of Magazine": "a charming romance intermingled with scientific fact and prophetic vision." The editorial then proceeded to elaborate on the value of each element. Gernsback conceded that, like other forms of literature, science fiction was a form of entertainment, "a charming romance," and appealing for that reason. However, because stories included "scientific fact," they offered the additional benefit of scientific education: "Not only do these amazing tales make tremendously interesting reading – they are also always instructive. They supply knowledge that we might not otherwise obtain – and they supply it in a very palatable form." Third, a story's "prophetic vision," firmly based on today's science, could provide useful ideas for inventors, so "Prophecies made in many of [these writers'] amazing stories are being realized – and have been realized."[5] He explained how science fiction made its predictions come true in a later editorial, "The Lure of Scientifiction": "The serious-minded scientifiction reader absorbs the knowledge contained in such stories with avidity, with the result that such stories prove an incentive in starting some one to work on a device or invention suggested by some author."[6] In these ways, unlike other types of literature, science fiction could enormously benefit the world, creating a more educated citizenry and wonderful new scientific advances inspired by its stories.

It is pointless to complain that these bold claims bore little relationship to the stories that Gernsback actually published in *Amazing Stories*, which only occasionally offered truly educational material and even more rarely presented provocative ideas that were not already commonplace, because this did nothing to diminish the impact of Gernsback's arguments. For even if most of his writers ignored his announced requirements in their stories, many young readers wholeheartedly embraced his ideas; and when some of them later began writing science fiction, they resolved to produce stories that would perfectly fulfill his agenda by providing intelligent new speculations firmly based on scientific knowledge. By the 1950s, the recognition emerged that these writers were specializing in a new subgenre of science fiction, "hard science fiction," dedicated to rigorously logical extrapolations of current science. So it is true that, in 1930, a person asked to provide examples of stories that matched Gernsback's claims might be hard pressed to find them – but by 1960, the same person could readily turn to stories by Poul Anderson, Arthur C. Clarke, Hal Clement, and others who were doing precisely what Gernsback had urged writers to do. In essence, Gernsback belatedly made his claims for science fiction come true.[7]

Moreover, advertising can be persuasive even if it is not exactly true, and Gernsback's proclamations could be regarded as unusually cunning ways to sell magazines within his marketing niche. In contrast to what he dismissed in "A New Sort of Magazine" as "the love story and the sex-appeal type of magazine," his science fiction magazine offered readers wholesome and educational entertainment; young people could learn useful scientific information instead of wasting their time reading tales of scantily clad women doing immoral things. And unlike the Westerns and detective stories found in "the usual fiction magazine" and "the adventure type" of magazine, his science fiction magazine was uniquely respectable; learned scientists were purportedly reading stories hoping to glean helpful insights that could lead them to scientific breakthroughs.[8] To drive this point home, Gernsback's later magazine *Science Wonder Stories* (which evolved into *Wonder Stories*) established an "editorial and advisory board" including "an imposing array of scientific authorities and educators," listed above each issue's editorial.[9] No other pulp magazine could claim that its stories were being reviewed by fourteen experts in astronomy, botany, electricity, mathematics, medicine, physics, and zoology, reinforcing the notion that reading science fiction magazines was an unusually productive and worthwhile activity – one that readers could enthusiastically recommend to friends and colleagues, unlike reading other pulp magazines that they might wish to hide from visitors. As he summed up the argument in a later *Wonder Stories* editorial: "the public at large should begin to know the benefits of Science Fiction and be turned from meaningless detective and love trash to the elevating and imaginary literature of Science Fiction."[10]

The effectiveness of Gernsback's marketing skills is evidenced by another phenomenon that he inspired and contributed to: the emergence of science fiction fandom. First, by publishing letters with readers' addresses in *Amazing Stories*, Gernsback provided a way for science fiction enthusiasts to get in touch with each other; then, as the next logical step, readers began to propose the formation of organizations to promote science fiction. One reader's letter, in the May 1928 issue of *Amazing Stories*, expressed surprise that the magazine itself had not taken this step: "I thought at first that you would take hold of [this idea], suggest a plan of organization, and get it started ... but it is now apparent that you are determined to leave it entirely in the hands of those of your readers who are interested enough to go ahead and organize the Science Club."[11] Rather quickly, such an organization actually sprung into existence; in the August 1929 issue of *Science Wonder Stories*, a reader named A. B. Maloire explained that he had been too busy to read all of the magazine's stories because "corresponding with members of the recently created Science Correspondence Club has taken up much of my time." This group of "twenty-five enthusiastic science fiction fans," he added, was presently "voting for officers"; a new Boston branch of the organization was announced in a later *Science Wonder Stories* letter.[12] This organization went on to publish what is generally regarded as the first science fiction "fanzine," an amateur magazine featuring reviews, articles, and stories, called *The Comet* and edited by a future editor of *Amazing Stories*, Ray Palmer. Many other groups and publications soon emerged; for example, a letter in the May 1930 issue of *Science Wonder Stories* announced the creation of a New York-based group, the Scienceers, and the June 1930 issue of *Wonder Stories* published the first of several letters from members of another group, the American Interplanetary Society.[13]

From the beginning, Gernsback recognized that such societies could help to make science fiction more popular and, not incidentally, sell more copies of his magazines. Thus, the editorial response to Maloire's letter supportively commented, "We are more than interested to learn about the Science Correspondence Club. Its idea is excellent and we wish to encourage it in all means within our power," while a later letter from another member to *Wonder Stories* expressed thanks for "the assistance and sincere cooperation of the Gernsback Publications" and "the wonderful help you have extended us."[14] Eventually, as more reports of independent clubs emerged, Gernsback decided to do what readers had long expected him to do: bring all these groups together into one vast organization under his magazine's supervision.

Accordingly, in the April 1934 issue of *Wonder Stories*, he announced the formation of the Science Fiction League, "a non-commercial membership organization ... for the betterment and promotion of scientific literature in all languages."[15] As part of a longer description of the League in the next issue, "The Science Fiction League," Gernsback unveiled its Executive Directors, an impressive team of published authors – Eando Binder, Edmond Hamilton, David H. Keller, P. Schuyler Miller, Clark Ashton Smith, and R. F. Starzl – as well as two prominent fans, Forrest J. Ackerman and Jack Darrow.[16] The group's announced mission was to "coördinate all who are interested in science fiction, into one comprehensive international group" that would "in due time become the parent organization of innumerable local science fiction clubs throughout the world."[17] While members of local chapters would "broadcast the gospel of Science Fiction," the League itself would offer "special LEAGUE meetings ... talks by prominent Science Fiction authorities, authors, writers, etc.... [and] exhibits or collections of Science Fiction literature and stories, so that members can get together and meet each other."[18]

One notes that Gernsback had vowed to create a genuinely international alliance of science fiction fans, and in fact he had already been making American science fiction popular in other nations by means of his magazine, as evidenced by letters in *Amazing Stories* from readers in India, Great Britain, and Canada, and letters in *Science Wonder Stories* from readers in Belgium and Mexico.[19] So it was not surprising that, in the months after Gernsback's announcement, the magazine heard about planned chapters in Great Britain, China, and the Philippines, though only the English chapter actually materialized.

For two years, Gernsback's *Wonder Stories* published regular reports on the League's chapters and activities, but when he temporarily abandoned the field and sold his magazine in 1936, the Science Fiction League officially dissipated. However, many chapters kept functioning as independent organizations, new societies emerged, and Gernsback's dream of a vast coalition of science fiction fans was achieved less formally in 1939, when several groups collectively staged the first World Science Fiction Convention in New York City; the alliance governing this now-annual event was eventually termed the World SF Society. In addition, by means of innumerable fanzines regularly mailed to interested subscribers, and fan reports in science fiction magazines, science fiction fans could stay in contact with each other, even if they were not members of official organizations.

Science fiction fandom would prove crucial to the growth and progress of American science fiction in innumerable ways.[20] Its ranks were a breeding ground for talented new writers like Ray Bradbury and Harlan Ellison; and, driven by their enthusiasm for science fiction, fans vigorously recruited new readers and tried to draw attention to writers. Fandom also bolstered the egos of science fiction writers; they may have spent most of their time laboring anonymously at day jobs while earning little from their writings, but they could receive an enthusiastic fan letter or serve as an honored guest at a science fiction convention and briefly feel like a star. Most significantly, the letters that fans sent to magazines, and fanzines they wrote and published, provided a forum for an intense, ongoing discussion of science fiction that called attention to its flaws and demanded better writing, contributing to small but steady improvements in its quality; thus, some regularly published writers of the 1930s, like Jack Williamson and Clifford D. Simak, matured and developed to become even more prominent in the 1940s, while many of their compatriots from the 1930s found that their unchanging work was no longer wanted. Similarly, some writers of the 1940s, like Robert A. Heinlein and Isaac Asimov, kept getting better and prospered even more in the 1950s, but lesser writers of that era who never improved gradually faded from view.

The criticisms of science fiction in letters and fanzines, interestingly, often focused on a particular form of science fiction that was becoming more and more popular with readers: the "space opera." As is the case with so many aspects of science fiction, the origins of this subgenre can be traced back to Gernsback, who in 1928 serialized a novel in *Amazing Stories*, E. E. "Doc" Smith's *The Skylark of Space*, now regarded as a pioneering work of space opera. These stories characteristically featured intrepid young heroes in spaceships who flew throughout the galaxy battling sinister aliens or space pirates with weapons ranging from planet-destroying rays to their fists. Smith went on to produce similar space adventures, as did many other writers like John W. Campbell Jr., Edmond Hamilton, Frank K. Kelly, Leslie F. Stone, and Jack Williamson. As readers clearly loved such stories, they became the most common form of magazine science fiction in the 1930s.[21]

Arguably, Gernsback should have seen this coming; even before Smith's novel appeared, a 1927 interview with his magazine's "youngest reader" had yielded the information "that he preferred stories of space and of inter-planetarian travel."[22] But, despite its popularity, space opera bore little relationship to Gernsback's agenda, usually offering no substantive scientific information or provocative new ideas. In 1932, he directly criticized the dubious science of space opera in a special editorial that introduced Campbell's story "Space Rays":

> When science fiction first came into being, it was taken most seriously by all authors. In practically all instances, authors laid the basis of their stories upon a solid scientific foundation. If an author made a statement as to certain future instrumentalities, he usually found it advisable to adhere closely to the possibilities of science as it was then known.
>
> Many modern science fiction authors have no such scruples. They do not hesitate to throw scientific plausibility overboard, and embark on a policy of what I might call scientific magic, in other words, science that is neither plausible, nor possible. Indeed, it overlaps the fairy tale, and often goes the fairy tale one better.... In the present offering, Mr. John W. Campbell, Jr., has no doubt realized this state of affairs and has proceeded in an earnest way to burlesque some of our rash authors to whom plausibility and possible science mean nothing. He pulls, magician-like, all sorts of impossible rays from his silk hat, much as a magician extracts rabbits.... I have gone to this length to preach a sermon in the hope that misguided authors will see the light, and hereafter stick to science as it is known, or as it may reasonably develop in the future.[23]

Clearly, Gernsback was imposing his own didactic message on a story with no satiric intent, but no doubt thought this was the gentlest way to inform Campbell and his colleagues that their colorful adventure stories were not the sort of science fiction he admired. In contrast, he made a special effort to praise a story that did not follow the usual pattern of space opera, Stanley G. Weinbaum's "A Martian Odyssey" (1934), by personally writing its introduction; Weinbaum, he wrote, "has written a science-fiction tale so new, so breezy, that it stands out head and shoulders over similar interplanetarian stories."[24]

Because innovative writers like Weinbaum were hard to find, Gernsback had also been striving to improve space opera by sponsoring contests in *Science Wonder Quarterly* (which became *Wonder Stories Quarterly*) to obtain new "Interplanetary Plots" that experienced authors could turn into stories. His instructions announced what he did not want, namely, stories like "Space Rays": "A plot submitted that simply relates a war between two planets, with a lot of rays and bloodshed, will receive little consideration." Instead, he wanted stories like "A Martian Odyssey," which offered "some original 'slant' on interplanetary travel, or of the conditions on other worlds."[25] Other members of the emerging science fiction community were, like Gernsback, similarly condemning routine space operas and calling for more imaginative approaches to science fiction. The very term "space opera" was coined by a fan, Wilson Tucker, while he was criticizing "the hacky, grinding, stinking, outworn space-ship yarn."[26] Another fan, Clyde F. Beck, whose writings were collected in 1937 as the first book of science fiction criticism, *Hammer and Tongs*, offered a similar complaint while explaining what constitutes

> the real reason for the great dearth in worthy writing in the contemporary "science fiction" magazines. There is an altogether deceptive appearance of easiness about it: seemingly one needs but to take the currently popular plot of pursuit, struggle, mystery, or intrigue, salt it with rockets or ray-guns, garnish it with a few strips of mathematics, pass it through interstellar space, the fourth dimension, the realm of the infinitely small – and behold, science fiction.[27]

None of these broadsides, however, diminished the burgeoning popularity of space opera, and this was actually helpful to science fiction – because even if the subgenre was not admired by dedicated fans, it did provide science fiction with a sense of identity and a characteristic plot, attracting numerous writers and readers who might later move on to more challenging material. Simak, for example, only wrote undistinguished space adventures in the 1930s, but later blossomed into an author who was widely admired for gentle, pastoral stories about aliens and robots. More importantly, space opera expanded the audience for science fiction, inspiring dozens of new magazines in the 1940s and 1950s – including a few, like *Planet Stories* (1939–55) and *Captain Future* (1940–4), which were exclusively devoted to space stories. It was also the form of science fiction that could be transferred most easily into other media: thus, two stories by Philip Francis Nowlan that Gernsback published in 1928, involving a present-day man named Anthony Rogers who awakens in the far future (collected in 1962 as *Armageddon*

2419 A.D.), became the basis for a popular comic strip, *Buck Rogers* (1929–67), that made him a space adventurer; this inspired a similar comic strip, *Flash Gordon* (1934–2003); and both comic strips became the basis of film serials (*Flash Gordon* [1936]; *Flash Gordon's Trip to Mars* [1938]; *Buck Rogers* [1939]; *Flash Gordon Conquers the Universe* [1940]). Comic books embraced space opera as well in popular comics like *Planet Comics* (1940–54), *Strange Adventures* (1950–73), and *Mystery in Space* (1951–66). Finally, in the 1950s, space opera ventured into film and television, represented by films like *This Island Earth* (1954) and *Forbidden Planet* (1956) and television series like *Space Patrol* (1950–5) and *Tom Corbett, Space Cadet* (1950–5). Like written space operas, these comic strips, serials, comic books, films, and television programs were often derided by fans, but they reached far more people than science fiction magazines and books, and hence served to strengthen the genre by increasing its visibility and popularity.

It will be recalled, though, that one element in Gernsback's campaign to promote science fiction was to make it respectable, and a genre dominated by space opera could not achieve that goal. Thus, to balance the bad image often projected by that subgenre, someone needed to establish and support an intellectual wing of science fiction, so there could still be stories to merit the attention of thoughtful adult readers. This role was played by editor John W. Campbell Jr., who assumed control of *Astounding Stories* in 1938, renamed the magazine *Astounding Science-Fiction*, and began writing editorials and articles conveying a new vision of science fiction and new reasons to value the genre.

As noted, Campbell began his career by writing exuberant space operas like the aforementioned "Space Rays" and *The Mightiest Machine* (1934–5), but was soon producing more interesting and imaginative stories under the pseudonym Don A. Stuart, including the elegiac "Twilight" (1934) and the scientific mystery "Who Goes There?" (1938), which inspired the 1951 film *The Thing* and two later remakes (1982, 2011). He was thus well prepared to take the field in new directions. True, Campbell still felt that science fiction could fulfill Gernsback's original goals – but it could transcend these priorities by offering more provocative and thought-provoking sorts of entertainment, education, and ideas. Thus, he wanted science fiction to be well-written literature: "In older science fiction, the Machine and the Great Idea predominated. Modern readers – and hence editors! – don't want that; they want stories of people living in a world where a Great Idea, or a series of them, and a Machine, or machines, form the background. But it is the man, not the idea or machine that is the essence."[28] Second, by offering readers stimulating puzzles to solve, science fiction did not simply teach them scientific facts, but rather how to think like a scientist: science fiction is "not the summer-vacation-snooze type of fun. More like the roller-coaster or mountain-climbing type, it presents a real mental challenge."[29] Finally, science fiction could intelligently examine not only new technologies, but the ways that they might affect future societies: by employing their "understanding of how political and social set-ups react to technological changes," science fiction writers could consider both "new and still undiscovered phenomena" and "what the results look like when applied ... to human society."[30] More broadly, science fiction could function as "a way of considering the past, present, and future from a different viewpoint, and taking a look at how else we *might* do things ... a convenient analog system for thinking about new scientific, social, and economic ideas – and for re-examining old ideas."[31] Unlike Gernsback, then, Campbell offered a literary agenda that even the most erudite readers could admire and appreciate.

Campbell had one advantage over Gernsback, who was largely describing a form of science fiction that had not yet appeared; not only had his own stories partially anticipated his ideas, but Campbell had attracted a writer in 1939, Robert A. Heinlein, who was already doing everything that Campbell wanted science fiction writers to do. In fact, Heinlein's work directly inspired some of Campbell's talking points; after examining Heinlein's Future History chart, for example, he wrote a 1941 editorial, "History to Come," that presented Heinlein's painstaking development of a consistent background as a model for other writers.[32] Campbell was also unlike the reticent Gernsback because he undertook, by means of voluminous correspondence and occasional meetings, to personally train his writers, ranging from veterans like Williamson to neophytes like Asimov, to produce the new sorts of stories that he preferred. Further, his impact extended beyond the writers who worked for *Astounding* because other writers like Philip K. Dick and Harlan Ellison, who read his editorials and the stories he published, started producing their own varieties of stimulating science fiction for adults even though they did not write for Campbell. Thus, by the late 1940s and early 1950s, there was an established cadre of talented, imaginative science fiction writers whose works functioned as exemplars of the deep, challenging literature that Campbell wanted – and these could be exported along with space opera to appeal to demanding as well as undemanding readers.

We can now understand precisely why American science fiction became widely recognized as the best science fiction in the world. It had a name that conveyed and imposed a special sense of identity, firmly associated with science; it was buttressed by arguments testifying to its unique value and significance; it was vigorously supported by armies of dedicated fans eager to both promote and critique its works; it was centered on a characteristic narrative that was exciting and colorful enough to attract a broad range of readers; and these adventures were accompanied by more distinguished stories rooted in a more challenging agenda that could appeal to literary connoisseurs. In contrast, the imaginative literatures of other nations lacked a recognized name, were not clearly associated with science, were not buttressed by arguments about their singular virtues, did not enjoy organized support, and were not anchored by an involving narrative pattern in alliance with more thought-provoking efforts. Hence, foreign science fiction could not resist the powerful juggernaut of American science fiction, which marginalized native traditions and forced writers to enlist in its ranks and emulate its strictures.

American science fiction's first triumphs came in Britain, where readers in the 1930s had already started reading American science fiction magazines and forming their own fan organizations like those in America; one participant was a young Arthur C. Clarke, who then became one of several British writers in the 1940s who focused their attention on the American market. Only after the trauma of World War II ended, however, could translators in France, Germany, Russia, Eastern Europe, and Japan start providing their fellow citizens with access to American science fiction in their own languages. What happened as a result can be exemplified by two popular series of publications in postwar France: the Fleuve Noir series presented French translations of American novels, while the accompanying Anticipation series featured French writers endeavoring to produce their own versions of American science fiction.[33]

Though its victory was thoroughgoing, however, the complete American domination of global science fiction was relatively brief. In America, around 1960, there arose a belief that the genre was somehow becoming exhausted, losing its strength; fan Earl Kemp's alarmist manifesto *Who Killed Science Fiction?* (1960) was the clearest signal of such concerns, but many others, who noted in particular the sudden demise of many science fiction magazines, felt that a grand era of science fiction history was coming to an end.[34] In the meantime, while new foreign writers were initially limited to imitating American models, some grew dissatisfied with science fiction's conventions and expectations, naturally looking back to their own national literatures, developing new ideas, and endeavoring to write science fiction that combined American priorities with their own distinctive styles. Such authors began to have an impact, on both America and the world, in the 1960s. In Britain, figures like J. G. Ballard and Michael Moorcock became leading figures in a new movement, the New Wave, demanding science fiction that featured daring stylistic experiments, less devotion to science, and more attention to contemporary human concerns. Elsewhere, writers like Poland's Stanislaw Lem and Russia's Boris and Arkady Strugatsky moved away from American influences to create imaginative novels that impressed readers throughout the world. Foreign science fiction filmmakers also attracted and influenced American viewers with innovative works like *Alphaville* (1965) and *Solaris* (1971). While American voices remained strong, science fiction in the 1960s and thereafter was becoming a truly global conversation, and the dividing lines between an American approach and a foreign approach to the genre were no longer quite as clear.[35]

Still, signs of American ascendancy remain visible to this day in all forms of science fiction: writers continue to respond to the agendas that Gernsback and Campbell promulgated; fans all over the world are still publishing fanzines (though these are now more often online) and holding conventions in the American manner; American space opera remains the quintessential form of science fiction; and American writers working in Campbell's tradition continue to attract most of the critical attention. Authors and critics in other nations may resent this lingering American influence; they may even attempt to deny that it exists, or condemn it as an atavistic remnant of earlier days that must be purged so the genre can progress; but it is hard to explain the success of science fiction as a whole without crediting the power of the provocative American ideas and activities that presided over its remarkable expansion and ongoing development.

NOTES

1 Consider, for example, the tone of Brian Stableford's response to my first article on Gernsback (Brian Aldiss, Brian Stableford, and Edward James, "On 'On the True History of Science Fiction,'" *Foundation: The Review of Science Fiction*, No. 47 [Winter 1989/1990]: 28–33).

2 At greatest length in *The Mechanics of Wonder: A History of the Idea of Science Fiction* (Liverpool: Liverpool University Press, 1998) and *Hugo Gernsback and the Century of Science Fiction* (Jefferson, NC: McFarland Publishers, 2007).

3 True, the term had been previously introduced by William Wilson in 1851, but no one noticed or remembered his work, as discussed in *The Mechanics of Wonder* (21). Also, in an early issue of *Amazing Stories*, a response to a letter, probably written by Associate Editor T. O'Conor Sloane, called Jules Verne "a sort of Shakespeare in science fiction" ("Discussions," *Amazing Stories*, 1 [January 1927], 974), a comment that officially qualifies as the first modern use of the term, though the reference went unnoticed.

4 The history of efforts to name science fiction is surveyed in Sam Moskowitz, "How Science Fiction Got Its Name," *Explorers of the Infinite: Shapers of Science Fiction* (Cleveland, OH: World Publishing Company, 1963), 313–33.

5 Hugo Gernsback, "A New Sort of Magazine," *Amazing Stories* 1.1 (April 1926): 3.

6 Gernsback, "The Lure of Scientifiction," *Amazing Stories* 1.3 (June 1926): 195.
7 I examine how the idea and subgenre of hard science fiction emerged in *Cosmic Engineers: A Study of Hard Science Fiction* (Westport, CT: Greenwood Press, 1996).
8 Gernsback, "A New Sort of Magazine," 3.
9 Gernsback, "Science Wonder Stories," *Science Wonder Stories* 1.1 (June 1929): 5.
10 Gernsback, "The Science Fiction League," *Wonder Stories* 5 (May 1934): 1062.
11 "Discussions," *Amazing Stories* 3.2 (May 1928): 188.
12 "The Reader Speaks," *Science Wonder Stories* 1.3 (August 1929): 283; "The Reader Speaks," *Science Wonder Stories*, 1.11 (April 1930): 1052.
13 "The Reader Speaks," *Science Wonder Stories*, 1.12 (May 1930): 1139; "The Reader Speaks," *Wonder Stories*, 2.1 (June 1930): 78.
14 "The Reader Speaks," *Science Wonder Stories* 1 (August 1929): 283; "The Reader Speaks," *Wonder Stories* 2.8 (January 1931): 908.
15 Gernsback, "The Science Fiction League: An Announcement," *Wonder Stories* 5.9 (April 1934): 933.
16 Gernsback, "The Science Fiction League," *Wonder Stories* 5.10 (May 1934): 1061. "Eando Binder" was a pseudonym used by two brothers: Earl and Otto Binder, thus "E"-and-"O."
17 Gernsback, "The Science Fiction League: An Announcement," 933.
18 Gernsback, "The Science Fiction League," 1062, 1064.
19 "Discussions," *Amazing Stories* 2.3 (June 1927): 307; "Discussions," *Amazing Stories* 2.4 (July 1927): 413–15; "The Reader Speaks," *Science Wonder Stories*, 1.4 (September 1929): 376; "The Reader Speaks," *Science Wonder Stories* 1.6 (November 1929): 569. Letters from Canada and Great Britain were actually commonplace in Gernsback's magazine, though letters from other countries remained rare.
20 For more on the importance of fandom in the history of science fiction, see also Chapter 11 of this volume, "Fandom and Fan Culture."
21 The history and evolution of space opera are further discussed in my "Space Opera," *The Cambridge Companion to Science Fiction*, edited by Edward James and Farah Mendlesohn (Cambridge and New York: Cambridge University Press, 2003), 197–208.
22 Cited in Gernsback, "Amazing Youth," *Amazing Stories* 2.7 (October 1927): 625.
23 Gernsback, "Reasonableness in Science Fiction," *Wonder Stories* 4.7 (December 1932): 585.
24 Gernsback, introduction to "A Martian Odyssey," *Wonder Stories* 6.2 (July 1934): 175 [unsigned].
25 "Wanted: Still More Plots," *Wonder Stories Quarterly* 3.4 (Summer 1932): 437 [author not given].
26 Wilson Tucker [writing as Bob Tucker], "Depts of the Interior" [*sic*], *Le Zombie* 4 (January 1941): 8.
27 Clyde F. Beck, *Hammer and Tongs* (Lakeport, CA: Futile Press, 1937), 17–18.
28 John W. Campbell Jr., "The Science of Science Fiction Writing," *Of Worlds Beyond*, edited by Lloyd Arthur Eshbach (Chicago, IL: Advent Publishers, 1964 [orig. 1947]), 92.

29 Campbell, "Introduction," *Analog 1*, edited by Campbell (Garden City, NJ: Doubleday and Company, 1963), xvi.

30 Campbell, "Introduction," *Venus Equilateral*, by George O. Smith (New York: Prime Press, 1947), 9–10.

31 Campbell, "Introduction," *Prologue to Analog*, edited by Campbell (Garden City, NJ: Doubleday and Company, 1962), 13.

32 Campbell, "History to Come," *Astounding Science-Fiction* 27.3 (May 1941): 5–6.

33 For an excellent study of the Anticipation series, see Bradford Lyau's *The Anticipation Novelists of 1950s French Science Fiction: Stepchildren of Voltaire* (Jefferson, NC: McFarland Publishers, 2010).

34 Earl Kemp, *Who Killed Science Fiction?: An Affectionate Autopsy* (Chicago, IL: Earl and Nancy Kemp, 1960).

35 For a more detailed history of the New Wave in American SF, see Chapter 2 of this volume.

2

DARREN HARRIS-FAIN

Dangerous Visions: New Wave and Post–New Wave Science Fiction

In 1952, noted editor John W. Campbell Jr. said that science fiction (SF), "unlike other literatures, assumes that change is the natural order of things."[1] Yet in literary terms American SF remained rather conservative from the late 1920s through the 1950s, seemingly unaffected by the formal experimentation associated with literary and artistic modernism. If early magazine SF had tended to resemble nineteenth-century Romanticism, perhaps appropriately given the genre's roots in Gothic fiction, the later magazine writers favored a realist approach. Just as Virginia Woolf had marked H. G. Wells, a deeply realist writer despite his early "scientific romances," as old-fashioned in her essays,[2] so too any contemporary critic perusing the American SF magazines of the first half of the century would have noted how distinctly their techniques differed from those of their more respectable literary cousins.

A similar conservatism governed much of the content of American SF. Viewed as having a large adolescent readership, the field strived to avoid offending the parents who paid the weekly allowances of their younger readers. Consequently, despite the many magazine covers showing scantily clad damsels in distress, the stories themselves were as free of sex as an elementary primer. Romance was occasionally present, but never anything as salacious as the covers might suggest. Likewise, while the stories often contained abundant action and adventure, the violence was generally bloodless. For instance, in both Robert E. Howard's *Almuric* (1939) and Ray Bradbury's "The Creatures That Time Forgot" (1946), heroic male protagonists employ both intelligence and physical courage in pursuit of their goals, along the way meeting women with whom they fall in love. Both protagonists fight others, but the violence is not detailed or explicit, and there is no sexual content whatsoever.

Although Golden Age SF was typically fantastic in nature, its treatment tended toward the straightforward, and favored a transparent style as well. In part, the magazines from which so much American SF of the first half of the twentieth century emerged favored such clarity because the pulps and their digest-sized successors catered not, by and large, to college-educated elites but to teenagers and adults with high school diplomas. Moreover, it did not take long for American SF writers, editors, and fans to claim that, if science fiction was less "literary" than what they came to call "mainstream" or "mundane" fiction, this was actually a virtue that allowed them to focus on traditional storytelling and ideas. Nor did SF characters tend to be as fully developed and rounded as the protagonists in literary fiction. The point of reading magazine SF before the 1950s was not typically to gain a better understanding of the human psyche; beyond escapism and entertainment, it was to gain a better understanding of the human condition, of humanity's place in the larger universe and its possible futures.

Occasionally, of course, American SF writers before 1960 did experiment with form and content. Philip José Farmer's "The Lovers" (1953) sent shock waves through the field for its depiction of sexuality, while Alfred Bester's experiments with typography and Freudian psychology in *The Demolished Man* the same year, as well as his later antiheroic protagonist in *The Stars My Destination* (1958),[3] foreshadowed later importations of modernist and postmodernist concerns and techniques into SF. Additionally, authors such as Theodore Sturgeon and especially Ray Bradbury were singled out as science fiction stylists of note, in contrast to the undistinguished writing that even many within the field admitted as typical.

But it was only in the 1960s that things truly began to change. Publications such as *The Magazine of Fantasy and Science Fiction* and *Galaxy* became increasingly open to new writers and approaches, and even some older writers began to explore new directions. While such authors as Farmer, Bester, Sturgeon, and Bradbury suggested new directions for American SF, it was with the generation who began their careers in the 1950s and 1960s that this change became most apparent.

The New Wave and Its Detractors

If the New Wave could be said to have a distinct origin, that would be England in 1964, when Michael Moorcock became editor of the magazine *New Worlds* and immediately began publishing experimental writers such as Brian Aldiss and J. G. Ballard. The term itself is borrowed from French cinema, and like its use there refers to the work of unconventional artists, most of them young. Innovative American writers who found a home in *New Worlds* in the 1960s included Thomas M. Disch and Norman Spinrad, whose controversial novel *Bug Jack Barron* (1969), serialized in the magazine, led to parliamentary denunciations and commercial bans.

The movement soon crossed the Atlantic, promoted by important figures in the genre, chief among them Judith Merril, whose extensive work as both editor and critic championed the values that would soon define the era (and who is even credited by some with the coining of the term "New Wave" itself). Merril's influential edited anthology *England Swings SF* (1968), along with Harlan Ellison's *Dangerous Visions* (1967), would both popularize New Wave authors and help solidify the New Wave as the new face of SF in the United States, as well as galvanize the reputations of her favored writers.[4]

The New Wave differed from traditional SF in both content and style. In content, writers felt freer to depict sex and violence, as well as drug use. To be sure, even literary fiction did not enjoy total artistic freedom in the United States until 1957, when the Supreme Court in *Roth v. United States* revised the legal definition of obscenity. Yet American SF was slower than mainstream literary fiction to exploit these new freedoms until the New Wave. Just as Hollywood pushed the boundaries of a moribund Production Code and then briefly eschewed all boundaries whatsoever with thanks to the new ratings system, many New Wave writers explored content and language that had previously been taboo within the field.

It is nonetheless misleading to think that the New Wave was *entirely* novel. In his memoir *The Way the Future Was* (1978), Frederik Pohl relates Harlan Ellison's efforts to recruit Pohl for an anthology titled *Dangerous Visions* intended to blow the field open. Pohl, as a magazine editor, had bought several stories from Ellison, and Ellison wanted to return the favor:

> ...Then Harlan called me up:
> "Fred, I want a story from you for *Dangerous Visions*, the kind of story that no editor dares to print."
> "Harlan, I don't know what kind of story that is."
> "Shit, man! Of course you do. Like you've been printing all along in *Galaxy*!"[5]

Pohl did contribute to the volume, and in fact he was hardly new to pushing boundaries himself, not just as an editor but also as an author, as shown in his comic story "Day Million" (1966), a gender-bending tale of a genetically engineered couple who enjoy virtual sex with each other although light years apart. Similarly, Pohl would demonstrate a greater willingness to experiment with narrative form, as in novels such as *Gateway* (1977), than many other writers of his generation, even if his roots in Golden Age science fiction remained obvious.

In 1961 one of the major figures of the Golden Age, Robert A. Heinlein, published a novel that would become a virtual bible of the counterculture, *Stranger in a Strange Land*. With its treatment of religion, sexuality, and altered states of consciousness, along with its social satire, the novel resonated with 1960s youth, even if its author was often baffled by his admirers. Religion, politics, and altered consciousness also feature in Frank Herbert's *Dune* (1965), and their presence as well as the novel's ecological concerns won it fans. Like Heinlein's novel, *Dune* is a transitional text, combining older SF trends (alien worlds, the hero, the superman, psionic powers) with newer ones.

These books are also noteworthy for how they achieved mainstream popularity. Heinlein's cult success was the first SF novel on the *New York Times* best-seller list, and his later novels enjoyed a mass audience. Herbert also enjoyed robust sales within and beyond the traditional science fiction market niche, as did Isaac Asimov, who late in his career expanded the universes of his Foundation and Robot stories into a long, interconnected series of sequels and prequels whose disturbing complexity belies the apparent simplicity of the earliest entries. Of course not every writer of the period broke with the Golden Age, nor was acclaim universally directed at New Wave writers. In 1964, Clifford D. Simak, who began his SF career in 1938, received the Hugo Award for his late novel *Way Station* (1963), and in 1966 Heinlein more or less returned to form with *The Moon Is a Harsh Mistress* (even if that novel did depict political revolution and unconventional marital arrangements). Nor did every younger writer ride the New Wave; notable exceptions include Alexei Panshin with *Rite of Passage* (1968) and Larry Niven with *Ringworld* (1970). As the history of art and politics has long demonstrated, just because revolutions occur does not mean that everyone supports them.

New Maps of Hell

The addition of sex, violence, and strong language in the New Wave is dwarfed by a newly contentious politics. Science fiction has always possessed a strong cautionary streak, but American SF, especially coming from the magazine tradition, had long been dominated by a sense that science and technology would ultimately lead to a better, brighter future. World War II – with its attendant horrors of the Holocaust and nuclear warfare – ushered in greater skepticism toward the dreams of mastery so often found in Golden Age SF. (The beginnings of this shift can already be felt in the name Kinglsey Amis chooses for his 1958 survey of the field of science fiction: *New Maps of Hell*.) The growing pessimism about humanity's present and future that permeated the New Wave scandalized many in the field. Reflecting Cold War tensions and contemporary ecological concerns, the New Wave, as Damien Broderick puts it, "peel[ed] open the ideological myth of supreme scientific competence and galactic manifest destiny."[6] Many in American SF, especially older readers, writers, and editors, denounced the New Wave as a betrayal of SF's core values, as did Lester del Rey in his history of the genre.[7] It should not be surprising that, in the late 1960s, real-world politics came to the fore in SF more prominently than ever before, represented most clearly in the June 1968 issue of *Galaxy*, which included two full-page ads: one with the names of SF writers who supported the war in Vietnam, the other with the names of those opposing it.

The differing political positions generally aligned with the debate in SF between optimistic and pessimistic views of humanity, its current condition, and its future prospects. As an example of such pessimism (albeit tempered with hope), consider three key stories by Ellison: "'Repent, Harlequin!' Said the Ticktockman" (1965), "I Have No Mouth, and I Must Scream" (1967), and "A Boy and His Dog" (1969). "Repent" depicts a dystopian future in which time is strictly regulated by a totalitarian government bent on efficiency and controlling its citizens, whose workings are disrupted by a colorful trickster. Although the Harlequin is quashed in much the same way as Winston Smith in George Orwell's *Nineteen Eighty-Four* (1949), to which the story alludes, his civil disobedience (the story also quotes Henry David Thoreau's classic essay on the subject) does have an effect. The central protagonist of "I Have No Mouth, and I Must Scream" also suffers for opposing a tyrannical force – in this case an earth-consuming, sentient supercomputer that tortures the five people it has preserved as perverse playthings. The computer, readers learn, is an amalgamation of the computers the superpowers constructed to wage their wars, and thus Ellison's story critiques the military-industrial complex in much the same way that "Repent" critiques a conformist consumer society. Both humanity's bellicose impulses and social conformity are the target of "A Boy and His Dog," set in a bleak postapocalyptic world of anarchy and sterility. Ellison's stories feature some of the stylistic experimentation commonly associated with the New Wave. "Repent" fragments the story's chronology, and along with its allusions, it employs a conversational style different from most SF before it – a style also found in Pohl's "Day Million." The central protagonist in "I Have No Mouth, and I Must Scream" is a classic unreliable narrator, and the narrator of "A Boy and His Dog" is also suspect because of his youth and ignorance.

It is hardly surprising that Ellison would be the one to propose a groundbreaking anthology of daring new work that challenged old restrictions and took advantage of new liberties, even if he (like many others) eschewed the designation "New Wave." *Dangerous Visions* (1967), featuring thirty-two original stories by both newcomers and veterans, was one of the most widely discussed books in SF's history, and also launched the publishing phenomenon of the original anthology, which remains popular in SF. Its sequel, *Again, Dangerous Visions* (1972), was even more ambitious, featuring nearly fifty individual pieces; a second sequel, *The Last Dangerous Visions*, was contracted but has never appeared.

Ellison also experimented with postmodernist techniques such as metafiction, particularly in his 1974 story "The Deathbird," whose self-reflexive elements rival those in a novel such as Donald Barthelme's *Snow White* (1967). Ellison was not alone in his experimentation with postmodern conventions – indeed, in many ways the conventions and concerns of postmodernism considerably blurred the distinctions between the world of the mainstream literary narrative and SF, as exemplified in what we might view today as the slipstream postmodernism of Thomas Pynchon, Walker Percy, and others, on the one hand, and the more obviously postmodern experiments of SF authors such as Samuel Delany, James Tiptree (Alice Sheldon), Philip K. Dick, and Ursula Le Guin on the other.

A key figure in this blurry middle ground is Kurt Vonnegut, whose story "The Big Space Fuck" appears in *Again, Dangerous Visions*. Having begun his career with SF stories and two novels in the 1950s, he took his satiric bent in a strongly postmodernist direction with *Cat's Cradle* (1963) and especially *Slaughterhouse-Five* (1969). *Cat's Cradle* draws on the absurdism and black humor typical of much postmodernist writing in its bitter satire of both religion and the military-industrial-academic complex, while the fiercely antiwar *Slaughterhouse-Five* employs metafiction and chronological fragmentation in depicting a man who becomes "unstuck in time," who meets a paperback SF writer named Kilgore Trout, and who believes he has been abducted by aliens. With this novel Vonnegut achieved literary fame and fortune, and he distanced himself from SF because of the critical disdain it still received and his desire to explore other subjects. However, in his 1965 novel *God Bless You, Mr. Rosewater*, the title character affectionately addresses a group of SF writers, saying they're the only ones who are truly discussing humanity's current challenges – and Vonnegut himself would ultimately return to SF in late works like *Galápagos* (1985) and *Timequake* (1997).

Although Kilgore Trout may have been inspired initially by Vonnegut's friend Theodore Sturgeon, Trout's work as described in chapter 5 of *Slaughterhouse-Five* – "His prose was frightful. Only his ideas were good" – is closer to that of their mutual contemporary Philip K. Dick. An incredibly imaginative writer, and famously prolific, Dick was not always the most accomplished stylist or skilled plotter, which perhaps prevented him from achieving the more mainstream success Vonnegut enjoyed. However, Dick's ideas alone assured him an audience, and in the second half of the twentieth century he became, along with Ursula K. Le Guin, the American SF writer most studied by literary critics, with his work adapted for motion pictures more than any other author in the field.

In the 1960s Dick published two major novels alongside many other intriguing ones. *The Man in the High Castle* (1962) is an alternate history in which the Axis powers win World War II and divide North America between them. A novel within the novel presents a utopian world in which the Axis powers lost – yet this alternate history within the alternate history does not quite depict our own history either, creating multiple layers of interpretation that are a pleasure to untangle. What makes Dick's novel distinctive is not only its startling depiction of an alternate world but its ambitious investigation into gnostic epistemology, a favorite Dickian theme. The true nature of reality is also a major consideration in *Do Androids Dream of Electric Sheep?* (1969), parts of which were used for the 1982 film *Blade Runner*. In the novel humanity has created lifelike artificial animals to replace species it has killed, and has even created androids who so resemble people that the difference is nearly impossible to discern. "What is real?" is obviously an important question here, but just as crucial is "What does it mean to be human?" Dick continued to pursue these questions across his career, even as his religious obsessions, visionary experiences, and experimentation with drugs led him to increasingly outré imaginings in the 1970s. His personal journals from this late period, which seek to understand his mystical experiences, have recently been collected in *The Exegesis of Philip K. Dick* (2011), while the ongoing rediscovery of his fiction by a new generation of scholars and the recent Library of America reprinting of his work have finally given Dick the imprimatur of literary success he never achieved while alive.[8]

Gender, Race, Politics, and Religion in the New Wave

Samuel R. Delany, another self-conscious stylist open to new forms and content in SF, has similarly since been recognized as a major figure in American literature. His first novel, *The Jewels of Aptor* (1962), initiates his career-long re-envisioning of gender and sexuality, including desexed astronauts in "Aye, and Gomorrah" (1967), first published in *Dangerous Visions*; people with three sexes in *The Einstein Intersection* (1967); and a sex-changing protagonist in *Trouble on Triton: An Ambiguous Heterotopia* (1976).[9] The latter is a fascinating depiction of a futuristic society of immense social and cultural variety, and it is worth noting how, as a gay African-American writer, Delany himself was emblematic of how American SF, long mostly the province of straight white males, was slowly becoming more diverse. Delany would prove to be an intersectional figure in the history of the genre in another sense as well; his literary criticism has been very influential in the academic subdiscipline of SF studies in such collections as *The Jewel-Hinged Jaw* (1977) and *Starboard Wine* (1984).

The new politics of gender and sexuality were also central to the novel that pushed Ursula K. Le Guin from the margins of the field to its center, *The Left Hand of Darkness* (1969), propelled as much by the quality of her prose as by her serious treatment of imaginative ideas. Its protagonist, Genly Ai, is a man from Earth sent as an envoy to an alien world where, for most of the year, the inhabitants are neither male nor female but instead strike Genly as possessing characteristics of both. Moreover, when in heat (referred to as a state of "kemmer" in the novel) they can become either. The novel's interest in byzantine political intrigues would be extended in her influential novel *The Dispossessed* (1974), whose experimental narrative structure contrasts a poor but egalitarian world governed by anarchist principles with a prosperous world with immense inequalities. Le Guin, like Delany, was eagerly taken up by academics interested in the genre as proof of SF's worthiness for scholarly investigation; the seventh issue of the new journal *Science Fiction Studies* would be devoted solely to her work, with articles by Darko Suvin, Fredric Jameson, and Le Guin herself.

Other writers also used SF to address the concerns of second-wave feminism. In 1972 Joanna Russ published a story titled "When It Changed" in *Again, Dangerous Visions*, in which a plague on a colonized planet kills all the men, leaving the surviving women to figure out how to reproduce without them. Generations later, male astronauts arrive, only to discover that the planet's all-female society does not need them. The men assert that sexual equality has finally been achieved on Earth, but their patriarchal condescension suggests otherwise. In contrast, not only is Russ's Whileaway egalitarian, but traditional gender roles have vanished. Russ returned to this world with *The Female Man* (1975), a postmodern novel in which four plot strands intertwine and interrelate, involving Joanna, an academic in contemporary America; Jeannine, a librarian in an alternate America where the Great Depression never ended; Jael, a warrior from a future in which the battle of the sexes has become literal; and Janet of Whileaway, who visits Joanna's world. Using various experimental techniques, including hostile "reviews" of the novel anticipating some of the criticism it would receive for its critique of gender politics, Russ encourages readers to question engrained notions of sex and gender.

A different type of gender play can be found in the career of James Tiptree, Jr. Because of fan conventions, which many writers attend, SF readers and writers have long experienced a close relationship. This makes private writers like Tiptree even more enigmatic, and until the author's identity was revealed in 1977, readers feverishly speculated as to who Tiptree actually was. They also tended to assume Tiptree was a man – Robert Silverberg even argued as much, based on what he considered Tiptree's masculine style – but in fact the mysterious author was Alice Sheldon, who drew on her earlier career with the Central Intelligence Agency to create an authorial persona that for years successfully hid both her identity and her gender. In retrospect, given her interest in women's points of view and her critique of masculine behavior in stories such as "The Women Men Don't See" (1973), "Houston, Houston, Do You Read?" (1976), and "The Screwfly Solution" (1977), readers came to appreciate Tiptree's ability to explore gender issues from an unusual perspective: that of a woman who wrote as a man. Since 1991, the Tiptree Award has been given to both male and female science fiction and fantasy authors whose works question conventional understandings of gender.

Similarly, in *Woman on the Edge of Time* (1976), Marge Piercy shows readers how the world could become either better or worse than the present through the story of a woman who is granted glimpses of both an egalitarian ecotopia and a nightmarish techno-dystopian future. Another example of feminist SF is Suzette Haden Elgin's *Native Tongue* (1984), which presents a dystopian future where women have been deprived of their rights – a concept similar to the premise of *The Handmaid's Tale* (1985) by Canadian author Margaret Atwood.[10] In Elgin's novel, female linguists, whose skills have been employed in communicating with aliens, create a secret language as a means of resisting patriarchal power. Resistance takes a different form in Sheri S. Tepper's *The Gate to Women's Country* (1988) – in this case, the rebuilding of society along gender lines following nuclear war, with women in charge and men relegated to soldiers and servants.

Tepper's novel explicitly critiques male aggression, a topic both male and female New Wave writers often examined in the context of the Vietnam War. Joe Haldeman's *The Forever War* (1974) depicts a future war in which humanity fights an alien race over vast distances, with the soldiers, traveling light years at great speeds, experiencing relativistic effects such that years and even centuries pass on Earth during their tours of duty. When they return home, "home" is no longer recognizable as the world they thought they were defending, analogous to the experiences of those who served in Vietnam, as Haldeman himself did as a combat engineer. While the novel superficially resembles Heinlein's *Starship Troopers* (1959), its gritty depiction of war's horrors and of soldiers serving a misunderstood cause contrasts with Heinlein's militarism. Although the novels' treatment of gender has received less attention, these also differ. Both present women in combat, but Heinlein depicts female soldiers as morally superior to men, whereas Haldeman's vision is more purely egalitarian.

Another implicit critique of the Vietnam conflict can be found in Le Guin's *The Word for World Is Forest* (1976). Here, human colonists on an alien world demonstrate a reckless disregard for the planet's indigenous populations, aided especially by the military. The novella also delves into ecological concerns and the evils of colonialism. Le Guin's treatment of these matters is heavily influenced by her background – her father was a noted anthropologist – and this influence is also apparent in her experimental 1985 novel *Always Coming Home*, an assemblage of multiple texts describing a postindustrial tribal culture. Like several of her contemporaries, she too addresses gender roles and the question of equality within the context of her elaborate world building.

The End of the New Wave and the Fragmentation of Science Fiction

While Haldeman and Le Guin presented less than positive depictions of the military in the 1970s, some writers a decade later would move in a different direction, perhaps reflecting the conservative turn the country took in the Reagan-Bush era. While SF writers have always told stories involving military forces, the presence of an increasing number of such works led to the recognition of "military science fiction" as a subgenre. Examples include David Drake's Hammer series starting in 1979 and Lois McMaster Bujold's Vorkosigan series beginning in 1986, as well as the most discussed SF novel with a military theme of the 1980s, Orson Scott Card's *Ender's Game* (1985). As in *The Forever War*, in *Ender's Game* humanity is fighting a war with an implacable alien race, but here a child genius is used for the military's purposes. In the process, Card investigates serious moral issues about the conduct of war and the exploitation of children for society's purposes.

As a kind of reflection of the era's "Star Wars" space-based militarization of America during its post-1970s conservative "rebirth," the war-themed SF novels of the 1980s like *Ender's Game* mark a kind of shift from the darker moral wranglings of the 1970s-era fictions of Haldeman and Le Guin and even, going back to the late 1960s, a work such as *The Moon Is a Harsh Mistress* by Heinlein. But this was no return to the sentiments of the Golden Age. As the New Wave era wound down in the wake of new directions in SF such as cyberpunk and, in the 1990s, steampunk, some of the key figures in American SF produced some of the movement's most complicated treatments of human morality – including treatments of race, class, gender, religion, and social justice – and, consequently, some of the most notable texts in the American SF tradition.

Other writers rose to prominence during this time, perhaps most notably Octavia E. Butler, at once the most prominent African-American woman in the history of the field and the post–New Wave author of SF most frequently taken up by scholars. In both her stories and her novels, characters grapple with complex ethical dilemmas – often, as in "Bloodchild" (1984) and her Xenogenesis trilogy (1987–9), at the intersection of race, gender, and alien contact. Inspiring the generation of black and women writers that followed, Butler's importance in the field of contemporary SF is undeniable; the MLA International Bibliography records countless articles devoted to her work, while a Butler bibliography gathering interviews and academic criticism for a 2006 issue of *Utopian Studies* (current only to 2006) is twenty pages long.[11]

Kim Stanley Robinson also emerged as an important writer during this post–New Wave period, beginning with a trilogy envisioning different futures for southern California that reflected environmentalist concerns, and then with his Mars trilogy (1992–6), a complex depiction of humanity's conquest of the red planet that encompasses science and technology, politics and culture. This anticapitalist interest in environmentalism and social justice runs across Robinson's career; still the most unapologetically utopian voice in contemporary science fiction, Robinson has continued to call for science-informed political change in the face of oncoming ecological catastrophe in such novels as the Science in the Capital trilogy (2004–7), *Galileo's Dream* (2009), and *2312* (2012).

With his novelette "The Lucky Strike" (1984) Robinson also explored alternate history, showing how the world might have been changed had the United States not dropped the atomic bomb on Hiroshima. In *The Years of Rice and Salt* (2002) Robinson considers an alternative hypothetical: What if the Black Death had killed off 99 percent of Europe's population in the fourteenth century, preventing the Native American genocide and leaving Europe an open space for colonization by Islamic and Chinese empires? Such works reflect a trend in the field; alternate histories in general grew in popularity during the 1980s and after, with some authors such as Harry Turtledove making them a specialty. Some writers explored historical subjects in other ways – either through traditional time travel, as in Butler's *Kindred* (1979) and Connie Willis's stories and novels about time-traveling historians, or through works depicting the science fictional in historical terms, as in Russ's "Souls" (1982).

And yet the future remained the chief concern of SF, and the growing prominence of computers led to the increasing treatment of this trope. Vernor Vinge's "True Names" (1981) anticipates our Internet world, but it was William Gibson's *Neuromancer* (1984) that truly launched the concept known as cyberspace and the movement known as cyberpunk, whose chief proponent, Bruce Sterling, edited *Mirrorshades: The Cyberpunk Anthology* (1986). A coinage drawn from both cybernetics and from punk music and fashion, it like the New Wave was controversial, with advocates hailing it as the future of SF and detractors decrying its world-weary cynicism. The cyberpunk movement, like the New Wave, framed itself as a revolutionary break with the past – only this time it was the orthodoxies of the New Wave itself that were being rebelled against.

But by this time American SF had become so diverse that, if one ignored cyberpunk, there were many other choices. In contrast to SF focusing more on social or psychological concerns, "hard science fiction" was rooted in the hard sciences. Authors such as Niven, Greg Bear, and David Brin mixed a solid grasp of science with accomplished storytelling. Nor were their fictions devoid of literary content, as one might often find among the early magazine writers. For instance, Gregory Benford's *Timescape* (1980) deals with difficult concepts in physics and yet at times possesses Faulknerian overtones.

One could say, then, that even if the experimentalism of the New Wave had passed, it had changed the field irrevocably by elevating the level of literary discourse, even among those who saw themselves as hard science storytellers. Writers emerged on the scene whose literary craftsmanship was equal to anything in the mainstream. Among them were John Crowley with *Engine Summer* (1979); Gene Wolfe with his subtle, allusive *Book of the New Sun* (1980–3); Dan Simmons with his Keats-inspired novels of the late 1980s and the 1990s; and Karen Joy Fowler with her enigmatic, ambiguous *Sarah Canary* (1991). Nor was literary sophistication limited to the novel, as demonstrated by stories such as John Kessel's postmodern "Buffalo" (1991), James Patrick Kelly's "Think Like a Dinosaur" (1995), and Fowler's "Standing Room Only" (1997), whose science fiction trope is apparent only on close reading. Although the magazines had declined from their heyday, at the same time, unlike with many other forms of fiction, the SF magazines continued to offer a paying market for short stories, as did original anthologies, and noteworthy short stories continued to appear.

Other forms of SF that emerged in an increasingly diverse market included those that addressed genetic engineering and the idea of transhumanism, as in Michael Swanwick's *Vacuum Flowers* (1987); science fiction with non-Western settings, as in Mike Resnick's "Kirinyaga" (1988) and Maureen McHugh's *China Mountain Zhang* (1992); and the revival of space opera, as in Vinge's *A Fire upon the Deep* (1992) and *A Deepness in the Sky* (1999) along with series by Brin, Bujold, and C. J. Cherryh. Another popular series, Anne McCaffrey's Pern novels, cannily incorporated fantasy scenarios into a science fiction setting, attracting both SF fans (especially women, long overlooked in a field dominated for much of its history by men) as well as the increasing number of fantasy enthusiasts in the 1970s and beyond. Meanwhile, tie-in novels related to popular SF media productions, especially *Star Trek* and *Star Wars*, sold thousands of copies to their respective fans – far more, perhaps, than even SF's most recognized and acclaimed writers. As has often been the case throughout the history of American SF, as the end of the century drew nearer, various parties expressed the concern that the field had exhausted every possible idea and story type – but the continued proliferation of new writers and ideas suggested that it had not yet finished exploring the future, and still had its own future ahead of it.

NOTES

1 John W. Campbell Jr., introduction, *The Astounding Science Fiction Anthology* (New York: Simon & Schuster, 1952), xiii.

2 In particular "Modern Novels" (1919) and its revised version, "Modern Fiction" (1925); "Mr Bennett and Mrs Brown" (1923); and "Character in Fiction" (1924).

3 First published in Great Britain in 1956 as *Tiger! Tiger!*

4 Merril's influence on the field, and in particular her interest in science fiction's potential for literary achievement, is further developed in Rob Latham's contribution to this volume, "American Slipstream."

5 Frederik Pohl, *The Way the Future Was: A Memoir* (New York: Ballantine-Del Rey, 1978), 298.

6 Damien Broderick, "New Wave and Backwash: 1960–1980," *The Cambridge Companion to Science Fiction*, edited by Edward James and Farah Mendlesohn (Cambridge: Cambridge University Press, 2003), 52.

7 Lester del Rey, *The World of Science Fiction, 1926–1976: The History of a Subculture* (New York: Ballantine, 1979).

8 Dick's relationship with the literary mainstream both before and after his death is also taken up by Latham's chapter.

9 Originally published as *Triton*. The subtitle alludes to Le Guin's 1974 novel *The Dispossessed: An Ambiguous Utopia.*

10 Both novels could be considered extrapolations of negative responses to the gains of Second Wave feminism, documented in Susan Faludi's *Backlash: The Undeclared War against American Women* (1991).

11 Butler's influence on the field of science fiction can also be felt in her frequent appearances in this volume; different aspects of her work are taken up at length in chapters 4, 5, 6, 13, and 15.

3

DAVID M. HIGGINS

American Science Fiction after 9/11

By the closing years of the twentieth century, after the climax of the Cold War, American science fiction reflected a prevalent sense that typical Western subjects were essentially victims of their own society and culture, colonized by vast networks of artificial simulacra, justified in their desire to break through to something more authentic (and recover the privilege of threatened masculine agency in the process). In the late 1990s, popular science fiction was dominated by awakening-from-simulacrum stories – exemplified by films like *The Matrix* (1999), *Dark City* (1998), and *The Truman Show* (1998) – which all presented narratives (with predecessors reaching back to Philip K. Dick's *Time Out of Joint* [1959] and beyond) in which the main characters found themselves trapped within a false or simulated world striving to gain access to some more real or authentic exterior.[1] Everyday life, in these narratives, was often portrayed as a kind of emasculating ensnarement within post-Fordist systems of command and control. Protagonists like Neo from *The Matrix* or Tyler Durden from *Fight Club* struggled against their externally imposed roles within boring and lifeless administrative white-collar jobs focused on keeping the late capitalist system running. There was a general sense in these films and stories that life had somehow become false or artificial, and science fiction literalized the metaphor of being trapped in an alienating system designed to keep one docile, numb, and plugged into an endless cycle of late capitalist production and consumption.

When 9/11 occurred, the tendency to use science fiction to portray life under late capitalism as deadening entrapment within enervating systems of control was radically transformed within popular SF imaginings. As Slavoj Žižek notes, the mythologized hard kernel of the real exterior to Western commodity culture was experienced directly when terrorists attacked the Pentagon and the World Trade Center towers.[2] Suddenly the seeming-outside of the late capitalist milieu came crashing inward, and this catastrophe itself was immediately commodified and propagated as consumer spectacle. Americans were terrified by the disaster of 9/11, yet this crisis intensified an already existing tendency within late capitalism to foster an environment of perpetual emergency in order to deploy fluid economic and military interventions in order to reinforce and protect the advantages enjoyed by the global capitalist elite.[3]

In the aftermath of 9/11, the yearning for an exterior authenticity in the face of enervating simulacra (reflected in films like *The Matrix*) is replaced by a simultaneous horror and fascination with the reality-effect of mediated disaster spectacles, and simulations (particularly simulated battles against terrorist threats in video games) become a widespread feature of social totality. American fantasy, as reflected in science fiction, moves away from defining the neoliberal subject as a victim of the commodity system in part because a greater and more productive victimization (the self under attack by terrorist threats) takes center stage, and with an omnipresent virtual enemy (the ever-shifting terrorist) a Cold War–style conflict between America and an external enemy again becomes possible. The location and identity of this enemy, however, is always radically uncertain, and in the context of ubiquitous globalizing information and technology advancements directed by the needs of late capitalism, distinctions between inside and outside seem to evaporate as space seemingly collapses into perpetual locality and time seemingly collapses into perpetual immediacy.

In short, two major trends characterize American SF after 9/11: First, the trope of the alien encounter (or alien invasion) is reformulated and redeployed during this period to address an environment of spectacular and indeterminate omnicrisis that can imaginatively encompass threats ranging from terrorism and biological attacks to natural disasters such as Hurricane Katrina. New iterations of the alien invasion narrative also enable SF to interrogate contemporary issues such as military intervention, surveillance, extraordinary rendition, and torture. Second, an intensification of technoscientific advancement and neoliberal capitalist expansion leads to a pervasive experience in the West during this time that many Americans (and others) are themselves living in a science fictional milieu. Science fiction therefore bleeds out of its traditional genre confines into nearly every aspect of life, and SF itself begins to register the difficulty of imagining *any* "outside" to the current regime of technoscientific and economic totality.

Alien Invasions

One of the most notable trends in American SF since 9/11 is the large-scale reemergence of the alien invasion or reverse colonization narrative. In 2005, for example, all three major networks released primetime sci-fi shows (NBC's *Surface*, CBS's *Threshold*, and ABC's *Invasion*) that focused on Earth as a target for alien attacks. Although the early seasons of *Star Trek: Enterprise* (2001–5) focus on exploration, at the beginning of season three, Earth experiences a catastrophic 9/11-style alien attack from the Xindi that transforms the show into an invasion-response narrative. These examples were overshadowed by even more successful invasion TV shows such as *Battlestar Galactica* (2003–9), *Falling Skies* (2011–), and *Fringe* (2008–13).

In science fiction cinema, there was a pronounced return to the alien invasion blockbuster, often in the form of remakes of 1950s alien invasion films. A short list of these films includes *Signs* (2002), *Alien Trespass* (2009), Steven Spielberg's *War of the Worlds* (2005), Scott Derrickson's remake of *The Day the Earth Stood Still* (2008), and a contemporary adaptation of *Invasion of the Body Snatchers* called *The Invasion* (2007). Other alien invasion films also include *The Mist* (2007), *Cloverfield* (2008), *Oblivion* (2013), *Man of Steel* (2013), *Pacific Rim* (2013), and *The Avengers* (2012). Marvel's comic universe was also invaded by shapeshifting alien Skrulls during *Secret Invasion* (2008–9), and DC launched its *New 52* line with a catastrophic invasion from the planet Apocalypse that united the new Justice League for the first time. After finishing her popular *Twilight* novels, Stephanie Meyer published her alien invasion narrative *The Host* in 2008, and this was adapted into a film in 2013. The popular video game series *Mass Effect* (2007–12) centers on the aggression of an ancient alien race called the Reapers, while countless other video games, such as *XCOM: Enemy Unknown* (2012) and *The Bureau: XCOM Declassified* (2013) also focus on alien invasions. If we extend our sense of the invasive alien to include viruses and infections, a wide variety of zombie franchises – such as *The Walking Dead*, *Resident Evil*, and Max Brooks' *World War Z* stories – can also be included in this list of invasion narratives.

In short, and unsurprisingly, American science fiction was fascinated with the traumatic spectacle of invasion in the years following 9/11. This is not to say that alien invasion stories weren't also present in the 1990s. *Independence Day* (1996), *The X-Files* (1993–2002), and *Men in Black* (1997) all focused on alien threats in the pre-9/11 context. The difference, however, is that the trope of alien invasion was appropriated in the post-9/11 period to directly address anxieties concerning terrorism, terrorist attacks, and America's war on terror, and aliens often functioned as direct allegories for terrorists. Indeed, given that the counterterrorism-action genre often relies on science fictional surveillance and security technologies, one might also reasonably include television shows like *24* (2001–10) and films such as *Skyfall* (2012) within the SF alien-as-terrorist genre as well.

Part of what is striking about post-9/11 alien invasion narratives is that the alien is often incomprehensibly difficult to understand. In *Cloverfield*

(2008), for example, a Godzilla-style alien monster attacks New York, and its origins and motivations are never revealed. This basic incomprehensibility of the alien invader reflects the challenges involved in understanding the complex causes of terrorism, and the portrayal of the alien invader as an absolute force of mindless hostility renders the alien/terrorist as an inhuman, monstrous enemy, more like a hostile force of nature than a politically motivated agent. Indeed, natural disasters are themselves reformulated as alien attacks after Hurricane Katrina in 2005; aliens create a cataclysmic tsunami to destroy Puerto Rico in *Surface,* and aquatic aliens invade Florida during a hurricane in *Invasion.* In a post-9/11 environment defined by a perpetual state of shifting emergency, terrorists, mindless alien monsters, and natural disasters often become imaginatively synonymous threats. Rather than battling an enemy with alternative but comprehensible motivations, SF protagonists wage war against the personified experience of terror itself. This is particularly true in superhero fictions like *Batman Begins* (2005), where the Scarecrow (a villain who uses drugs to cause hallucinogenic fear) functions as a literal agent of terror, and also in Geoff Johns' run on the relaunch of *Green Lantern* (2004–13), which resurrects the totalitarian antihero Hal Jordan (who had previously died trying to remake the universe in his own image) to wage unending police actions against the fear-wielding Sinestro Corps.

As Robert A. Saunders observes, post-9/11 zombie narratives often represent the threat of terrorism in much the same way as aliens or natural disasters.[4] Alongside incomprehensible aliens and other dangers, however, zombies after 9/11 are often stripped of their particular reference to specific cultural anxieties as they grow to represent the generalized threat of perpetual crisis in a broader sense. Certain specific zombie films like *World War Z* (2013) reflect fears of ecological catastrophe or out-of-control biomedical experimentation, but the prevalence of the zombie threat more generally invokes what Michael Hardt and Antonio Negri refer to as "omnicrisis" – a permanent state of exception and the corresponding continual fear of invasion (from without and/or within) that enables global elites to deploy emergency powers in the name of a presumed greater good.[5] In many zombie narratives, such as the *Resident Evil* films (2002–12), the question of what has caused the zombie outbreak (and what exactly the zombies represent) is dramatically overshadowed by the imperative to respond and survive; zombies are a ubiquitous danger, and their status as absolute abject monsters opens the doorway for spectacular retributive violence uncorrupted by critical consideration or ethical remorse.

Some zombie narratives, like AMC's *The Walking Dead* (2010–), utilize the threat of catastrophe in order to attempt to dramatize a reconstitution of the nuclear family and threatened paternal authority. In the face of overwhelming outside danger, families must come together, and estranged parents can (or should) reconcile their differences under paternal guidance for the sake of protecting their children. This story is echoed throughout post-911 invasion stories, particularly in 24, in Steven Spielberg's *War of the Worlds*, and also in almost every SF television show produced by J. J. Abrams. In *Alias* (2001–6), Sydney Bristow is constantly pressured under emergency circumstances to reconcile with her estranged father figures (Jack Bristow and Arvin Sloane); in *Lost* (2004–10), broken families are always under pressure to reform, and John Locke's central story centers on whether he should (or should not) trust his biological and metaphysical fathers; in *Fringe* (2008–13), Peter Bishop's complicated relationships with the multiple versions of his father (Walter Bishop) are generally resolved through coming together in the face of emergency circumstances. Interestingly, attempts to reconstitute oedipal family bonds in the face of crisis often fail spectacularly in post-9/11 invasion stories: Jack Bauer from 24, for example, is always motivated to rescue estranged family members who often die or dramatically betray him. In such instances, the oedipal family bond becomes yet another site of perpetual omnicrisis, a structure constantly under attack from without and within, and the affective pleasure offered by the narrative of such attacks is often the male protagonist's unrestricted license to undertake extraordinary measures to defend the family rather than a successful harmonious reestablishment of secure familial relations.

American men are often represented as victims in post-9/11 alien invasion narratives, and part of what's interesting about the shift in imperial ideology that occurs after 9/11 is that America as a whole is able to occupy the subject position of the victim in order to draw on a kind of sacred power of reactionary violence in the service of the expansion of its global advantage. This was also true during the Cold War, when the United States was able to imagine itself as under attack from Soviet forces and acting to defend and liberate Third World countries in the name of their own supposed freedom to operate free market economies. Yet even during this time, America was never able to imagine itself as the absolute victim (and thus the bearer of absolute moral authority) in the way that became available in the aftermath of 9/11.

Occupying the position of the victim enables America to imaginatively decolonize its own imperial privilege, and this is observable in the way that American subjects are invited to self-identify in fantastic narratives as members of developing or colonized groups who are striving to liberate and expand their own agency. In both the *Mass Effect* trilogy and in *Star Trek: Enterprise*, for example, humans (embodied by American cultural norms) are framed as members of a disadvantaged species striving to achieve greater privilege in galactic civilization. In James Cameron's *Avatar* (2009), humans as a whole may represent dominant corporate forces exploiting developing worlds, but viewers are invited to identify with a hero (Jake Sully) who joins the Na'vi (literally wearing their skin) in order to fight a battle for decolonization. *The Hunger Games* trilogy similarly invites readers and viewers to position themselves in identification with subaltern subjects who have been dominated and exploited by a corrupt Capitol and who must ultimately fight an anticolonial battle of liberation against oppressive forces. Occupying the position of the colonized subject enables the protagonist in such stories to self-identify as a kind of fantastical hyper-victim entitled to absolute revenge in the face of external oppression: Captain Archer gets his hands dirty in the battle against the Xindi, Shepard has the option to make dark choices in his fight against the Reapers, Jake Sully and the Na'vi wage a dramatic revolution against Earth's Resources Development Administration, and the traumas experienced by Katniss Everdeen emotionally justify nearly any revenge she might wish to exact from President Snow.

In this imaginative environment, complex ethical questions about the responsibilities associated with one's own privilege and agency are subsumed in the face of the overwhelming need to respond to crisis. *Star Trek Into Darkness* (2013), for example, begins with a scene that invokes classic debates around the Federation's Prime Directive to avoid intervention in the development of non-spacefaring species. Soon, however, just as with the Xindi attack in *Enterprise*, the advent of a devastating terrorist offensive obviates the need for ethical analysis and demands instead an immediate response. "I don't know what I'm supposed to do," Kirk says when Spock questions the ethical basis of his counterterrorism strategies, "I just know what I *can* do." In the face of an alien invasion, a zombie attack, a natural disaster, or any other sort of threat, the imperative for immediate counteraction overshadows other considerations, and self-identification as a victim opens the doorway to an unlimited range of reactionary responses. Americans are invited to feel good about knowing what *can* be done in response to crises, and the question of what *should* be done is often rendered inconsequential.

Enrica Picarelli and M. Carmen Gomez-Galisteo propose that *The X-Files* may have captured the zeitgeist of the 1990s in its particular flavor of paranoia regarding alien invasion; in this series, mastery over one's own body and mind are under constant threat of subversion from alien forces often acting in concert with shadowy government forces.[6] *The X-Files* therefore reflects a larger postwar American trend Timothy Melley calls "agency panic," or an "intense anxiety about an apparent loss of autonomy or self-control – the conviction that one's actions are being controlled by someone else, that one has been 'constructed' by powerful external agents."[7] Alien invasion stories after 9/11 often (but not always) reflect similar forms of agency panic, yet negative attitudes concerning government authority become more complex; shadowy government agencies are typically framed as vital and necessary, for example, in the battles against external intrusions (cf. *Threshold*, 24, *Fringe*, *The Avengers*), and authoritarian military and government power are portrayed as indispensable in the face of potential threats.

One unusual transformation that occurs, however, is an exploration (rather than paranoid rejection) of the precarious nature of human subjectivity; in many post-9/11 narratives, the radical contingency of the self becomes a commonplace narrative element. In *Battlestar Galactica* (2003–9), for example, a story that begins from the premise of invasion and infiltration quickly develops into a much more radical challenge to the idea that clear boundaries exist between humans and their alien antagonists. Several human characters in *BSG* discover that they have actually always-already been Cylons without their own knowledge, and rather than framing this revelation as abjectly horrific (as *The X-Files* might have), the series interrogates the basic differentiation between humans and Cylons, opening the space for radically shifting modes of identification and exploring the possibility that the self/other binary that structures the show's central conflict may be artificially constituted, and therefore able to be transcended.

The Contemporary Novum

More than a decade after the events of 9/11, American science fiction again turns its attention to *The Matrix*, but not in the medium of SF film. One of the opening pages of the April 2014 issue of *National Geographic* features an advertisement for the Kia K900 that showcases the car on a white background as Morpheus (Lawrence Fishburne) gestures inexplicably toward it. This magazine ad was one aspect of a larger Kia campaign for the K900, including the 2014 Super Bowl commercial "The Truth," in which Morpheus invites a pair of car owners to choose between the "blue key" of what they have previously considered to be luxury and the "red key" of the more radical unexpected luxury of the K900. Once they have chosen the red key, the male driver is so impressed with the car that he says, "this is unreal," to which Morpheus replies, "no, it's *very* real," before bursting into operatic song in order to demonstrate the unreal *reality* of the luxury the K900 has to offer – an extreme luxury that ultimately destroys several city blocks in a *Matrix*-style catastrophe of computer-generated explosions as the car accelerates toward the horizon.

The Matrix's Agent Smith (Hugo Weaving) also appears in a 2013 commercial advertising GE's medical hardware and software technologies. The commercial's message proclaims that "brilliant machines are transforming the way we work," and rather than revealing a fear of the post-Fordist technosocial organization of everyday life (as the original films did), the advertisement celebrates an increasingly technologized approach to human health care mediated by intelligent computers. Gone is the fear that robots will subjugate humans and turn them into living batteries; now Agent Smith is an unironic representative of the technoscientific future emerging thanks to progressive corporate research and advancement.

In both cases, the commercials deploy references to *The Matrix* in order to suggest that Americans are living in a science fictional future today. Both commercials also strip away the sense that this techno-luxurious future might have a sinister dystopian aspect – there is no cause for rebellion, and the desire to break free from a totalizing system of simulation designed to pacify and contain counterhegemonic resistance is notably absent. Now, these commercials suggest, we are living in the Matrix, and its myriad consumer benefits are fantastic to behold and purchase.

In conjunction with the renewal of the alien invasion trope, a parallel distinctive development in American science fiction after 9/11 (as exemplified by these *Matrix* commercials) is a pervasive feeling that contemporary life under globalized capitalism itself feels science fictional. Mark Bould and Sherryl Vint propose in *The Routledge Concise History of Science Fiction* that SF as a distinct genre in the new millennium "is disappearing, its images diffusing into contemporary culture and the boundaries that once kept it 'pure' and 'separate' eroding."[8] One symptom of this erosion of the distinction between SF and contemporary life is the emergence of slipstream fictions that blur the boundaries between mainstream literature, science fiction, and fantasy. Literary authors such as Aimee Bender, Rebecca Goldstein, Jonathan Lethem, Steven Millhauser, Shirley Jackson, and Richard Powers each use science fictional or fantastic elements in their fictions, and a variety of mainstream authors have turned toward science fiction as a means of exploring and critiquing America's response to crisis and disaster. Examples of such works include Philip Roth's *The Plot Against America* (2004), Paul Auster's *Man in the Dark* (2008), George Saunders' *The Brief and Frightening Reign of Phil* (2005), Michael Chabon's *The Yiddish Policeman's Union* (2007), and Cormac McCarthy's *The Road* (2006). These literary artists are joined by genre writers who write fantastic fictions that also blur traditional genre boundaries, including Ted Chiang, Kelly Link, Benjamin Rosenbaum, and Jeff VanderMeer (among many others).[9]

Slipstream fiction blurs genre boundaries in literary productions just as commercials such as the GE and K900 examples mix the boundaries between realism and science fiction in advertising. On a much larger level, however, the sense of the science fictionalization of everyday life in the aftermath of 9/11 is symptomatic of a new expansion in the global reach of capitalism and the interpenetration of capitalist economic and social norms into diverse areas of day-to-day existence.

Jaak Tomberg proposes that contemporary life often now seems to possess a science fictional flavor because "the contemporary technocultural context ... *behaves as if there were no outside of any kind.*"[10] In this observation, he draws on Hardt and Negri, who suggest that imperial capitalism has always thrived through a process of liquidating boundaries to its own expansion while organizing and managing differential regimes of access to its rewards and benefits. Hardt and Negri propose that imperial capitalism (or Empire) is now approaching its "ideal form" where "there is no outside to the world market: the entire globe is its domain."[11] As global capital unceasingly internalizes its exterior, science fiction's novum, which had previously been localized in alternate times (the future) or spaces (other worlds), now becomes internalized within the fabric of everyday life. As Tomberg notes,

> the high-tech scientific developments of contemporary late-capitalist culture have now become so smoothly and thoroughly integrated into our understanding of the everyday environment that their near-natural and unnoticeable presence and their almost intimate closeness and speed of development are no longer worthy of note as distinctively novel. It is not that people have become too used to technology or that technology is no longer a figure for the source of cognitive estrangement; it is rather that we now stand too close to it, unable to maintain the distance necessary to confine this estrangement to a separate cognitive realm.[12]

Tomberg observes that William Gibson's movement away from cyberpunk futures toward narratives set in a cognitively estranging science fictional present (*Pattern Recognition, Spook Country,* and *Zero History*) reflects the complex ways the estrangement-effect of the science fictional novum has become simultaneously banal and shocking within the operations of late capitalist totality. Gibson's efforts to represent the contemporary world inevitably capture a science fictional feel because nearly every aspect of contemporary life "is now a figure for the infinitely ungraspable late-capitalist world-system."[13] (277).

As Brian Massumi notes, late capitalist totality in its perpetual expansion has depended on a continuous atmosphere of indeterminate crisis in order to organize biopolitical subjectivity in ever more fluid and diverse formations. Since at least the Kennedy assassination, an environment of perpetual (yet generic) threat has enabled greater expansions of elite political and economic power while at the same time inviting consumers to take refuge from crisis in the illusory security of the commodity form. Human health may be precarious, but GE can create "brilliant machines" to help steward your medical care (at least according to Agent Smith), and if you own the K900, you will be driving in perfect safety and luxury (with Morpheus singing opera in the back seat) while the rest of the world explodes around you. As Massumi demonstrates, this socioeconomic regime, which he calls "the perpetual imminence of the accident," was operative in the decades prior to 9/11.[14] The 9/11 attacks simply took the situation to a new level by amplifying the volume of the spectacle and enabling ever-greater deployments of technoscientific hegemony in response to the threat of perpetual accident or disaster.

If, as Hardt and Negri suggest, Empire has capitalized on an environment of perpetual crisis in order to fold its exterior inward and to territorialize the entire globe within its domain, science fiction registers this contemporary ubiquity of Empire through the internalization of the novum (as Tomberg outlines). The outside seems to have collapsed inward, the future feels like it is now, and the novum seems immanent; it becomes difficult to imagine science fictional futures that radically differ from the present. Indeed, as Bould and Vint propose in an echo of Žižek and Fredric Jameson, science fiction in the contemporary moment finds it "easier to imagine the end of the world than the end of capitalism."[15] Dystopian postapocalyptic imaginings proliferate in contemporary science fiction, and global capital's unchecked technoscientific advancements are often the cause of the world's collapse: Canadian Margaret Atwood's critically acclaimed *MaddAddam* trilogy, for example, imagines the apocalypse as the consequence of genetic engineering, while Max Brooks' *World War Z* frames a dystopian zombie pandemic as the rise of the world's repressed underclasses catalyzed by catastrophic environmental degradation and pollution. Yet even when late capitalism breeds its own apocalypse, capitalism often continues to operate beyond the collapse of Western society. In Paolo Bacigalupi's *The Windup Girl* (2009), corporate gene hunters scour the world for genetic patents in the aftermath of an environmental collapse caused by irresponsible genetic engineering. Similarly, David Mitchell's *Cloud Atlas* (2004), which was adapted into a big-budget Hollywood film by Lana and Andy Wachowski and Tom Tykwer in 2012, presents a postapocalyptic future in which the world has been severely damaged by environmental catastrophe, and the fabricant clones who are created to serve humanity and survive in dangerous environments are subjugated and exploited through debt slavery in a corrupt social and economic corpocracy.

Bould and Vint propose that even fictions that contemplate SF futures with an eye toward economics, such as Canadian-British SF author Cory Doctorow's *Down and Out in the Magic Kingdom* (2003), Tricia Sullivan's *Maud* (2004), and David Marusek's *Counting Heads* (2005), often approach capitalist totality with a "comical or satirical edge."[16] Science fictions that extrapolate a more radical break with late capitalist norms are rare and have become more unusual. As Colin Milburn argues, most popular science fictions (such as those found in contemporary advertising) neutralize the radical potentials of speculative futurity by suggesting that the futures we need are already present – you don't need to gaze toward the future to find green technologies, because a science fictional Prius is available today at your local Toyota dealership! Milburn suggests that some science fictions, most notably Kim Stanley Robinson's Mars trilogy and his Science in the Capitol novels, actively resist this failure to imagine postcapitalist futures by taking up Jameson's challenge to "think the break" from hollow visions of the present-as-future in order to contemplate radical alternative social, political, and economic lifeworlds that might disrupt the norms of late capitalist totality.[17]

If Tomberg is partially correct in his assertion that "we now stand too close" to the science fictional novum and that we are therefore "unable to maintain the distance necessary to confine this estrangement to a separate cognitive realm," it is vital to note that the subjects who optimistically experience science fiction's interpenetration with contemporary life are often the same ones who benefit from its expansive hegemony. Although Empire may invite everyone across the globe to identify as cosmopolitan neighbors, it nonetheless regulates access to its advantages in favor of a privileged elite, and science fictions written from the margins of such access foreground the conditions of repression and exploitation that constitute Empire's biopolitical regime. Certain futures may seem hypervisible in the immanent contemporary landscape of iPhones, Priuses, and medical technologies, yet as Avery Gordon argues, such hypervisibility is itself the function of a system of image production that is "wedded to conjoined mechanisms that systematically render certain groups of people apparently privately poor, uneducated, ill, and disenfranchised."[18] As Malisa Kurtz suggests, the cardboard signifiers of evacuated futurity that saturate neoliberal culture serve as "a means of hiding and refusing to confront the structures of inequality that persist."[19]

Postcolonial science fictions excavate and illuminate such obscured structures of inequality and return our attention to the darker aspects of Empire's slippery regime of exploitation and differential inclusion. A wide variety of postcolonial science fictions have emerged in the years following 9/11 from authors across the globe. Postcolonial SF authors with American backgrounds (in a broad sense), such as Karen Tei Yamashita, Larissa Lai, Aliette de Bodard, Tananarive Due, Nalo Hopkinson, Nnedi Okorafor, Andrea Hairston, Eden Robinson, Sheree R. Thomas, and Nisi Shawl challenge the very notion of what it means to write American science fiction, and they stand alongside a growing number of indigenous futurists (such as Gerald Visenor, Sherman Alexie, Zainab Amadahy, Celu Amberstone, Diane Glancy, Misha Nogha, Simon J. Ortiz, Robert Sullivan, and Gerry William) and global SF writers (including Ian McDonald, Vandana Singh, Guillermo Lavin, Rosaura Sanchez, Beatrice Pita, Kenji Siratori, Lauren Beukes, and many others) who each in various ways deploy representational strategies that critique the hegemony of technocapitalist Empire and reveal its obscured operations.

Conclusion

In the aftermath of the so-called Great Recession of 2008–9, a predicament in the operations of late capitalism that revealed a continuity of neoliberal crisis response strategies uniting the Bush and Obama regimes, some popular science fictions turned their attentions toward the problem of global wealth inequality. Certain examples, such as DC Comics' simultaneous launch of *The Green Team* (about a group of teenage superhero trillionaires) and *The Movement* (focusing on Occupy-style hactivist heroes) offer little more than a mass media commodification of the tensions between the global elite and the global poor. In a similarly disappointing vein, Skye from Marvel's *Agents of SHIELD*, who begins as a hacktivist for a grassroots group called Rising Tide, quickly sacrifices her commitment to radical social and economic justice as she learns that SHIELD's totalitarian interventions are well-meaning and necessary in the face of the omnicrisis posed by alien and superhuman threats. Marvel proved willing to explore SHIELD's totalitarian interventionist overtones in *Captain America: The Winter Soldier* (2014), yet SHIELD's mission (and by extension the unilateral intervention policies of the United States in the face of perpetual terror) is ultimately portrayed as a valorous cause corrupted from within by neo-Nazi HYDRA terrorists. In addition, Marvel tragically (and predictably) rejected China Mieville's pitch for *Scrap Iron Man*, a Marxist response to the celebration of technoscientific capitalist elitism embodied by Tony Stark, which would have featured global laborers banding together to build collectively operated power-armor suits to deploy in the battle against worldwide economic injustice (including those perpetrated by Stark himself).

In contrast to such fictions that either frame the struggle for wealth equality in superficial ways (or that minimize the importance of economic injustice through references to the larger threat of lurking indefinite global catastrophe), Neill Blomkamp's *Elysium* (2013) (coproduced by Hollywood and Blomkamp's own South African production company) explores issues such as global poverty (and the exploitation of the global poor by the global elite), the imperialist economics of territorial borders and immigration restrictions, the use of unsanctioned military contractors to perform the dirty work of the global elite, and the complex politics of citizenship and belonging, particularly in relation to inequities of access to privileged medical resources. In spite of what many regard as the film's one-dimensional character development, *Elysium* presents a world in which increasing wealth inequality has created a small hyper-rich capitalist elite who are insulated from the global poor through powerful border controls and a differentiation between economic classes enforced through state citizenship. Unlike *The Purge* (another wealth inequality SF film from the summer of 2013), *Elysium* maps the economics of the relationship between the elite and the impoverished in a way that resonates with existing global economic conditions. Although *Elysium* feels somewhat forced and heavy-handed in its treatment of such issues, it stands out (particularly among spectacle-ridden summer SF blockbusters) for its willingness to cognitively map the conditions of inequality operating in the post-9/11 global milieu and for its courage and creativity in imagining modes of resistance that move beyond simply staging the spectacle of economic conflict for the purpose of elite economic gain.

NOTES

1 For more on the awakening-from-simulacrum parabola, see my "Coded Transmissions: Gender and Genre Reception in *The Matrix*" in Brian Attebery and Veronica Hollinger, eds., *Parabolas of Science Fiction* (Middletown, CT: Wesleyan University Press, 2008), 143–60.

2 Cf. Slavoj Žižek, *Welcome to the Desert of the Real* (London and New York: Verso, 2002).

3 For more on the deployment of fear to organize late capitalist subjectivity in the decades prior to 9/11, see Brian Massumi's "Everywhere You Want to Be: Introduction to Fear" in Brian Massumi, ed., *The Politics of Everyday Fear* (Minneapolis: University of Minnesota Press, 1993), 3–37.

4 Robert Saunders, "Undead Spaces: Fear, Globalization, and the Popular Geopolitics of Zombiism," *Geopolitics* 17 (2012): 80–104.

5 Michael Hardt and Antonio Negri, *Empire* (Cambridge, MA: Harvard University Press, 2000), 189.

6 Enrica Picarelli and M. Carmen Gomez-Galisteo, "Be Fearful: *The X-Files'* Post-9/11 Legacy," *Science Fiction Film and Television* 6:1 (Spring 2013): 71–85.

7 Timothy Melley, *Empire of Conspiracy: The Culture of Paranoia in Postwar America* (Ithaca, NY and London: Cornell University Press, 2000), 12.

8 Mark Bould and Sherryl Vint, *The Routledge Concise History of Science Fiction* (London and New York: Routledge, 2011), 183.

9 For further discussion of slipstream science fiction, see Chapter 7 in this volume.

10 Jaak Tomberg, "On the 'Double Vision' of Realism and SF Estrangement in William Gibson's *Bigend Trilogy*," *Science Fiction Studies* 40:2 (July 2013): 274.

11 Hardt and Negri, 190.

12 Tomberg, 277.

13 Ibid.

14 Massumi, 10.

15 Bould and Vint, 184.

16 Ibid.

17 Colin Milburn, "Greener on the Other Side: Science Fiction and the Problem of Green Nanotechnology," *Configurations* 20:1–2 (Winter–Spring 2012): 87.

18 Avery Gordon, *Ghostly Matters: Haunting and the Sociological Imagination* (Minneapolis: University of Minnesota Press, 2008), 17.

19 Malisa Kurtz, "Specters of Cyberpunk: Haunted Spaces in Lauren Beukes's *Moxyland* and *Zoo City*," *Paradoxa* 25 (2013): 70.

4

LISA YASZEK

Afrofuturism in American Science Fiction

At first glance, the history of American science fiction (SF) seems fairly straightforward – and overwhelmingly white. The usual narrative for this history begins in the nineteenth century with the proto-SF experiments of writers Nathaniel Hawthorne and Edgar Allan Poe, extends through the turn-of-the-century technoutopias of Edward Bellamy and Charlotte Perkins Gilman, and comes to full fruition in the twentieth-century specialist SF magazines edited by Hugo Gernsback and John W. Campbell. And yet, while these authors and editors were indeed pioneers in the creation of American SF (and, as some have claimed, in the creation of SF as a distinctly American genre), they were by no means alone in their desire to write amazing stories about the relations of science, technology, and society. For nearly two hundred years African Americans have used a mode of speculative fiction called "Afrofuturism" to dramatize the issues most important to people of color living in a technocultural world, and to create a sense of wonder about the futures that might emerge from scientific and social change.

Cultural critic Mark Dery defines Afrofuturism as "speculative fiction that treats African-American themes and addresses African-American concerns in the context of 20th century technoculture – and more generally, African-American signification that appropriates images of technology and a pros-thetically enhanced future" to explore how people of color might radically change the social and political world.[1] Afrofuturist stories can be identified by three characteristics. First, Afrofuturists use their chosen genre to par-ticipate in what Toni Morrison calls the black Atlantic intellectual project of reclaiming American history by demonstrating how African slaves and their descendants experienced conditions of homelessness, alienation, and dislocation that embody what Nietzsche described as the founding condi-tions of modernity.[2] Second, Afrofuturists draw on the historic experience of Afrodiasporic people who survived and changed such conditions to cre-ate what Kodwo Eshun calls tales of "chronopolitical intervention" that multiply readers' understanding of what it might mean to live in a variety of raced futures.[3] Finally, Afrofuturists locate the possibility of these new futures in the figure of the black genius: a young (and traditionally male) "scientist-inventor who uses the products of his genius to save himself, his friends and his community" from white oppression.[4] Indeed, it is precisely his experience of alienation that leads the black genius to create things that change the course of history forever.

All the major elements of Afrofuturism appear in what is considered the first African-American SF story: Martin Delany's *Blake or the Huts of America*. Initially serialized in *The AngloAfrican Magazine* (January–July 1859) and then published in its entirety in *The Weekly Anglo-African* (November 1861–May 1862), *Blake* relates the adventures of Henry Holland, a free black West Indian who is kidnapped and sold into slavery in Maryland under the name Henry Blake. When his wife is sold away to a Cuban plantation owner, Blake takes action. First, he teaches his wife's family astronomy and compass navigation techniques "necessary to guide you from a land of slavery ... to a land of liberty."[5] Then he escapes to Cuba and liberates his wife. Along the way, Blake sows the seeds of revolution amongst other slaves and creates a Grand Council of free blacks. By combining the agricultural expertise of Africans with the technocultural ability of Afrodiasporic people who quickly adopt "all the usages of civilized life, attaining wherever practicable every position in society," Blake and his Council plan to build a transcontinental cotton empire that will undermine the U.S. South's economic might and dismantle slavery.[6] As such, *Blake* performs what we might call the first act of chronopolitical intervention in American letters; dramatizing both how Afrodiasporic people are alienated from modernity and how they might use their technoscientific genius to change the world.[7]

But – in a move that would set the tone for nearly a century of Afrofuturist SF to come – Delany ends his story on a profoundly ambivalent note, asking if there will ever be this kind of glorious future, or indeed any future, for black people in the modern world. Delany's heroes dream of utopia, but *Blake* ends with members of the Great Council preparing for an all-out race war they seem unlikely to win. Despite his misgivings, the most vocal advocate of military action is Blake himself. As he tells the Council: "I am for war – war against the whites.... May God forgive me for the wickedness, as my conscience admonished and rebuked me.... But my determination is fixed, I will never leave you."[8] Thus Delany insists that black people have the talent to compete in a technoscientific global economy. To deny them this opportunity is to halt the natural progression of capitalism, turning nonviolent economic and technocultural competition into apocalyptic military battle.

The themes that first appear in *Blake* come together most forcefully in a group of texts published between 1880 and 1940. This period marked the consolidation of American SF as a popular genre complete with its own authors, publishing venues, and stylistic rules. For the most part, however, Afrofuturists did not place their stories in white-owned specialist SF magazines such as *Amazing Stories* or *Weird Tales*, preferring instead to publish in black-owned venues such as *The Crisis* and *The Pittsburgh Courier*.[9] The reasons for this were both political and aesthetic. Black authors were hesitant to publish serious stories about the future of race relations in magazines featuring lurid images of planets, scantily clad women, and bug-eyed monsters. Such concerns were amplified by the tendency of SF pulp authors to craft racist futures. For example, while Stanley G. Weinbaum's 1934 "A Martian Odyssey" is celebrated as one of the first stories to treat the alien other sympathetically, it does so at the expense of black people. Weinbaum's characters know that the Martian they encounter is intelligent precisely because his knowledge classification systems are more complex than those of the "Negritoes" back on Earth who are "too primitive to understand that rain water and sea water are just different aspects of the same thing."[10] Finally, even if Afrofuturist writers were willing to risk the bad political match to reach new audiences, they would have been stymied by pulp magazine editorial practices, which encouraged authors to spin fantastic tales of race war – but only if those stories were told as far-future space operas where issues of race were either metaphorically displaced onto human-alien relations or eclipsed by detailed descriptions of brilliant men inventing and deploying "spaceships armed with marvelous ray-guns and the like" to conquer whatever enemy they faced.[11]

Regardless of where it was published, Afrofuturist fiction of this period increasingly resembled its specialist SF counterpart in two ways. First, the figure of the technoscientific genius became increasingly central to such fiction. Edward A. Johnson's *Light Ahead for the Negro* (1904), Roger Sherman Tracy's *The White Man's Burden: A Satirical Forecast* (1915), Pauline Hopkins's *Of One Blood* (1903), and George S. Schuyler's *Black Empire* (1936–8) treat such genius in a general way, as the birthright of Afrodiasporic people everywhere. Meanwhile, Sutton E. Griggs's *Imperium in Imperio* (1899), Hopkins's *Of One Blood* (1903), and Schuyler's *Black No More* (1932) and *Black Empire* (1936–8) feature individual scientist-inventors who are brilliant creators in their own right. Taken together these tales demonstrate the evolution of Afrofuturist storytelling. In *Blake*, Delany included technoscientific ability as one of his hero's many attributes and imagined a future where blacks would use modern agricultural and economic techniques to command political attention. Turn-of-the-century

Afrofuturists took these ideas a step further, casting lead characters as scientists and engineers who actively create the theories, techniques, and things that can change race relations forever.

Early Afrofuturism also paralleled early specialist SF in that artists from both traditions insisted discovery and invention are crucial to the creation of new futures. While the near future focus of most Afrofuturist stories from this period meant that authors generally did not speculate about what a black-designed spaceship, ray gun, or intergalactic civilization might look like, they did provide readers with equally thrilling descriptions of their Earthly equivalents. Tracy's *White Man's Burden* and Schuyler's *Black Empire* describe a whole host of new military technologies including bioweapons, television-like viewing systems, electric artillery, and disintegrator beams. Along with Griggs and Hopkins, Tracy also imagined that blacks might construct elaborate hidden (usually subterranean) cities to protect them against human enemies and natural disaster alike. But black invention did not stop with wartime technologies; Johnson, Schuyler, and Hopkins also prophesied that Afrodiasporic people would make civilian life better with new communication technologies, wide-scale hydroponics, and death-defying medical practices. While some of these inventions were entirely fabulous, others were not: Johnson predicted the regular use of wireless communication two decades before Richard H. Ranger patented the wireless photoradiogram and Schuyler wrote about fax machines twenty-five years before Xerox patented the first commercial version. Like their counterparts in specialist SF, African-American authors extrapolated carefully from current scientific and social trends to create plausible high-tech futures.

Yet Afrofuturism remained distinct from specialist SF in its sustained consideration of race as a central factor informing the relations of science and society. Perhaps not surprisingly, black authors interested in speculating about the future often did so by extrapolating from African-American engagements with science and technology. Sometimes this engagement was general, as in the case of W. E. B. Du Bois, who began writing fiction (including the 1920 SF story "The Comet" and the 1928 fantasy novel *Dark Princess*) to raise awareness about the complexity of black life in America when he could not secure funding for his sociological research into that same topic.[12] At other times it was more direct, as in the case of Pauline Hopkins, whose novel *Of One Blood* dramatizes the theories of black racial superiority first offered by Martin Delany to counter the white supremacy inherent in mainstream nineteenth-century racial science.[13] Even more explicitly, Griggs's *Imperium* revolves around a "negro scientist who won an international reputation by his skill and erudition" and who uses the funds raised by his "book of science" to create an

African-American shadow empire within the United States.[14] Readers were likely to recognize this scientist as an homage to Benjamin Banneker, the Revolutionary era free black scientist-inventor who used the proceeds of his bestselling almanac to fund abolitionist causes.[15] Taken together, such stories show how early Afrofuturists expanded the black Atlantic intellectual project by reclaiming the history of African Americans as creative technoscientific subjects.

This does not mean that such authors abandoned the project of demonstrating black social and political alienation. Instead they brought these two areas of historical recovery together in their representations of black genius. As Dr. Henry Belsidus, the mastermind behind the global revolution described in Schuler's *Black Empire*, eloquently puts it:

> We are going to out-think and out-scheme the white people.... I have the organization already ... scattered all over the world; young Negroes [who are] intellectuals, scientists, engineers. They are mentally the equal of the whites. They possess superior energy, superior vitality, they have superior, or perhaps I should say more intense, hatred and resentment, that fuel which operates the juggernaut of conquest.... You will see in your time a great Negro nation in Africa, all-powerful, dictating to the white world.[16]

For Schuyler, technoscientific ability is a trait bestowed naturally to individuals regardless of race. The expression of that ability, however, is shaped by historical circumstance. Here, two centuries of slavery and racial oppression have honed black genius in such a way that it is no longer a tool to increase human knowledge or build better futures for all. Instead, it becomes a tool of black conquest that might well simply reverse and amplify historic modes of racial injustice.

Finally, early Afrofuturism departed from specialist SF in its pessimism about the ability of black genius to secure any future for black people whatsoever. Like Delany before them, Griggs, Hopkins, and Du Bois end their stories on the brink of massive race wars that no one is likely to win. Tracy's far-future African utopia seems to be an exception to this general pattern, but as readers soon learn, it is a fragile community built on three millennia of racial conflict and perpetually threatened by barbaric white outsiders. Ambivalence about the use of black genius to foster military action is perhaps most evident in Schuyler's *Black Empire*. Dr. Belsidus may be the brilliant mastermind behind a successful black revolution, but he is also terrifyingly amoral, amassing the funds for his revolution by murdering rich white women and enlisting talented young blacks to his cause at gunpoint. In case readers miss the point, Schuyler also ends each section of his story with the image of Belsidus's girlfriend weeping for all the lives lost in the creation of his new world order. As such, Schuyler and his contemporaries anticipate the cautionary "if this goes on" tale that would become central to the specialist SF magazines at the American mid-century.[17]

Given that so many early Afrofuturist texts anticipate later developments in specialist SF, it is perhaps no surprise that since the 1960s, many African-American authors have chosen to call the genre their own. The first generation of Afrofuturist SF authors – including Octavia E. Butler, Samuel R. Delany, Charles Saunders, and Steve Barnes – published and continue to publish regularly with SF specialist magazines such as *Asimov's* and *The Magazine of Fantasy and Science Fiction* and presses such as Dell and Ace. Collectively speaking, all these authors have been nominated for or have won most of the major SF and fantasy awards, including the Hugo, the Nebula, and the World Fantasy Awards.[18] Subsequent Afrofuturist SF authors have built upon the work of their predecessors with the creation of dedicated Afrofuturist anthologies such as Sherree R. Thomas's *Dark Matter* series and Milton R. Davis and Charles Saunders's *Griots: A Sword and Soul* collection. They have also established dedicated author collectives such as the Carl Brandon Society, writing prizes such as the Kindred and Parallax Awards, and events such as Tananarive Due's Black to the Future conferences and Joseph Wheeler III's OnyxCon.

Afrofuturist participation in the contemporary SF community can be attributed to two factors. Like their white counterparts, black authors often fondly remember growing up in a world saturated by comics, children's fantasy literature, and science fiction films. Indeed, Butler claims her career was directly inspired by her childhood experience with a "terrible movie" called *Devil Girl From Mars*: "As I was watching the movie, I had a series of revelations. The first was that 'Geez, I can write a better story than that.' And then I thought.... 'Somebody got paid for writing that awful story.' So I was off and writing."[19] Such efforts were likely facilitated by changing aesthetic priorities within SF. Authors and editors associated with the New Wave movement of the 1960s argued that classic SF story types and tropes – including the far future, gadget-oriented space opera, and the inevitably evil, racialized alien other – were grossly outdated and have little to do with the scientific or social realities of the modern era. Instead, they called for new modes of speculative fiction that emphasized the soft sciences over their hard counterparts and that engaged politically charged and previously taboo subjects. As such, the SF community was finally ready to embrace the kind of fiction African-American authors had been writing since Martin Delany.

And indeed, contemporary Afrofuturists continue to explore many of the same themes that interested their predecessors. Stories including Delany's *Babel-17* (1966) and *Trouble on Triton* (1976), Butler's "Bloodchild" (1984) and *Lilith's Brood* trilogy (1987–9), Derrick Bell's "The Space Traders" (1992), Walter Mosely's *Futureland* (2001), Barnes's *Charisma* (2003), Andrea Hairston's *Mindscape* (2006), and Balogun Ojetade's edited anthology *Steamfunk!* (2013) all invoke the specter of race war. Bell, Mosely, and Barnes figure this in classic Afrofuturist terms as a near-future conflict pitting light-skinned people against their dark counterparts, while the authors featured in *Steamfunk!* set such conflict in an alternate turn-of-the-century America. Meanwhile, Delany and Hairston project race war into far futures where humans colonize new worlds and survive massive natural disasters, but still cannot figure out how to get along with one another. Finally, Butler extrapolates from African-American history to show how human-alien encounters might lead to violence in the name of racial purity. Taken together, such stories serve as Eshun's acts of chronopolitical intervention, reminding readers how easily the racial animosity and alienation marking African-American history might resurface in the future.

Afrofuturist authors also continue to commemorate the history of African-American technoscientific innovation with stories of ethnic geniuses who save their people from destruction while building strange but hopeful new futures. Delany's *Babel-17* and *Stars in My Pocket Like Grains of Sand* (1984), Mosely's *Futureland*, Bill Campbell's *Sunshine Patriots* (2004), and Ojetade's *Steamfunk!* (2013) imagine this might be accomplished by brilliant individuals who use novel combinations of old and new technologies. Meanwhile, Hairston's *Mindscape* and Butler's Patternmaster series (1976–84) and *Fledgling* (2005) show how marginalized people might work collectively to engineer new strains of humanity that are better equipped to negotiate the harsh environmental and social realities of their worlds. Like Schuyler before them, contemporary Afrofuturists often attach complex moral and ethical dilemmas to their representations of black genius, asking readers to consider how social relations influence the deployment of genius and to evaluate whether or not such responses are appropriate to the goal of justice for all.

But the accomplishments of African Americans in the twentieth and early twenty-first centuries also inspire black authors to innovate upon the traditions forged by their predecessors. For example, rather than ending their stories on the brink of race war, contemporary Afrofuturists often shift focus to ask what might happen in the aftermath of such war. This question is particularly central to Butler's "Bloodchild," which is set in a far future where space-faring humans wage war on the bug-like T'lic, only to lose that war and be enslaved by the aliens, who see human men as "convenient, big, warm-blooded animals" perfect for carrying their offspring to term.[20] The story begins in a period much like that of American Reconstruction; the

T'lic have just released humans from slavery and the two races are trying to find a way to live together. When Butler's protagonist – the human teenager Gan, whose family is bound to the alien politician T'Gatoi, leader of the movement to secure equality between the races – sees an interspecies childbirth go wrong, he picks up a gun and sets out, in seemingly classic pulp SF fashion, to destroy T'Gatoi and her people.

But that is not what happens. Instead, Gan and T'Gatoi sit down in their kitchen to talk out their issues. The human boy admits that he is afraid to experience pregnancy and childbirth, while the alien politician reluctantly admits that she is afraid to educate humans about what has always been "a private thing" for her people.[21] Once they acknowledge their fears, Butler's characters agree to move forward and make the baby that they believe will represent a better future for both races. Here then, Butler's story invokes a very different part of American-American history – the history of women's behind-the-scenes work in the civil rights movement, fostering interpersonal relations between whites and blacks in the private sphere of the home – to show how communication might be the greatest weapon of all in ending race war forever.[22]

Other authors imagine that new sciences and technologies might end racial animosity altogether. In *Trouble on Triton* (1976), Delany extrapolates from what were then still relatively new developments in sex change surgery to imagine a future where advanced medical technologies make both gender and race a matter of choice. As the Tritonian government worker Sam explains, earlier in life he was a "blonde, blue-eyed (and terribly myopic) waitress" attracted to women who were themselves attracted to "the six-foot plus Wallunda and Katanga immigrants" living in her neighborhood.[23] Rather than pining away or taking out her anger on the racial other with whom she initially sees herself in competition, Sam decides to get an operation that transforms her into a happy, successful black man. While individual characters such as the Martian-born Bron believe that the best societies are those based on forms of "natural" biological difference and planets such as Earth are willing to go to war for such beliefs, Delany insists that the inhabitants of Triton are happier – and their world better – precisely because they have detached race (and gender) from nature. In this particular future, race might well still be a sexual fetish for some Tritonians, but because it is so fluid, detached from both personal identity and collective history, it no longer functions as a system of oppression or as an excuse for bellicose behavior.

Contemporary Afrofuturists also update the classic character of the black genius by connecting that character to both Eurowestern science and African or Afrodiasporic "magic." Nalo Hopkinson's edited collection *Mojo: Conjure*

Stories (2003), Nisi Shawl's *Filter House* (2008), Hairston's *Redwood and Wildfire* (2011), and Ojetade*'s Steamfunk!* all insist that the mundane and supernatural worlds coexist on a continuum and that much of what white Eurowesterners describe as magic is black scientific practice. For instance, Benjamin Montgomery, the genius at the center of Ronald T. Jones's alternate history "Benjamin's Freedom Magic," defends the free black republic of Delany against incursion by the slave-holding Grand Confederacy with magnet-based artillery that operates so efficiently that Confederate soldiers assume they are up against "satanic weapons" forged through "African voodoo."[24] But Montgomery actually creates these weapons by pursuing an abandoned line of Eurowestern inquiry. Here then, "magic" turns out to be a matter of perspective, fueled by the failure of white Americans to recognize black technological prowess.

Meanwhile, in "Rite of Passage: Blood and Iron," Ojetade rewrites the story of John Henry to cast the American folklore hero as a real-life superhero, created by the African god Ogun to defend Afrodiasporic people against an array of natural and supernatural enemies. While Ojetade never provides readers with a plausible explanation for Ogun, Henry's transformation from human to superhero is surprisingly mundane: he gains incredible strength by training in a subterranean gymnasium where he must survive a "deadly obstacle course" comprised of "thick, iron chains" and cannonballs while imbibing energy drinks comprised of blackstrap molasses, ground-up bullets, and "a little bit of this and a little bit of that thrown in fo' good measure."[25] As Ojetade points out elsewhere, stories such as "Benjamin's Freedom Magic" and "Rite of Passage" do the classic Afrofuturist work of reclaiming yet another aspect of African-American history: the centuries-old tradition of Afrodiasporic people who used "voodoo, stage-magic, fortune telling, and mesmerism" to support their families, create community, and advance the cause of civil rights.[26] Such stories also contribute to the ongoing development of SF as a living genre: by telling tales that merge Eurowestern and African ways of knowing the world, Afrofuturists prove SF luminary Arthur C. Clarke's famous claim that "any sufficiently advanced technology is indistinguishable from magic."

The appeal of Afrofuturism is perhaps best illustrated by the use of Afrofuturist themes and techniques on the part of authors who are not themselves historic African Americans. This is particularly evident in the work of Kenyan-Canadian Minister Faust and Caribbean-born Tobias Buckell and Nalo Hopkinson, all of whom have either been nominated for or have won major SF awards for their groundbreaking explorations of science, technology, and race as those relations have developed outside the United States. Additionally, Hopkinson has introduced American SF readers to other non-U.S. Afrodiasporic authors in her edited collections *Whispers from the Cotton Tree Root: Caribbean Fabulist Fiction* (2000) and *So Long Been Dreaming: Postcolonial Science Fiction and Fantasy* (2004, with Uppinder Mehan). The past two decades have also marked an increasing interest in Afrofuturism on the part of white SF authors. For example, Paul Di Filippo's short story collection *Ribofunk!* (1996) invokes the history of American slavery and the black nationalist dream of an independent Afrodiasporic nation-state to imagine how new biotechnologies might lead to the re- and deconstruction of racial hierarchies. Meanwhile, Kathleen Ann Goonan's *Crescent City Rhapsody* (2000) explores how the intellectual perspectives and political tactics associated with the history of African American magic might help black people – and indeed, all people – negotiate the brave new world of nanotechnology.

But perhaps the most exciting new work in Afrofuturist SF comes from Nigerian-American Nnedi Okorafor, an award-winning novelist whose fiction has been celebrated by the American and African SF communities alike.[27] A first-generation American with strong ties to her family's home continent, Okorafor uses the techniques of Afrofuturism to explore how Africans grapple with the lingering alienation of their various colonial pasts while combining Eurowestern and African technoscientific traditions to build new futures. These interests come together particularly clearly in the short story "Hello Moto," which revolves around the adventures of Rain, a brilliant Nigerian woman who creates three cybernetically and magically enhanced wigs designed to transform the young inventor and her best friends into a new breed of caring and generous political leaders who will "cure the deep seated culture of corruption" plaguing their country.[28]

But this future is not meant to be. When Rain's friends use the wigs for personal gain, leaving a trail of death and destruction in their wake, Okorafor's protagonist realizes that "when you mix juju with technology, you give up control" and allow history to repeat itself.[29] To "Right Her Great Wrong," Rain creates a magically infused computer virus (triggered by the cellphone ringtone "Hello Moto") that she hopes will destroy the wigs forever.[30] Unfortunately, things go wrong once again and the story ends with all three women transformed into vampires, waiting to tear each other to pieces. Like her historic African-American counterparts, Okorafor uses classic SF tropes to stake claims for black people as authoritative subjects of technocultural modernity while asking us to carefully consider the ethics of technoscientific genius and its creations. Furthermore, like other contemporary Afrofuturists, she asks readers to consider how black genius might be predicated on both Eurowestern and African ways of knowing the world. As such, Okorafor demonstrates that while Afrofuturism might have begun as a specifically American art form, it has evolved into a global language that enables people to talk about the relations of science, technology, and race across centuries, continents, and cultures.

NOTES

1 Mark Dery, *Flame Wars: The Discourse of Cyberculture* (Durham, NC: Duke University Press, 1994), 136.
2 Morrison, quoted in P. Gilroy, *Small Acts: Thoughts on the Politics of Black Cultures* (London: Serpent's Tail, 1993), 178.
3 Kodwo Eshun, "Further Considerations on Afrofuturism," *CR: The New Centennial Review* 3.2 (Summer 2003): 298.
4 Lisa Yaszek, "The Bannekerade: Genius, Madness and Magic in Black Science Fiction," in I. Lavender III (ed.), *Black and Brown Planets* (Jackson: University of Mississippi Press, 2014): 15–30.
5 Martin Delany, *Blake or the Huts of America* (1859–62) (Boston, MA: Beacon Press, 2000), 134.
6 Ibid., 262.
7 As Mark Bould points out, this fictional vision of black industrial and commercial dominance reiterates many of the Heinleinian "engineering" solutions that Delany proposed in his political writing. For further discussion, see Mark Bould, "Revolutionary African-American SF before Black Power SF," *Extrapolation* 51.1 (2010): 53–81.
8 Delany, *Blake or the Huts of America*, 290–1.
9 As Samuel R. Delany notes, there might very well have been black authors publishing speculative fiction in white-owned turn-of-the-century magazines. Such magazines conducted most of their business by mail, so it would have been impossible to know an author's race unless s/he announced it publicly. What we do know for certain is that authors associated with these magazines did not write stories for them that addressed racial issues in meaningful ways. For further discussion, see Samuel R. Delany, "Racism and Science Fiction," in Sheree Renée Thomas, ed., *Dark Matter: A Century of Speculative Fiction from the African Diaspora* (New York: Aspect, 2000), 383–97.
10 Stanley G. Weinbaum, "A Martian Odyssey" (1934), in Arthur B. Evans et al., eds., *The Wesleyan Anthology of Science Fiction* (Middletown, CT: Wesleyan University Press, 2010), 145.
11 Brian Stableford, "Future War" (December 14, 2012), in John Clute and David Langford, eds., *The Encyclopedia of Science Fiction*, 3rd ed., accessed October 10, 2013, http://www.sf-encyclopedia.com/entry/future_war.
12 For further discussion, see Maria Farland, "W.E.B. Du Bois, Anthropometric Science, and the Limits of Racial Uplift," *American Quarterly* 58.4 (December 2006): 1017–44.
13 For further discussion, see M. Reid, "Utopia Is in the Blood: The Bodily Utopias of Martin R. Delany and Pauline Hopkins," *Utopian Studies* 22.1 (2011): 91–103.
14 S. E. Griggs, *Imperium in Imperio* (1899) (Greenbook Publications, 2010), 94.
15 For further discussion, see Yaszek, "The Bannekerade."

16   George S. Schuyler, *Black Empire* (originally published as *Black Internationale* and *Black Empire*, 1936–8) (Boston, MA: Northeastern University Press, 1991), 15.

17   The "if this goes on" tale is named after a Robert Heinlein story of the same title, which first appeared in *Astounding Science Fiction* in 1940 and has been reprinted numerous times since.

18   The accomplishments of these pioneering black SF authors have also been recognized outside the SF community in the form of Butler's MacArthur Foundation "Genius Grant," Delany's Stonewall Book Award, and Barnes's NAACP Image Award.

19   Octavia E. Butler, "'Devil Girl From Mars': Why I Write Science Fiction" (October 4, 1998), *MIT Media in Transition Project*, accessed October 21, 2013, http://web.mit.edu/comm-forum/papers/butler.html.

20   Octavia E. Butler, "Bloodchild" (1984), in P. Sargent, ed., *Women of Wonder: The Contemporary Years* (San Diego, CA: Harcourt Brace, 1995), 127.

21   Ibid., 140.

22   For further discussion of women's work in the American civil rights movement, see K. L. Nasstrom, "Down to Now: Memory, Narrative, and Women's Leadership in the Civil Rights Movement in Atlanta, Georgia," *Gender and History* 11 (April 1999): 113–44, and C. M. Payne, "Men Led, but Women Organized: Movement Participation of Women in the Mississippi Delta," in G. West and R. L. Blumberg, eds., *Women and Social Protest* (New York: Oxford University Press, 1990), 156–63.

23   Samuel R. Delany, *Trouble on Triton: An Ambiguous Heterotopia* (New York: Bantam, 1976), 149.

24   Ronald T. Jones, "Benjamin's Freedom Magic," in Balogun Ojetade, ed., *Steamfunk!* (MVmedia, LLC., 2013), n. p.

25   Balogun Ojetade, "Rite of Passage: Blood and Iron," in Balogun Ojetade, ed., *Steamfunk!* (MVmedia, LLC., 2013), n. p.

26   Balogun Ojetade, "Steamfunk Enchanters: Black Magicians, Conjurers, and Soothsayers in the Age of Steam" (January 23, 2013), *Chronicles of Harriet*, accessed October 28, 2013, http://chroniclesofharriet.com/2013/01/23/steamfunk-enchanters/.

27   Okorafor's awards include the World Fantasy Award and the Carl Brandon Parallax Award as well as the Wole Soyinka Prize for Literature in Africa, and her fiction appears in Western anthologies such as *Eclipse 3: New Science Fiction and Fantasy* and *Dark Matter II: Raising the Bones* as well as the first-ever anthology of African SF, *AfroSF: Science Fiction by African Writers*.

28   Nnedi Okorafor, "Hello, Moto" (November 2, 2011), *Tor.com: Stories and Comics*, accessed October 28, 2013, http://www.tor.com/stories/2011/11/hello-moto.

29   Ibid.

30   Ibid.

5

ALEXIS LOTHIAN

Feminist and Queer Science Fiction in America

What would a world without gender be like? How might radical changes in the structuring of family and reproduction affect individuals, relationships, societies? How could technology alter the experience of love and desire? Science fiction has often been stereotyped as a genre oriented around masculine themes – and yet, since the nineteenth century, speculative visions of alternate futures, pasts, and elsewheres have provided individual and collective spaces in which to reimagine the workings of gender, sexuality, love, and desire in both political and personal worlds. As multiple feminist, gay, lesbian, bisexual, transgender, and queer movements and cultures have challenged the conventions, expectations, and power structures that surround gender and sexuality in American culture, writers and fans of science fiction have raised questions and posed critiques about the futures of gender, sex, technology, patriarchy, and reproduction in endlessly inventive ways.

Feminist science fiction has a specific genre history, both a part of and parallel to what L. Timmel Duchamp has called "malestream" science fiction.[1] This chapter offers a starting point for exploring its broad universe. It begins with two sections on science fiction's historical intersections with feminist movements, looking at speculative explorations of women's roles as they have been constrained by patriarchal social and familial structures. The venerable tradition of the feminist utopia is followed by a discussion of science fiction's diverse varieties of feminist critique. The next two sections address speculative representations of reproductive and erotic frameworks outside the hegemony of heterosexuality, as they have been explored in science fiction's conversation with queer theory and activism's insistence that neither sexual orientation, gender roles, nor biological sex itself can be taken for granted. Finally, we turn to cultural institutions that have supported and perpetuated feminist science fiction not just as a literary genre but as a social and intellectual world. As diverse and filled with debate as feminist movements and theories themselves, the field of discourse that Joan Haran and Katie King name "science fiction feminisms" has been as much a social scene mediated by letters, 'zines, conventions, and academic organizations as it has been the work of writers and cultural producers exploring the issues of most concern to them as individuals.[2]

Worlds of Women: Gendering Utopia

In the United States, the use of fictional speculation to challenge gender norms has a history that predates pulp magazines' coinage of the term "science fiction," reaching back to the utopian imaginings of nineteenth-century progressive movements. Charlotte Perkins Gilman is the best remembered of the late nineteenth- and early twentieth-century feminist writers who deployed science fictional ideas in pursuit of gender equity, but recovery work by scholars like Carol Kessler and Darby Lewes has shown that American women were creating utopian narratives on feminist themes as early as Mary Griffith's 1836 "Three Hundred Years Hence." Gilman's 1915 *Herland* imagined a manless utopia; it captured feminist imaginations when it was republished in 1979, by which time the idea of women-dominated or women-only societies had become a trope in both feminist and nonfeminist science fiction writing (Justine Larbalestier's *The Battle of the Sexes in Science Fiction* discusses this history in depth). *Herland* created a vision of a hidden country in which women reproduce by mystical parthenogenesis, discovered by a trio of American men whose reactions allow Gilman to carry out a comprehensive critique of masculinity. An earlier utopia by Mary Bradley Lane, *Mizora* (1880), depicts another women-only country, in which an aristocratic Russian woman discovers a perfected society buried underground in Antarctica. For both writers, along with their contemporaries in white middle-class first-wave feminism, utopian speculation was a means of proving that women's liberation would advance national governance in both public and private spheres, especially if technology could be developed to free women from the burden of domestic labor.

Both Gilman and Lane suggest that the values of femininity, constructed at the turn of the twentieth century as domestic and connected to education and the nurture of children, could have the potential to change the world for the better. In Lane, feminine virtue accrues to the idea of universal education, combined with the technological elimination of manual labor; in Gilman, an ecological concern for the cultivation of landscape is a primary focus. Both versions of utopian feminism route through American nationalist ideals of melting-pot democracy: In *With Her in Ourland*, the sequel to *Herland*, and in *Mizora* alike, utopian citizens visit the United States and find it much more progressive than hierarchical Europe, though with a long way to go. Race is also a central feature of the way Lane, Gilman, and their contemporaries in both the United States and the United Kingdom imagined utopia being achieved.[3] Herlanders are white and blond, despite their geographical location in an amorphous South American location surrounded by "savage" peoples who cannot understand their advanced technology; disability and antisocial behavior have been eliminated through strict eugenic control (which, like the idea of human parthenogenesis itself, has obvious ties to white supremacist fantasies of "pure" reproduction). Mizorans, located at the South Pole, have similarly developed a eugenic technology that enables "dark complexion" to be banished. In these precursors to feminist science fiction, white middle-class American femininity is envisioned as a maternal reproductive model to be imperially exported across the world.[4]

The all-women landscapes of early feminist utopia make no mention of the possibility of erotic connections between women. Yet their notions of women's mutual care and love for land were characteristic of the lesbian feminist utopian fiction that emerged in the 1970s and 1980s, creating images of women's self-sufficient erotic spaces outside of – and sometimes at war with – patriarchal society. Sally Miller Gearhart's *The Wanderground* (1979) depicted a peaceful lesbian society that had escaped a patriarchal world, reminiscent of the "women's land" movements of the 1970s;[5] Katherine V. Forrest's *Daughters of A Coral Dawn* (1984) imagined a group of genetically superior women leaving the planet to create their own world. French feminist writer Monique Wittig created a speculative lesbian erotic world in her experimental 1971 fiction *Les Guérillères*, drawing on her philosophy (which would later influence Judith Butler's 1990 *Gender Trouble*) that women outside of the matrix of heterosexuality would have the potential to become something entirely different than women defined in relationship to men.[6] These utopian works updated Lane and Gilman's notion that women without men might have an inherent capacity to create a better world, though they and the movements that created them were later fiercely critiqued for the gender essentialism in their presumption that sexuality between women could provide a kind of redemption from the violence of dominant patriarchal heterosexuality – as well as for a racial exclusivity that we might see as of a piece with first wave feminist utopians' commitment to eugenics. A decade later, Nicola Griffith's *Ammonite* (1993) used fiction to reimagine a women-only world incorporating those critiques in a novel that highlighted cultural diversity, conflict, and a range of gender presentations on a planet where all the people happen to be women.[7]

Challenging the World Machine: Science Fiction as Feminist Critique

The second wave of feminism in the 1960s and 1970s brought intersections between civil rights and women's liberation to the forefront of American culture. Consciousness-raising groups offered women space to connect personal experience with larger social, political, and cultural concerns, and feminist theory and fiction exploded both within and beyond the science fiction genre. Among the most acute science fictional articulations of women's experiences of exclusion – and of the lack of awareness most men had of those experiences – was James Tiptree, Jr.'s 1973 "The Women Men Don't See," which shows an ordinary mother and daughter leaving Earth because they feel less alienated among unknown extraterrestrial beings than in their regular lives in the "chinks" of the patriarchal "world-machine" (134). Its title is given an added irony by the later exposure of Tiptree as the male pseudonym of Alice Bradley Sheldon.[8] Yet even prior to the second wave, within the genre and community of twentieth-century American science fiction, women writers often explored the ways technological and social change would affect women's experience within patriarchal society, even when their work was not explicitly feminist. Lisa Yaszek argues in *Galactic Suburbia* (2008) that mid-century women science fiction writers who transposed the gender expectations of the mid-twentieth century onto galactic futures were creating a ground on which to critique those restrictive modalities of gender and technology. In 1944, C. L. Moore published "No Woman Born," a subtly feminist version of the popular trope in which men create an automaton to be their perfect, obedient woman. Moore's Deirdre, a dancer transmuted into robotic form, develops a posthuman femininity beyond the comprehension of the men who previously had power over her. Judith Merril's 1948 "That Only a Mother" also has a protagonist in a traditional role within patriarchy, a wife and mother who responds to her daughter's radiation-induced mutation. Though sometimes dismissed by later feminists for its emphasis on feminine domesticity, the story offers a complex view of family, love, and disability through the voice of a woman who is prepared to open herself up to a different view than her husband's normative social one. Bringing the language and consciousness of the feminist movement to these domestic concerns, Pamela Zoline's "The Heat Death of the Universe" (1967) depicts a housewife's interior landscape in collapse, drawing ambiguously on science fiction tropes to create a speculative version of Betty Friedan's *The Feminine Mystique* in its focus on the pressures exerted on women by the excess of domestic labor.[9]

Political backlash against feminist incursions into the public sphere led many writers to imagine dystopian visions of women's futures in the

1970s and 1980s. *Walk to the End of the World* (1974) by Suzy McKee Charnas portrayed women as "Fems" reduced to the status of slaves after a catastrophic war.[10] Margaret Atwood's 1986 *The Handmaid's Tale* influentially imagined the United States as a religious state in which fertile women's bodies become public property. Utopia and dystopia blend in intricate dialectics through the multiple worlds and storylines in Joanna Russ's 1975 *The Female Man*, one of the most complex feminist science fiction works of this period. The novel grew out of Russ's 1972 short story "When It Changed," itself a nuanced take on a not-quite-utopian women-only society facing conflict at the prospect of returning men. Narration in *The Female Man* switches among four characters who share the same genetics but live in different timelines, allowing Russ to comment on the role of the feminist movement in American history and culture. Jeannine lives in a world without feminism, in which the Great Depression carried on into the 1970s; Janet, protagonist of "When It Changed," lives happily with her wife and daughter on the planet of Whileaway, a world that has rebuilt itself after a plague that destroyed the male population; Joanna is the voice of Russ's now, struggling with the restrictive requirements of womanhood and her desire to be a "female man"; and Jael, her body modified for combat, is a fighter in a shooting war between the sexes that she insists will be required for patriarchy ever to be overcome (which Jael claims is in fact the *true*, forgotten prehistory of Janet's Whileaway utopia).

Science fictional feminist critiques have often focused intensively on gendered power relations as experienced by white, middle-class American women; other axes of oppression and difference remain marginal, though Russ's later work in feminist theory highlights the centrality of race, class, and ability to any analysis of gender, whether it is named or not. Octavia Butler's 1995 *Parable of the Sower* is one example of a feminist science fiction work whose critiques, rooted in black feminism, highlight the intersectionality of multiple forms of oppression. Lauren Olamina, a young black woman living within a very realistic dystopian extrapolation of the neoliberal policies of late twentieth- and early twenty-first-century U.S. politics, experiences racism, sexism, and the effects of a science fictional disability that causes her to feel any pain that she observes. Lauren creates a religion called Earthseed and uses it to build a community that challenges the oppressive world in which she lives. Earthseed's credo is that God is Change, people must shape god, and the best goal for god-shaping is to leave the planet Earth: as in politicized science fiction itself, the suggestion is that imagining the world otherwise might be the first step in transforming it.[11]

Queering Reproduction: Beyond Male and Female

The potential transformation of reproduction, the biological process that serves as the presumptive basis for our sex-gender system, has been crucial for science fictional explorations of gender and sexuality. All-female worlds, with various degrees of utopian aspiration, have imagined parthenogenetic reproduction (Gilman) or processes by which ova are merged to create new life (Gearhart, Russ). The feminist dystopias of the 1970s and 1980s focus on the ways patriarchal society has exerted reproductive control by reducing women to reproductive machines. Alternate modes of reproduction were imagined as ways out of this bind; in 1978's *Motherlines*, Charnas's escapees from the postapocalyptic patriarchy memorably make use of horse semen to kickstart their reproductive functions. Other writers – beginning with England's Mary Shelley, often named the progenitor of science fiction itself – have imagined scientific and technological interventions into reproductive processes through the creation of clones, androids, and robots, raising questions about what it means to be human.

Alterations to the process of childbearing have been among the most widespread technological innovations imagined by feminist writers. In 1970, Shulamith Firestone's Marxist-feminist critique, *The Dialectic of Sex*, posited that women's liberation from the bodily work of childbearing (along with the elimination of family and childhood as we know them) would be necessary for a true feminist revolution. Firestone's version of science fictional radical feminism was taken up by Marge Piercy, whose 1976 *Woman on the Edge of Time* features – among several interlocking timelines whose reality is called into question – a future community in which children are gestated in artificial wombs and reared collectively, and in which male-bodied people can also participate in the work of breastfeeding. The idea is framed as a necessary – but melancholic – leap forward into a truly egalitarian utopia:

> Finally there was that one thing we had to give up too, the only power we ever had, in return for no more power for anyone. The original production: the power to give birth. Cause as long as we were biologically enchained, we'd never be equal. And males never would be humanized to be loving and tender. So we all became mothers. Every child has three. To break the nuclear bonding.[12]

Technological replacements for the uterus also appear in less explicitly feminist work, such as Lois McMaster Bujold's Vorkosigan saga, in which the increasing prevalence of uterine replicators within a conservative, aristocratically organized society begin to shift its prevalent gender expectations slowly over time. In conversation with one another, these works highlight the complex interactions of technology and social structures. In Bujold the uterine replicator makes for a slow increase in women's autonomy while maintaining a structure based on heterosexual kinship ties.[13] In Piercy, on the other hand, the breaking down of biological sex roles is part of the creation of a queer society in which the nongendered pronoun "per" is universal and both binary gender and heterosexuality have become an outdated irrelevance.

Perhaps the most famous work of feminist science fiction, *The Left Hand of Darkness* by Ursula K. Le Guin (1968) imagines a society in which biological sex itself is radically altered. Often shorthanded as a "genderless" world, Le Guin's Gethenians' lives are organized around a month-long biological sexual cycle in which they are either in a latent (somer) or sexually active (kemmer) phase. In the kemmer phase, any Gethenian may temporarily take on male or female physical sexual characteristics; individuals who bear such characteristics permanently are known as "perverts" and shunned. *The Left Hand of Darkness* has inspired vigorous criticism and conversation about what gender is and does, both among science fiction fans and feminist scholars, yet it has also inspired critique. The story is told through the voice of Genly Ai, a heterosexual man from a far-future earth, who finds Gethenian gender impossible to comprehend; many critics, Le Guin herself among them, have castigated the voice in which the story is told for its repetition of masculinist tropes such as the use of "he" to signify a generic and supposedly non-gendered human pronoun (Le Guin, 1989). In a 1995 story set in the same universe, "Coming of Age in Karhide," Le Guin writes from a Gethenian perspective in which she complicates her initial vision, particularly the way she had assumed that a kemmer phase in which one partner's male or female pheromones bring out the opposite sex in the other would restrict the Gethenians to heterosexual coupling.

Feminist and queer explorations of alternative sex/gender structures have explored the complex ways biology affects culture – sometimes accepting and sometimes rejecting the idea that biology might be a determining factor in gendered experience. Melissa Scott's *1995 Shadow Man* takes its central premise from real-world research on sexual biologies: Anne Fausto-Sterling, the feminist biologist and theorist of science, whose 1993 article "The Five Sexes: How Male and Female are Not Enough" argued that human biology might support a five-sex structure. Scott's novel assumes that the relationship between biology and culture is significant but not straightforward, and explores how different cultures might accept or reject the radically increased appearance of intersex human bodies. A more disturbing representation of sex and gender altered at the level of biology is Octavia Butler's Xenogenesis trilogy (1987's *Dawn*, 1988's *Adulthood Rites*, and 1989's *Imago*, collected as *Lilith's Brood* in 2000), which imagines that the human race destroys itself in war and is rescued by an alien species called the Oankali. The Oankali have three sexes, one of which (ooloi) has an organ for genetic engineering; through the three volumes of Butler's trilogy, the protagonist Lilith Iyapo and the community of human survivors she leads must grapple with what it means for humans to lose their humanness and accept alien domination if they are to live on. The tripartite gender structure of the Oankali and the eventual Oankali-human hybrids has been read as offering as a queer imaginary – one that suggests that the norm of heterosexuality need not be carried into the future.[14] The Oankali's verdict on humanity as genetically unsustainable, coupled with their ability to ineluctably seduce humans through their bioengineering capacities, make it clear that Butler's meditation on power, nature, and consent is no utopia, however.

Speculating Desire: Science Fiction Sexualities

This chapter so far should have made it clear that readers looking to find representations of nonheterosexual sexualities will discover a rich landscape in feminist science fiction. Yet, with exceptions such as the lesbian feminist utopian writings discussed earlier, the concerns of gay, lesbian, and queer political movements have not often been found explicitly in American science fiction. Instead, heterosexuality has been presumed to be the natural outlet for human – and even alien – desire.[15] Theodore Sturgeon published one of the earliest sympathetic depictions of male homosexuality in science fiction in "The World Well Lost" (published in *Universe* in 1952). The story imagines mysterious, male alien "loverbirds" escaping from a homophobic planet with the help of a closeted astronaut; critics have rightly celebrated the text for its progressive vision of cross-species queer connection, yet its basic structure involves the re-installation of 1950s homophobia within an imagined future. As Wendy Pearson has explored in several essays and as many of the works discussed earlier make clear, science fiction has not always had to focus on images of same-sex desire in order to create the possibility of imaginative spaces in which gender and sexuality could be lived and thought in different ways.[16]

American science fiction's most extensive and sustained engagement with queer cultures and theories can be found in the work of Samuel R. Delany. Engaged also with the larger conversation of feminist science fiction, Delany wrote *Trouble on Triton* (1976), *Stars in My Pocket Like Grains of Sand* (1984), and many more novels while also participating in queer sexual, social, and intellectual communities in the United States – as he documents in his memoir *The Motion of Light in Water*. Delany's 1984 work of fantasy, "The Tale of Plagues and Carnivals," was one of the first works of fiction to deal with the early experience of the AIDS crisis in New York City's gay male subculture. In *Trouble on Triton*, Delany draws on Michel Foucault's idea of "heterotopia" to imagine a world in which any desire, so long as it is consensual, can be fulfilled.[17] The protagonist, Bron Helstrom, changes gender in the middle of the novel; though Bron is a throwback to male chauvinism and does not find his sex change satisfying, Delany creates a speculative infrastructure in which transition for biological affirmation of characters' felt gender becomes routine. *Stars in My Pocket Like Grains of Sand* has a same-sex couple at its heart, but the text's exploration of alternate sexual and gender configurations extends far beyond their gendered bodies. The protagonist, Marq Dyeth, has a sexuality organized around his desire for hands, especially bitten fingernails, a fetish about which Delany has written extensively in memoir; the narration offers a lyric paean to the "wondrous and exciting" "structure of desire" that this creates for Marq (340). Queer ideas run through the very language of the novel (*he* is the pronoun for the object of sexual desire at the moment of desiring), its imagined technology (the central couple are found to be one another's "perfect erotic object – out to about seven decimal places" [166]) and, of course, the processes of reproduction (Marq is raised in a "nurture stream" comprising humans and lizard-like alien evelm with five total genders involved and "no direct egg-and-sperm relations" between generations [118]).

The established literary canon of science fiction contains only a small proportion of the cultural production that has centered on possibilities for gender and desire beyond the heterosexual. Science fiction in film and television has been a particular focus for gay and lesbian fans wishing to see themselves represented in popular visions of the future. The long-running Gaylaxian campaign to bring a homosexual character to the technological utopian future of *Star Trek* has been unsuccessful,[18] but 2011's adaptation of the British series *Torchwood* brought one of the first out queer protagonists to American science fiction television in the person of the omnisexual Captain Jack. And fans, both heterosexual and queer, of pop cultural science fiction have been creating grassroots homoerotic narratives since the 1970s in slash fan fiction that imagines queer relationships between popular characters from genre media. As Joanna Russ wrote in 1985's "Pornography by Women for Women with Love," *Star Trek* was an incredibly important text for many women fans of science fiction, and in slash fan fiction, art, and remix video they developed a space for exploring speculative erotics in a feminist and queer realm. Even when it was not erotic, fan fiction and other forms of fan creativity gave marginalized viewers a space to create their own visions of media texts, opening up the possibility of feminist reinterpretation – though feminist, queer, and science fictional production is only a small corner of the massive online world of fan culture in the 2010s. Additionally, gay and lesbian independent filmmakers have integrated science fiction themes in a variety of ways, notably Lizzie Borden's 1985 *Born in Flames*, which shows a cross-racial lesbian uprising against the sexism of a future socialist society, and Canadian John Greyson's 1993 *Zero Patience*, which makes use of the time-traveling figure of Sir Richard Burton, along with a ghost, to explode homophobic scientific mythologies about the rise of AIDS.

Building a World: Queer and Feminist Science Fiction Off the Page

To think about feminist and queer science fiction purely from the perspective of textual production is to think about it in a relatively impoverished way. Feminist science fiction is also a community and a world that has invited readers, writers, fans, and scholars into new ways of understanding, thinking, and living gender and sexuality. This imagined community has often been lived purely through published fiction, as L. Timmel Duchamp discusses in "The Grand Conversation" (2004), yet it also has an infrastructure and institutions of its own, into which diverse explorations of queerness, race, disability, and other forms of social and embodied difference have been fostered. Academic feminist and queer theory are often, especially in summary articles like this one, figured as critical approaches that can be applied to science fiction. Yet academia has also been a world-building pillar for feminist science fiction's development, even as the intersection of two fields marginal to the canon has meant that its proponents have sometimes had precarious experiences in the academy. Feminist science fiction scholarship merges intellectual work done inside and outside the institution, and can be said to include the science-fiction-infused science studies work of Donna Haraway, whose "Cyborg Manifesto" (1991) drew extensively from the work of Octavia Butler and other science fiction writers, as much as the genre theory and history developed in journals like *Science Fiction Studies*, *Extrapolation*, and *FemSpec*.

As Helen Merrick documents in *The Secret Feminist Cabal* (2009), science fiction feminisms now have a grassroots infrastructure with a forty-year, ever-changing history in the parallel and sometimes intersecting universes of fandom, publishing, and academia. In the 1970s, feminist fanzines, including Jeanne Gomoll's *Janus* and Amanda Bankier's *The Witch and the Chameleon*, opened up spaces for conversation in which authors and fans alike participated.[19] The 1975 "Women in Science Fiction" issue of the 'zine *Khatru*, edited by Jeff Smith and reissued with additional material in 1993, is a microcosm of the debates and worlds of feminist science fiction at this instigating moment. Conventions have been another prong of science fiction feminism's formation as a culture and a world. Madison-based Gomoll began the feminist convention WisCon, inspired by the limitations on discussion created by singular "women in science fiction" panels at fan conventions; the 38th WisCon was held in 2014. WisCon and similar conventions (such as Diversicon and Think Galacticon) have served as a hub for ongoing online and print-based discussions of how feminist analysis and feminist science fiction can best integrate race, queer, and gender non-conforming perspectives, class, and disability. And the intersection of feminist theorizing with science fiction is not only focused on fan communities; black feminist organizers at the Allied Media Conference, which brings together activists working for media justice, use Octavia Butler's work as a gathering point from which to focus the speculative, world-changing energies of radical activists.[20]

If one side of feminist and queer science fiction real-world world building is amateur creativity and grassroots activism, another is publishing – bringing into print the work of authors whose creative texts challenge and explore what might be possible for gender as it intersects with other modes of difference. In 1991, at WisCon, the Tiptree Award was founded to honor science fiction that did these things, in critical response to the ecosystem of science fiction awards that structure the genre's publishing industry: the Clarke, Campbell, Hugo awards, all named after men (the Nebula being the nongendered star system exception). The Tiptree has, in the twenty-four years since its inception, become more than an award; "Tiptree" is an adjective that signals a particular kind of story, a particular kind of tradition, thanks not only to the award but to the work the Tiptree Motherboard has done in keeping older works of feminist science fiction in print. Yet the world of mainstream publishing is a difficult place, in the early twenty-first century, in which to bring out work that proposes the kind of challenge to norms that queer and feminist science fiction ought to do. And so participants in the feminist science fiction world have also begun to create institutional structures that will give this kind of writing space to flourish. Founded by author and critic L. Timmel Duchamp, Aqueduct Press's tagline is "Bringing challenging feminist science fiction to the demanding reader" and its name and logo highlight the ways this kind of work can feel as necessary as water to the thirsty. Aqueduct's first publication was in 2004; it has published more than fifty books since, of which three have been winners of the Tiptree Award. Mindful political knowledge production and preservation perpetuates and expands the radical explorations of queer and feminist science fiction – through fiction, theory, and conversations on paper, in digital form, and in person.

Note: Thanks to Lauren Shoemaker for research assistance in the compiling of this chapter.

NOTES

1   L. Timmel Duchamp, *The Grand Conversation* (Seattle, WA: Aqueduct Press, 2004).
2   Joan Haran and Katie King, "Science Fiction Feminisms, Feminist Science Fictions and Feminist Sustainability," in *Ada: A Journal of Gender, New Media and Technology* 3 (November 2013).
3   For a British example, see Elizabeth Burgoyne Corbett's 1889 *New Amazonia*.
4   White utopian feminism is not the only story of women's fictional speculation at this historical moment; African-American writer Pauline Hopkins, for example, was engaging questions of gender and race in her 1903 speculative fiction *Of One Blood*.
5   Ariel Levy's 2009 *New Yorker* article "Lesbian Nation" offers an accessible introduction to these movements.
6   Monique Wittig, "The Straight Mind," in *The Straight Mind and Other Essays* (Boston, MA: Beacon Press, 1992).
7   See Nicola Griffith and Kelley Eskridge, "War Machine, Time Machine," in Wendy Gay Pearson, Veronica Hollinger, and Joan Gordon, eds., *Queer Universes* (Chicago, IL: Liverpool University Press, 2008).
8   See Julie Phillips's outstanding biography, *James Tiptree, Jr.: The Double Life of Alice B Sheldon* (London: Picador, 2006).
9   See Mary Papke's "A Space of Her Own: Pamela Zoline's 'The Heat Death of the Universe,'" in Justine Larbalestier, ed., *Daughters of Earth: Feminist Science Fiction in the Twentieth Century* (Middletown, CT: Wesleyan University Press, 2006), 144–59.
10 English writer Katharine Burdekin had earlier explored this theme, under the male pseudonym Murray Constantine, in 1937's *Swastika Night*.
11 The Parables series is discussed in more detail in the closing chapter of this volume, "After America."
12 Marge Piercy, *Woman on the Edge of Time* (London: Women's Press, 2000), 105.
13 See Lucy Baker's analysis of reproduction in Bujold in "A Curious Doubled Existence: Birth Here and in Lois McMaster Bujold's Vorkosigan Saga," in *Ada: A Journal of Gender, New Media and Technology* 3 (November 2013).
14 See Patricia Melzer, *Alien Constructions: Science Fiction and Feminist Thought* (Austin: University of Texas Press, 2006).
15 See Wendy Pearson's "Science Fiction and Queer Theory," in Edward James and Farah Mendlesohn, eds., *The Cambridge Companion to Science Fiction* (Cambridge University Press, 2003), 149–60.
16 See, for instance, Wendy Pearson's "Alien Cryptographies: The View From Queer," *Science Fiction Studies* 26 (March 1999): 1–22 and "Towards a Queer Genealogy of SF," in Wendy Gay, Veronica Hollinger, and Joan Gordon Pearson, eds., *Queer Universes: Sexualities in Science Fiction* (Liverpool: Liverpool University Press, 2008), 71–100.
17 Michel Foucault, "Of Other Spaces," *Diacritics* 16 (April 1986): 22–7.

18 The campaign is detailed in Henry Jenkins, "'Out of the Closet and Into the Universe': Queers and *Star Trek*," in John Tulloch and Henry Jenkins, eds., *Science Fiction Audiences: Watching Doctor Who and Star Trek* (New York: Routledge, 1995).

19 See Roxanne Samer's interview with Gomoll and Bankier in Alexis Lothian, ed., *The WisCon Chronicles Volume 6: Futures of Feminism and Fandom* (Seattle, WA: Aqueduct Press, 2012), 2–17.

20 See Moya Bailey's 2013 interview with Adrienne Maree Brown in "'Shaping God': The Power of Octavia Butler's Black Feminist and Womanist SciFi Visions in the Shaping of a New World – An Interview with Adrienne Maree Brown," *Ada: A Journal of Gender, New Media and Technology* 3 (November 2013).

6

MARK BOULD

The Futures Market: American Utopias

In 1979, Darko Suvin asserted that "strictly and precisely speaking, utopia is not a genre but the *sociopolitical subgenre of science fiction*."[1] Just twenty-five years earlier, Glen Negley and J. Max Patrick had claimed, with equal confidence, that SF was "a bastard literary device" with "about the same resemblance to utopian speculation that the tales of Horatio Alger bore to the economic theories of Adam Smith."[2] While both these combative displays of cultural capital are clearly the products of specific historical conjunctures, taken together they also indicate the complexity of the relationship between SF and utopian fiction. Suvin himself notes the paradox of the older form being a subset of the younger, explaining that "it can be seen as such only now that SF has expanded into its modern phase, 'looking backward' from its englobing of utopia," while noting that this "expansion was in some not always direct ways a continuation of classical and nineteenth-century utopian literature."[3] However, even as Suvin emphasized the formal distinctions and hierarchical relationship between these intertwined genres, so a fresh understanding of utopia was emerging, largely in response to Ernst Bloch's weighty elaboration of the principle of hope. Bloch argued that the "world is full of propensity towards something ... and this intended something means fulfillment of the intending" in "a world which is more adequate for us, without degrading suffering, anxiety, self-alienation, nothingness."[4] Bloch describes this latent futurity in terms of *Heimat*, an "*anticipated* state of reconciliation with conditions of possibility that do not as yet exist, and indeed *will* not exist until present conditions have been radically reconceptualised so that they can be transformed into something as yet impossible to define."[5] Traces of utopian hope can be identified in a vast array of texts and practices, far beyond the literary tradition Negley and Patrick championed and Suvin reduced to a subset of SF.

Although this chapter will at times evoke Blochian hope, and its opening section will note several experiments in living, intentional communities and other utopian cultural practices, as well as a number of distinctly un-science-fictional texts, it will take "utopia" primarily to refer to literature that speculates about social organization and transformation, including satires and dystopias that exaggerate rather than negate elements of their real-world context. Such speculations are to be understood as discourses about change – as fluid evocations of possibility rather than static plans for a perfected world. Combining pessimism of the intellect with optimism of the will, they aspire to a world better than the unhomely ruin we continue daily to make.

Utopianism in the Americas before Bellamy

The relationship between utopia and the Americas dates back nearly a thousand years, to the text known variously as *Gayanashagowa* (The Great Binding Law), *Kaianerekowa Hotinonsionne* (The Great Law of Peace of the Longhouse People), or *The Constitution of the Iroquois Nations* (that is, the Haudenosaunee nations of Oneida, Mohawk, Cayuga, Onondaga, the Seneca, and, from 1722, Tuscarora),[6] which details an ideal political system (aspects of it are often said to underpin the U.S. constitution and the UN Charter). However, the destruction of indigenous cultures by European colonization of the continent makes it difficult to determine how widespread utopian sentiments and narratives were in their largely oral traditions.[7]

In terms of the colonizing powers, this relationship can be dated to Thomas More's *Utopia* (1516). Raphael Hythloday, the traveler who tells the narrator all about the eponymous isle, is identified as one of Amerigo Vespucci's crewmen; set ashore in Brazil, he ventured on by himself to discover the community King Utopus founded. Throughout the Enlightenment, Europeans continued to project utopian desires onto the New World. For example, Gilbert Imlay's *A Topographical Description of the Western Territory of North America* (1792) reputedly inspired a number of intentional communities, such as the Pantisocracy proposed by Samuel Taylor Coleridge and Robert Southey and outlined in the former's *Lectures on Revealed Religion* (1795).[8] Frances Brooke's *The History of Emily Montagu* (1769), the first novel written in Canada (albeit by a visiting Englishwoman), depicts First Nations culture so as to critique European gender relations, while Robert Bage's *Hermsprong: or, Man As He Is Not* (1796) features a young settler raised by indigenous peoples so as to emphasize unnatural and hypocritical aspects of English society.

The utopian tradition produced by colonists can be dated from John Winthrop's "A Model of Christian Charity" sermon (1630). This early exercise in American exceptionalism instructed the Massachusetts Bay settlers that their Puritan colony would be, paraphrasing the Sermon on the Mount, "a city upon a hill," that is, an exemplar of Christian virtue for the whole world to see (despite the colony's patriarchal authoritarianism, religious intolerance, growing antagonism toward indigenous peoples, and tolerance of slavery, limited forms of democratic republicanism did emerge there). In a similar vein, John Cotton's *Abstract of Lawes of New England, As they are now established* (1641) outlined and argued for the adoption of a system of laws based on a particular interpretation of the Bible.[9] A century later, Reverend William Smith's tract "A General Idea of the College of Mirania" (1753) proposed a fictional college of liberal arts and sciences, which practiced greater religious tolerance than these earlier Christian examples, and which attempted to include indigenous peoples and new immigrants in its community. Among the many settlements and intentional communities that developed during European colonization, perhaps a more hopeful oppositional vision can be seen in the efforts of German mystic Christian Gottlieb Priber, who in the 1730s and 1740s found Cherokee allies for his idea of a communal society without private property, which welcomed criminals, debtors, and runaway slaves.

The interrelation of utopian fiction, intentional communities, and political activism in the New World is well demonstrated by the example of Frances Wright, a feminist, abolitionist, anticlerical, anticapitalist campaigner for reproductive, educational, and workers' rights. Born in Scotland in 1795, she became a U.S. citizen in 1825. In the same year, influenced by Robert Owens's New Harmony settlement, she founded the egalitarian, interracial Nashoba commune in Tennessee, with the intention of preparing slaves for emancipation. After Nashoba collapsed, she ensured the former slaves' relocation to Haiti, where they could live as free men and women. Her well-regarded *Views of Society and Manners in America* (1821) evinces a democratic humanitarianism, and her 1833–6 lecture tours on abolition and women's health were popular and influential – but her utopian novel, *A Few Days in Athens, being the translation of a Greek manuscript discovered in Herculaneum* (1822), which espouses an Epicurean philosophy, proved far more controversial.

Throughout the nineteenth century, a large number of American utopian texts – not all of them science fictional – were published, including Herman Melville's *Typee* (1846), James Fenimore Cooper's *The Crater; or, Vulcan's Peak* (1847), Nathaniel Hawthorne's *The Blithedale Romance* (1852), Henry David Thoreau's *Walden; or, Life in the Woods* (1854), Elizabeth Stuart Phelps's *The Gates Ajar* (1868), Mark Twain's *A Connecticut Yankee in King Arthur's Court* (1889), and Charles M. Sheldon's *In His Steps: "What Would Jesus Do?"* (1896). None, however, would have the galvanizing effect on American utopianism of Edward Bellamy's best-selling *Looking Backward,*

2000–1887 (1888). In addition to the 165 or more Bellamy clubs formed to discuss and promote its ideas, which provided the basis for the Nationalist Party and thus influenced the Populist Party, it also prompted an outpouring of more than two hundred utopian novels before the century's end.

In Bellamy's novel, late nineteenth-century Bostonian Julian West wakes from hypnotic slumber a century into a post-scarcity – if not exactly socialist – future, where Dr. Leete and his daughter, Edith, explain the workings of their egalitarian (if bourgeois, white, patriarchal, and consumerist) society and how it came to be. At times Bellamy clearly echoes Karl Marx, recognizing the astonishing productive forces unleashed by the capitalist mode of production while simultaneously decrying the anarchic wastefulness of blind and remorseless competition, with its unavoidable crises of overproduction and systemic immiseration of human lives. He also describes wages as mere exchange value, and profit (surplus value) as a plutocratic tax on workers' labor. Central to his utopia is the reorganization of production so that it provides equal incomes for all rather than profits for a few. However, although Bellamy grants that workers' fears of subordination to an inhuman corporate tyranny is not unreasonable, he denies any role in this transformation to labor or socialist activism. To him, workers are a confused, rudderless mass, lacking in understanding, and their mass action is merely epiphenomenal. The real driver of change is the increasing concentration of capital into national monopolies that ultimately merge with, and somehow become subordinate to, the state: the great trusts give way to The Great Trust, and the chaos of capitalist competition is replaced, nonviolently, with benevolent management. Everyone works for the sole remaining capitalist – the state – and in this utterly reasonable meritocracy, everyone pursues the socially necessary labor best suited to their abilities.

However, this is not a world without contradictions. Although monadic individualism has given way to intersubjectivity, and social alienation to social responsibility, the organization of labor is predicated on a belief that the majority of workers are indifferently skilled and thus competitive hierarchies – organized around social standing rather than income differentials – must be maintained, perpetuating precarity (albeit of position rather than physical well-being). The universal income freed women from financial dependence on men, and marriage from the cash nexus capitalism imposes on all social relations. Even so, monogamous heterosexuality remains the norm, and the freedom enjoyed by women is that of being mothers not only to their own children but also to the coming future world. At the same time, liberated from the distortions of economic necessity, sexual selection produces eugenic improvements, and utopia is dominated by a racial hierarchy, with peoples of color needing white civilization to uplift them.

From Bellamy and into Genre SF

William Dean Howells's *A Traveler from Altruria: A Romance* (1892–3) and its sequels respond to Bellamy's urban plenitude with a pastoral vision of Christian socialism. In contrast, Ignatius Donnelly's *Caesar's Column: A Story of the Twentieth Century* (1890) and Jack London's *The Iron Heel* (1908) react to Bellamy's abstract dialecticism by foregrounding the violence inherent to capital's extraction of surplus value and to the authoritarian terror with which oligarchies maintain a socioeconomic order beneficial to themselves, and the revolutionary action necessary to transform the mode and relations of production. King Camp Gillette's *The Human Drift* (1894) argues for public ownership of industry and mass relocation to a new city in the Niagara region to benefit from abundant hydroelectric power – an idea reiterated in his *World Corporation* (1910) and *The People's Corporation* (1924), cowritten by Upton Sinclair, as well as in Philip Nowlan and Dick Calkins' *Buck Rogers* daily comic strip (from 1929). Upton Sinclair's *The Millennium: A Comedy of the Year 2000* (1924, based on an unproduced 1907 play) replaces revolution with the destruction of almost all human life, apart from a bunch of plutocrats who must then progress through a succession of modes of production, from slavery to feudalism to capitalism to cooperative socialism.[10] A number of socialist SF writers were active in the genre magazines, including Harl Vincent, the Futurian group,[11] Chan Davis, Howard Fast, and Mack Reynolds (who wrote a pair of replies to Bellamy, *Looking Backward from 2000* [1973] and *Equality in the Year 2000* [1977]). David H. Wheeler's nonfiction *Our Industrial Utopia and Its Unhappy Citizens* (1895) champions capitalism, as do Ayn Rand's *Atlas Shrugged* (1957), Ben Bova's *Kinsman* stories (1965–79), and Larry Niven and Jerry Pournelle's *Oath of Fealty* (1981). While some genre SF suggests a need to restrain capitalist excesses, this typically takes the form not of democratic control but of technocratic management and engineering interventions, as in Robert A. Heinlein's "The Roads Must Roll" (1940) and George O. Smith's *Venus Equilateral* stories (1942–7). More commonly, from Hugo Gernsback's *Ralph 124C 41+: A Romance of the Year 2660* (1911–12) onward, SF normalizes capitalism by assuming its endless, unquestioned perpetuation, a tendency that leads Bruce Sterling's *Schismatrix* (1985), for example, to treat neoliberal economics as if they are laws of physics.

Equality (1897), Bellamy's sequel to *Looking Backward*, broadened the scope of women's activities from shopping and maternity, giving Edith a job in scientific agriculture, and addressed the total absence of peoples of color from its future Boston by indicating that they live equal, but segregated, lives. A strong feminist utopian tradition, including Mary Griffith's

Three Hundred Years Hence (1836) and Mary E. Bradley Lane's *Mizora: A Prophecy* (1880–1), preceded Bellamy, and flourished again in his wake, in novels such as Alice Ilgenfritz Jones and Ella Marchant's *Unveiling a Parallel* (1893) and Charlotte Perkins Gilman's *Moving the Mountain* (1911), *Herland* (1915), and *With Her in Ourland* (1916). In the following decades, as the U.S. magazine-and-paperback tradition consolidated, utopian elements would continue to occur in SF by women – C. L. Moore, Leigh Brackett, Judith Merril, Carol Emshwiller, and others[12] – but a fully fledged feminist utopianism would not emerge until the remarkable flourishing that stretched from the late 1960s to the mid-1980s, and spilled out of genre SF.[13]

Among the utopias by women published in the early SF pulps[14] are Leslie F. Stone's pastoral "Letter of the Twenty-Fourth Century" (1929) and Lilith Lorraine's socialist-feminist "Into the 28th Century" (1930). The latter argues for winnowing the dross from all the races and then uniting these various strains through intermarriage to form a superior humanity. While problematic in terms of its misapprehensions of biology and evolution, not uncommon in eugenic thought, it nonetheless refuses the notion of a hierarchy of races and advocates a color-blind future. On the rare occasions pulp SF engaged with race other than merely to repeat racist stereotypes or jingoistic colonial adventure narratives, it tended to disappear peoples of color entirely on the grounds that race was no longer an issue, or achieved the same effect by displacing explorations of race onto aliens or robots.

African-American Utopianism

There is a strong tradition of African-American utopian fiction both in and outside genre SF. Frances E. W. Harper's *Iola Leroy, or, Shadows Uplifted* (1892) charts the separation of an African-American family, first by slavery and then by the Civil War, and the reunion of the survivors during Reconstruction. The light-skinned protagonist refuses to pass for white or to marry into a white family, choosing instead – like her brother and her eventual husband, both of whom could also pass – to work for the individual and collective uplift of their own people. This refusal of white privilege and wealth in favor of black identity, and the accompanying elevation of family and community over competitive individualism and of gradualist reform over radical action, are utopian prefigurations of "a brighter coming day."[15] Pauline Hopkins's *Of One Blood, or, The Hidden Self* (1902–3) is more overtly science fictional: an African American on an archaeological expedition in Ethiopia discovers both a hidden ancient city of superscience *and* that he represents the long prophesied return of an ancient ruler destined to produce a global dynasty that will displace white supremacist modernity. Edward Augustus Johnson's *Light Ahead for the Negro* (1904) depicts a rationally planned, corporate utopia a century in the future, which affirms the philanthropy of white, antiracist sympathizers, while simultaneously depicting African Americans (who do not actually appear in the novel) as pliable, docile, and in need of charitable white guidance. Roger Sherman Tracy's *The White Man's Burden: A Satirical Forecast* (1915) is rather less supine. Although the reader is left with only a vague sense of what its fifty-first-century anarchist African utopia is like, its satirical inversions of white supremacism are sharply critical of the Jim Crow era: a single drop of polluting white blood is enough to transform a person of color into a debased criminal; the white race is doomed because of its taste for domination. An even more devastatingly satirical take on Jim Crow is George S. Schuyler's *Black No More* (1932). Extrapolating from ubiquitous hair-straightening and skin-lightening nostrums, Schuyler introduces a scientific process for turning black people white, and pursues its consequences with absurdist rigor. In addition to satirizing assimilationist, separatist, and other black radical discourses, the novel takes acerbic delight in excoriating different races and classes for their various investments in the maintenance of the color line, while exposing its lunacies and hypocrisies. The novel ends with "white" people darkening their skins so as not to be mistaken for lightened "black" people, a practice that the latter group, of course, also then adopts.

In Sutton E. Griggs's *Imperium in Imperio* (1899), soon after the declaration of the Spanish-American war, an African-American postmaster is murdered by white supremacists. Knowing that the government will do nothing to protect black citizens but nonetheless call on them to defend the nation, a secret African-American organization declares war on white America. They plan a mass relocation to, and the fortification and secession of, Texas. The novel ends on the cusp of an apocalyptic war, as does W. E. B. Du Bois's *Dark Princess: A Romance* (1928), in which the Great Central Committee of Yellow, Brown and Black announces a timetable for global revolution against Euro-American imperialism and white supremacism. Schuyler's *Black Empire* (1936–8) goes further, depicting the global war necessary for Afrodiasporic peoples to free themselves and build a superscience utopia in Africa.

A similar cycle of novels emerged in the 1960s and 1970s, although they could only go as far as the opening shots of a revolutionary race war and were incapable of imagining the utopian future that might come after. Among the key examples of this cycle are John A. Williams's *The Man Who Cried I Am* (1967), *Sons of Darkness, Sons of Light* (1969), and *Captain Blackman*

(1972), which move from realist *roman à clef* to a pulpier and more didactic mode; Julian Moreau's superscience revenge fantasy *The Black Commandos* (1967); Sam Greenlee's hardboiled thriller, *The Spook Who Sat by the Door* (1969); Blyden Jackson's Frantz Fanon-inspired *Operation Burning Candle* (1973); and Chester Himes's apocalyptic satire, *Plan B* (written 1969–72; published 1983).[16] Nivi-kofi A. Ealey's *The Militants* (1974) begins in a similar mode, but soon abandons revolutionary action and, unable to imagine a postrevolutionary future, instead figures *Heimat* in the sleazily banal terms of the prerevolutionary world: an interracial ménage-a-trois in a commodity-laden, swanky new apartment. Faced with the same problem, William Melvin Kelley's *A Different Drummer* (1962) displaces the violence of revolution into a symbolic refusal: one day, Tucker Caliban sows his land with salt, burns down his house, and, with his wife and child, departs the Southern state to which his ancestors were brought as slaves; a mass black exodus ensues, resolutely unexplained but far from inexplicable.[17]

From Dystopian Satire to Critical Utopia to Critical Dystopia

While utopian designs are often equated with the Stalinist and Nazi regimes that successfully co-opted utopian desire into the service of the totalitarian state, the totalizing capitalist world system has been equally effective at channeling such desires into the prescribed channels of commodity consumption. This is evident in advertising, entertainment,[18] the corporate utopias of the 1939 New York World's Fair,[19] and "those living maps of restrictive pleasure which carry the passive consuming audience along in a totally managed environment, Disneyland and Disneyworld."[20] In response to such developments, Tom Moylan argues, utopian critique transformed into dystopian critique through the mid-twentieth century.

The 1950s, for example, saw the development of dystopian satires or comic infernos, most strongly associated with *Galaxy* magazine, which would extrapolate contemporary trends – corporate culture, mass media, suburban lifestyles, consumerism – to absurd extremes. Frederik Pohl and Cyril M. Kornbluth's *The Space Merchants* (1953) depicts a future of unconstrained corporate power, ubiquitous advertising, and promotional campaigns in which anything goes. Ann Warren Griffith's "Captive Audience" (1953) and Garen Drussai's "Woman's Work" (1956) take on advertising and consumer cultures from within the domestic realm to which the postwar backlash had returned many women. Ray Bradbury's *Fahrenheit 451* (1953) depicts a media-saturated, post-literate suburbia, and in Pohl's "The Midas Plague" (1954), the production of commodities has accelerated to the point where the poorer one is the greater the daily quota of manufactured goods one is legally obliged to consume. Bernard Wolfe's *Limbo* (1952) concatenates anxieties about nuclear war, cybernetics, psychoanalysis, masculinity, and feminism in a devastating portrait of Cold War culture. Philip K. Dick, in such novels as *Time Out of Joint* (1959), *Martian Time-Slip* (1962), *The Three Stigmata of Palmer Eldritch* (1964), *Do Androids Dream of Electric Sheep?* (1968), *Ubik* (1969), and *A Scanner Darkly* (1977), captured the tawdry crumbling landscape of monopoly capitalism – suburban alienation, disempowering corporate culture, the false promise of the commodity – as it transformed into simulacral multinational capitalism.

The countercultural politics of the 1960s and 1970s foregrounded the incongruities between an era of relative affluence and its multiple modes of oppression, thus reinvigorating utopia. These tensions are evident in the liberal-humanist *Star Trek* (1966–9), which has been interpreted by some as depicting an egalitarian, even socialist, future, while others have been more critical of the ways the United Federation of Planets can be seen to extend white patriarchal imperialism into the future and the galaxy. *Star Trek: The Next Generation* (1987–94) would perfectly capture this contradiction with the introduction of the Borg, whose relentless drive to assimilate all other species into their collective is either opposite to, or exactly the same as, the goal of the Federation.

Many of the feminist works noted earlier overlapped with a queer utopianism, evident in Theodore Sturgeon's *Venus Plus X* (1960) and African American Samuel R. Delany's *Dhalgren* (1975) and *Triton: An Ambiguous Heterotopia* (1976), and with the ecological concerns of Harry Harrison's *Make Room! Make Room!* (1966) and Ernest Callenbach's *Ecotopia: The Notebooks and Reports of William Weston* (1974). Moylan argues that at the heart of this new burst of utopian SF is the critical utopia, exemplified by Russ's *The Female Man*, Le Guin's *The Dispossessed*, Piercy's *Woman on the Edge of Time*, and Delany's *Triton*. Such novels negate the dystopian negation of utopia that dominated the postwar decades, and reclaim utopian energies from the totalizing structures of patriarchal capitalism and compulsory heterosexuality while building on the feminist perception that the personal is political to offer visions of tumultuous, diverse, sensually fulfilling non-alienation. A fresh emphasis on the transition to utopia and the forces arrayed against such social change, along with depictions within a single novel of several alternative worlds, create a much stronger sense of utopia's incompletion, of utopia as a historical process, endlessly unfolding without teleology or end-point as a constantly fought-for asymptote to perfection.

Ronald Reagan's election signaled the imposition of a grand utopian scheme – the neoliberal ideological fantasy that, once deregulated, capitalism could become a friction-free system delivering social justice, equality, and trickle-down wealth to all – that banished Keynesian ameliorations of capitalism and, accompanied by backlash politics, overturned many of the relatively small advances made by leftist, feminist, queer, and civil rights activism since the war. William Gibson's *Neuromancer* (1984) offers a remarkably compelling vision of the future neoliberalism entailed: the nation-state withers away while global economic systems serve the interests of corporations and their compradors; massive ecological disaster is just part of the background noise; the marginalized, precarious majority scrabble a hard living in the ruins; and collective resistance is replaced by the privatized dissent of subcultural posturing and dabbling in grey and black economies. The nearest thing to Blochian traces of hope are the opportunities to practice professional skills – whether as hacker or street samurai – that a short-term contract might offer, and the disembodied exhilaration the protagonist experiences when his virtual avatar flies free in cyberspace. Such archetypal cyberpunk fictions as *Neuromancer* and Neal Stephenson's *Snow Crash* (1992) depict a common dystopian spatiality of (complexly) segregated locations that articulate economic and social power in terms of class, race, and gender, but they nevertheless offer their putative outsider figures access to the realm of power through masculinized hacker skills. *Red Spider, White Web* (1990) by Misha (Metis-Cree) retains this spatiality but significantly reworks it by refusing the virtual realm. She insists on the material struggles of her artist-characters not only to survive in the polarized world of unrestrained multinational capital – a choice between living in the subterranean, working-class Dogton, succumbing to the blandishments the corporate elite's domed, amusement-park city Mickey-san, or scrabbling a hand-to-mouth existence in the polluted, postindustrial ruins outside the city – but also to produce artworks that resist commodification and retain a genuinely critical capacity.

In the context of this new dystopianism, Moylan identifies a number of works – Kim Stanley Robinson's *Gold Coast* (1988), Marge Piercy's *He, She and It* (1991), and African American Octavia E. Butler's *The Parable of the Sower* (1993) and *The Parable of the Talents* (1998) – as critical dystopias; within these dystopian texts and the settings they delineate, "voice and space" is given to "dispossessed and denied subjects," and the opportunity to move beyond mere survival to the potential creation of "a social reality that is shaped by an impulse to human self-determination and ecological health" is explored.[21] The middle volume of a thematic trilogy, coming between the postapocalyptic pastoral of *The Wild Shore* (1984) and the critical utopia of *Pacific Edge* (1990), *Gold Coast* depicts a near future of increasingly militarized corporate capital, wearying commodity culture, and middle-class precarity. While the protagonist becomes involved in direct action against outposts of the military-industrial complex, uncovering layers of corporate conspiracy that stand in for a cognitive mapping of the operations of multinational capitalism, he also writes a history of the long degradation of Orange County, summoning from the past an impossible *Heimat*. Robinson's Mars trilogy (1993–6) transforms the critical dystopian balance as the interplanetary gulf between a ravaged Earth and a terraforming Mars permits some respite from capitalism, a harried breathing space in which different social and economic arrangements can be tried and tested; and as Mars becomes increasingly habitable, such alternatives render it increasingly a home. His *2312* (2012) has a rather bleaker view of human expansion into the solar system, but at the same time celebrates human creativity and, like Delany's *Triton*, the sheer dazzling diversity of lifestyles and cultures people might build once freed from capitalist immiseration and alienation. With a similar sentiment and radically different approach, Delany's *Through the Valley of the Nest of Spiders* (2012) focuses in intimate, sometimes pornographic, detail on a queer relationship that spans seventy years of a twenty-first century that gradually, if sketchily, becomes a world rather different to our own.

The embrace of difference represented by such novels is central to the anticapitalist politics of the 1990s and the new millennium, and to the utopias of the same period. African-American/Tsalagi Zainab Amadahy's *The Moons of Palmares* (1997), Dennis Danvers's *The Fourth World* (2000), and Rosaura Sánchez and Beatrice Pita's *Lunar Braceros, 2125–2148* (2009) are critical dystopias that draw inspiration from the largely indigenous Zapatista uprising and its resistance to neoliberalism. In 2000, British author China Miéville announced that the elusive, mutating, category-transgressing New Weird was intimately tied to the anticapitalist alter-globalization movement – that it was a fiction responding to and expressing the opening of the world to radical possibilities, registering the "another world is possible" slogan of the 1999 protests against the World Trade Organization in Seattle.[22] The post-genre tumult, not restricted to those identified with the New Weird, saw many emerging writers working with, and across old distinctions between, SF, fantasy, and horror, often introducing myth and/or magic into SF or historical scenarios, such as: Larissa Lai's *When Fox Is a Thousand* (1995) and *Salt Fish Girl* (2002); Nalo Hopkinson's *Brown Girl in the Ring* (1998), *Midnight Robber* (2000), and *The Salt Roads* (2003); Colson Whitehead's *The Intuitionist* (1999); Junot Díaz's *The Brief Wondrous Life of Oscar Wao* (2007); Nnedi Okorafor's *Who Fears Death* (2010); Andrea Hairston's *Redwood and Wildfire* (2011); Kameron Hurley's *Bel Dame Apocrypha* (2011–12); G. Willow Wilson's *Alif the Unseen* (2012); and

Amadahy's *Resistance* (2013). While such novels might not initially seem to be utopian, they nonetheless draw on other knowledges – indigenous, African, Caribbean, Asian, Islamic, female, queer – to defy the deadening diktats of (eco-catastrophic, white supremacist, patriarchal, heteronormative) capitalist realism.²³ They re-enchant the world, and restore *Heimat* to its place at the center of our desires and demands for the better world we need urgently to build.

NOTES

1   Darko Suvin, *Metamorphoses of Science Fiction: On the Poetics and History of a Literary Genre* (New Haven, CT: Yale University Press, 1979), 61.
2   Glen Negley and J. Max Patrick, eds., *The Quest for Utopia: An Anthology of Imaginary Societies* (College Park, MD: McGrath, 1971), 588.
3   Suvin, *Metamorphoses of Science Fiction*, 61.
4   Ernst Bloch, *The Principle of Hope, volume one*, trans. Neville Plaice, Stephen Plaice, and Paul Knight (Cambridge, MA: The MIT Press, 1986), 18.
5   Jamie Owen Daniel, "Reclaiming the 'Terrain of Fantasy': Speculations on Ernst Bloch, Memory, and the Resurgence of Nationalism," in Jamie Owen Daniel and Tom Moylan, eds., *Not Yet: Reconsidering Ernst Bloch* (London: Verso, 1997), 53–62, at p. 59 emphasis in original.
6   Variant translations are available at http://www.indigenouspeople.net/iroqcon.htm and http://www.manataka.org/page135.html.
7   B. C. Mohrbacher, in "The Whole World is Coming: The 1890 Ghost Dance Movement as Utopia." *Utopian Studies* 7.1 (1996): 75–85, intriguingly interprets the *Nanissáanah* (Ghost Dance) that developed in response to the teachings of Wovoka (Nevada Pauite) and spread to other nations, including the Lakota Sioux, as a utopian practice of cultural renewal and spiritual revitalization in the face of colonial genocide. It prompted violent repression by the U.S. military, including the 1890 massacre at Wounded Knee. In the counterfactual *The Indians Won* (1970), Martin Cruz Smith (part Pueblo, Senecu del Sur, and Yaqui) depicts a rather different sequel to the 1876 Battle of Little Big Horn, which includes an early appearance of Wovoka's prophecies and results in the establishment of a successful indigenous nation alongside the United States. Pamela Sargent's *Climb the Wind* (1998) follows a similar pattern, while Eric Flint's *1812: The Rivers of War* (2005) and *1824: The Arkansas War* (2006) takes an even earlier historical divergence to postulate an alternative world in which a confederacy of indigenous nations, welcoming to runaway slaves and other peoples of color, is established in the Arkansas Territory. In Sesshu Foster's *Atomik Aztex* (2005), the Aztecs defeated European invaders, but there is a leaky border between their alternate world and our own.
8   The successful founding of a North American Pantisocracy is possibly the earliest point of historical divergence in William Gibson and Bruce Sterling's dystopian steampunk alternative history, *The Difference Engine* (1990).
9   Nathaniel Hawthorne's *The Scarlet Letter* (1850) can be understood as a dystopian depiction of this culture, the metaphoric potential of which was further developed in Arthur Miller's anti-McCarthyist *The Crucible* (1953).

10 Sinclair also wrote utopian fiction as part of his End Poverty in California campaign to seize the Democratic gubernatorial nomination for socialist ends, and in support of the related national campaign, in the pamphlets *I, Governor of California – and How I Ended Poverty* (1933), and *We, People of America, and how we ended poverty: a true story of the future* (1933). Robert A. Heinlein worked for the EPIC campaign, and traces of Sinclair's socialism can be discerned in his first novel, unpublished until 2004, *For Us the Living: A Comedy of Customs.* In Chris Bachelder's *US!* (2006), Sinclair appears, repeatedly resurrected and assassinated, as a constant, socialist reminder of American failings.

11 The Futurian group included Isaac Asimov, James Blish, Virginia Kidd, Damon Knight, Cyril M. Kornbluth, Robert A. W. Lowndes, Judith Merril, John B. Michel, Frederik Pohl, and Donald Wollheim.

12 See Lisa Yaszek, *Galactic Suburbia: Recovering Women's Science Fiction* (Columbus: The Ohio State University Press, 2008).

13 Key works include Ursula K. Le Guin's *The Left Hand of Darkness* (1969), *The Dispossessed: An Ambiguous Utopia* (1974) and *Always Coming Home* (1985); Joanna Russ's "When It Changed" (1972), *The Female Man* (1975) and *The Two of Them* (1978); Marge Piercy's *Woman on the Edge of Time* (1976); James Tiptree, Jr's "The Women Men Don't See" (1973); and "Houston, Houston, Do You Read?" (1976); Suzy McKee Charnas's *Holdfast Chronicles* (1974–99); Suzette Haden Elgin's *Coyote Jones* series (1970–86) and *Native Tongue* trilogy (1984–94); Pamela Sargent's *The Shore of Women* (1986); Sally Miller Gearhart's *The Wanderground: Stories of the Hill Women* (1979); Katherine V. Forrest's *Daughters of A Coral Dawn* (1984); Joan Slonczewski's *Elysium Chronicles* (1986–2000); Sheri S. Tepper *The Gate to Women's Country* (1988); and Canadian Margaret Atwood's *The Handmaid's Tale* (1985). This tradition continues to evolve, though without quite the same critical mass, in such novels as Nicola Griffith's *Ammonite* (1993), Tricia Sullivan's *Maul* (2003), and L. Timmel Duchamp's *Marq'ssan Cycle* (2005–8). For more on the relationship between feminism, utopianism, and SF, see Alexis Lothian's contribution to this volume in the previous chapter.

14 See Jane L. Donawerth, "Science Fiction by Women in the Early Pulps, 1926–1930," in Jane L. Donawerth and Carol A. Kolmerten, eds., *Utopian and Science Fiction: Worlds of Difference* (Liverpool: Liverpool University Press, 1994), 137–52.

15 Frances E. W. Harper, *Iola* (London: X Press, 1994), 193.

16 Afrofuturism's utopian valences are further discussed in Lisa Yaszek's chapter in this volume (Chapter 4).

17 For a fuller discussion of these African-American fictions, see Mark Bould, "Revolutionary African-American SF before Black Power," *Extrapolation* 51.1 (2010): 53–81 and "Come Alive By Saying No: An Introduction to Black Power SF," *Science Fiction Studies* 102 (2007): 220–40. Several white novelists contributed to this cycle, not all of them opportunistic scaremongers, and it is significant that it is one of them, Warren Miller, who is able to imagine a postrevolutionary America. However, his *The Siege of Harlem* (1964), set seventy-five years after Harlem's secession, only hints at the nature of its Afrocentric, black pride utopia, focusing instead on recounting the events of the revolution as a bedtime story for the community's children. Equally sympathetic to black liberation,

Mack Reynolds's *North Africa* trilogy (1961–78) pieces together a postcolonial, pan-African utopia, without Schuyler's revenge fantasy and in a far more *reasonable* tone, but focuses on the social engineering skills of educated African Americans rather than on Africans, most of whom have to be duped into pursuing radical transformation.

18 See Richard Dyer, "Entertainment and Utopia," in *Only Entertainment* (London: Routledge, 1992), 17–34.

19 See H. Bruce Franklin, "America as Science Fiction: 1939," *Science-Fiction Studies* 26 (1982): 38–50.

20 Tom Moylan, *Demand the Impossible: Science Fiction and the Utopian Imagination* (London: Methuen, 1986), 8.

21 Tom Moylan, *Scraps of the Untainted Sky: Science Fiction, Utopia, Dystopia* (Boulder, CO: Westview, 2000), 189.

22 For more on the New Weird as "post-Seattle" fiction, see China Miéville, "Long Live the New Weird," *The Third Alternative* 35 (2003): 3. The manifesto and the New Weird as a literary movement is further discussed in Roger Luckhurst's contribution to this volume, "American Weird."

23 On capitalist realism, see Mark Fisher, *Capitalist Realism: Is There No Alternative?* (Ropley: Zero, 2009).

PART II

Media and Form

7

ROB LATHAM

American Slipstream: Science Fiction and Literary Respectability

Because the genre developed in the pulp (and later digest) magazines, American science fiction was essentially segregated from the body of so-called mainstream literature from the 1920s onward.[1] Before that time, what we would now call works of science fiction appeared in the "general" pulps (i.e., magazines that had not yet begun to specialize in "category" genres such as SF or detective stories), yet science fiction was still largely seen as popular reading material by contrast with more serious kinds of writing. Like the nineteenth-century dime novel, pulp fiction was marked from the outset as a "lowbrow" form, geared for working-class readers or immigrants still learning to master English.[2] Even in Great Britain, which did not have a significant native tradition of magazine SF before the 1950s, the "scientific romance" pioneered by H. G. Wells was also viewed as distinct from the more prestigious realistic novel. Though Wells had a substantial reputation among the literary elite, he was "seen as a man who had achieved great success *in spite of* the character of his work; his feat in winning respect for extravagant fantasies was considered almost paradoxical; a freak performance which could not stand as a precedent."[3] The ugly split between Wells and Henry James over aesthetic priorities, with Wells championing the novel of ideas while James defended the novel of character, served to mark speculative writing as inferior in Britain as indelibly as the gaudy covers of the pulp magazines exiled American SF writers to a literary "ghetto."[4] Further reinforcing this separation, no substantial market for book-length SF – outside of serial publication in the pulps – existed prior to the 1950s.

The emergence of such a market, combined with a widespread awareness of the growing role of modern technoscience in the postwar world, raised the cultural visibility of SF during that decade. Yet while this led to occasional crossover successes (Ray Bradbury's early work, for example, was embraced by literary intellectuals),[5] the vast majority of genre writers continued to labor in a marginal (and increasingly unstable) magazine market. Some SF themes – especially depictions of the onset or aftermath of atomic warfare – were catapulted into the mainstream because of their resonance with prevailing social concerns, and works on the subject by genre and non-genre writers alike achieved bestseller status during the 1950s and early 1960s. Meanwhile, some prominent SF editors and commentators, such as Judith Merril and Damon Knight, were working to raise the literary standards of the field, with Merril in particular arguing for a broader sense of its horizons than that encompassed by the publishing category "science fiction." In her annual "Year's Best S-F" anthology series, which commenced in 1956, Merril sought to popularize the alternative term "speculative fiction" as a way of displaying the affiliation between genre SF and a range of non-realist work by more "literary" talents, from John Steinbeck and Bernard Malamud to André Maurois and Eugène Ionesco.

During the 1960s, the advent of the so-called New Wave seemed to vindicate Merril's strategy, as a new generation of writers and editors, chafing at the constraints of the magazine tradition, embraced the experimental novels of William S. Burroughs as forerunners of a more aesthetically challenging and socially conscious science fiction. New markets, such as all-original anthologies, offered stout competition to the magazines, and book editors grew bolder in their willingness to solicit unconventional material, giving ambitious young authors fresh venues for publication.[6] At the same time, figures such as Kurt Vonnegut and Thomas Pynchon enjoyed mainstream success with novels that, while not published as science fiction, drew heavily on the resources of the genre. These novels had a significant readership among SF writers and fans, with Vonnegut's *Cat's Cradle* (1963) and *Slaughterhouse-5* (1969) being nominated for Hugo Awards and Pynchon's *Gravity's Rainbow* (1973) for a Nebula Award. Yet with the exception of a very few SF titles – such as Frank Herbert's *Dune* (1965) or Samuel R. Delany's *Dhalgren* (1975), which became best sellers among counterculture readers – the traffic mostly flowed in one direction: from the mainstream into the genre. Major SF authors such as Philip K. Dick and Robert Silverberg, despite producing increasingly complex and provocative work, continued to be shut out of the larger literary marketplace.

By 1989, if one is to judge by Bruce Sterling's column in the July issue of the fanzine *Science Fiction Eye*, the genre's situation looked dire indeed. While at one time it might have offered readers "a real grip on the chrome-plated handles of the Atomic Age," Sterling asserted, it now seemed little better than "a dream that failed," a "self-perpetuating commercial power-structure" giving off a strong "reek of decay."[7] Much more responsive to the concerns of serious readers, including serious SF readers dissatisfied with the state of the field, was a new genre Sterling called "slipstream." Slipstream was a kind of writing that "set its face against consensus reality," often by deploying surreal or other avant-garde techniques, and that as a consequence made readers "feel very strange; the way that living in the twentieth century makes you feel, if you are a person of a certain sensibility."[8] Though it sometimes featured elements of speculative fiction, it was very different from the New Wave movement in that its authors generally "kn[e]w or care[d] little or nothing about SF."[9] The provisional list of slipstream titles featured in the essay was an admittedly motley assortment of texts with little in common save Sterling's sense that they were all addressing the palpable weirdness of the contemporary world in a bolder and more engaging way than genre SF could presently muster. The list, while making some token efforts at internationalism (e.g., Günter Grass, Gabriel García Márquez, J. M. Coetzee, Angela Carter), was dominated by American writers – though these ranged from postmodern experimentalists (Pynchon, William Gaddis) to edgier genre talents (Thomas M. Disch, Jack Womack) to realist novelists who sometimes dabbled in the fantastic (Walker Percy, Toni Morrison).

For all its claims to gaze beyond SF's borders to descry the contours of an emerging field, however, the essay was, as Paweł Frelik has argued, "overdetermined by intra-sf concerns" spawned by the genre's persistent anxiety about its literary legitimacy.[10] In Frelik's analysis, there have always been slipstream texts – that is, fiction that "falls through the cracks of exclusionary definitions of sf"[11] – since the inception of the genre as a marketing category in the 1920s. Merril's efforts, during the 1950s, to expand the bounds of SF to include "speculative" material emanating from other sources was simply a different historical inflection of the same basic impulse animating Sterling's essay. Yet Frelik also acknowledges that the advent of postmodernism in the 1960s gave this recurring impulse a particular new urgency, considering how this aesthetic movement challenged traditional distinctions between high art and mass culture (indeed, Sterling's essay had flirted with the phrase "Novels of Postmodern Sensibility" before settling on "slipstream" as a more convenient term that operates as "a parody of 'mainstream'" in the SF lexicon).[12] In Victoria de Zwaan's view, the very existence of such a label, despite the incoherence of Sterling's list of representative texts, is evidence of the ongoing "postmodernization of sf"[13] – even though Sterling was eager to see slipstream as "definitely not SF" and "essentially alien to what [he] consider[ed] SF's intrinsic virtues" of scientific accuracy and rigorous extrapolation.[14] In Doug Davis's words, slipstream "is the fiction that happens at the intersection of SF and postmodernism."[15]

As noted earlier, the 1960s–1970s was an era when a number of novelists – now usually characterized as postmodernist – began to be embraced by those segments of the SF community eager to break with the genre's pulp past. The fact that many of these postmodern authors borrowed liberally from SF's classic repertoire of images and themes was taken as proof that the field had generated a popular iconography and a technocultural vocabulary that spoke powerfully to contemporary readers. And, indeed, novels such as Ishmael Reed's *Mumbo Jumbo* (1972) and Joseph McElroy's *Plus* (1976), while considerably more structurally experimental than most genre SF, show a clear familiarity with SF themes and plots.

Plus is a novel told from the perspective of "Imp Plus," a disembodied human brain sent into orbit on a monitoring mission; initially afflicted with a kind of amnesia, Imp Plus gradually grows into a self-confident cyborg entity, intricately enmeshed with the technologies of its orbital platform, that finally risks its life in an attempt at deep space exploration. While this brief summary might make the novel sound like a fairly conventional space adventure, its dense manner of telling – a fusion of abstruse technocratic jargon and visionary prose poetry – clearly set it off from hard-SF tales with similar storylines. Indeed, probably because of the lingering low-art status of the genre at the time, McElroy refused to describe the novel as science fiction,[16] but this dismissive attitude was not necessarily shared by other postmodern novelists. Reed, by contrast, expressly praised SF in *Mumbo Jumbo*, a delirious extravaganza chronicling the mythic struggle between a secret society of repressive monotheists, the Atonists, and a liberating, animistic force called "Jes Grew" – a battle that features, among other things, an attempt by the former faction to infiltrate, undermine, and coopt the latter via the deployment of a "Talking Android." Critical of both "official" histories and canonical cultural forms, which are seen as mere tools of Atonist power, the narrator suggests that "the Nursery Rhyme and the book of Science Fiction" – because they embrace fantastic possibilities and thus defamiliarize the given world – "might be more revolutionary than any number of tracts, pamphlets, [or] manifestoes."[17] Despite their convergence with SF, however, neither of these novels had a broad genre readership at the time (although Reed's does appear on Sterling's slipstream list).

Aside from Vonnegut's works, the postmodern novel that enjoyed the warmest reception within the SF field was probably *Gravity's Rainbow*, which is clearly deeply conversant with the pulp tradition, even if its fantasies of technological transcendence are subjected to a merciless deconstruction over the course of the story. A poisonous paean to the romance of rocketry in the twentieth century, Pynchon's novel is steeped in both the hard facts of aerospace engineering and the poetic reveries surrounding human flight, especially the dream of interplanetary travel. Yet it links this soaring aspiration to the brutal reality of mechanized death via the Nazi V-2 program, with the rockets raining down on London serving as prefigurations of the postwar world of ICBMs and Mutual Assured Destruction.

Pynchon's corrosive vision of the perversion of transcendence into annihilation achieves its apotheosis in the protagonist's fantasies of a "Rocket-City," where "dioramas on the theme 'The Promise of Space Travel'" are mere ideological window dressing on a totalitarian dystopia.[18] Moreover, Pynchon's oneiric evocations of this "City of the Future" are redolent with the imagery of pulp-era covers featuring "swoop-façaded and balconied skyscrapers …, classy airships of all descriptions drifting in the boom and hush of the city abysses."[19] Among its manifold allusions to SF-related materials, *Gravity's Rainbow* also mobilizes comic books – the protagonist is an avid reader of *Plastic Man* and at one point imagines himself a member of a superhero gang called the "Floundering Four" – along with the early futuristic films of Fritz Lang. Pynchon's attitude toward these materials is ambivalent, at times almost fannish, at others viciously satirical – and it is likely that the latter posture is what caused a more conventional work of hard SF, Arthur C. Clarke's *Rendezvous with Rama* (1973), to beat out *Gravity's Rainbow* for the "best novel" Nebula.

By the end of the 1970s, according to Brian McHale, the interchange between SF and postmodernism had become so extensive that "a feedback loop began to operate," with postmodern novels growing increasingly "science-fictionalized" while SF texts were reciprocally "postmodernized."[20] There is definitely something to this argument: classics of cyberpunk SF such as William Gibson's *Neuromancer* (1984) show obvious debts to postmodern writers, especially Burroughs and Pynchon, while Kathy Acker's *Empire of the Senseless* (1988) literally borrows from Gibson's novel in generating its playful intertextual collage.[21] Meanwhile, a few neglected SF writers, in particular Philip K. Dick, were posthumously canonized as postmodernists *avant la lettre*, with Dick's work being rereleased by mainstream publishers and, often, reshelved in the Literature section of bookstores.

Yet McHale's hopeful vision of an ongoing mutual concord between SF and postmodern writing has been sharply contested by novelist Jonathan Lethem in a 1998 article for the *Village Voice*, ominously entitled "The Squandered Promise of Science Fiction." In Lethem's reckoning, the nomination of *Gravity's Rainbow* for a Nebula "stands as a hidden tombstone marking the death of the hope that science fiction was about to merge with the mainstream." The victory of Clarke's novel signaled a "retrenchment" behind the "genre-ghetto walls" – a defensive move away from mainstream respectability toward "a reactionary SF as artistically dire as it was comfortingly familiar." This retreat occurred just as literary novelists such as Pynchon, McElroy, and Don De Lillo were producing a sophisticated new breed of SF that spoke to a wider readership. Thus, writers with artistic ambition who remained within the genre were compelled to subsist "in a twilight world, neither respectable nor commercially viable. Their work drowns in a sea of garbage in bookstores, while much of SF's promise is realized elsewhere by writers too savvy or oblivious to bother with its stigmatized identity."[22] Understandably controversial within the SF genre, Lethem's essay does manage to capture a dynamic that has characterized literary production since at least the 1990s: younger authors who grew up reading both SF by the likes of Dick and mainstream postmodern novels by the likes of Pynchon – authors such as Lethem himself, say – no longer feel the need ritualistically to disavow any connection with the genre (as McElroy did two decades earlier), but they also do not feel compelled to publish within its borders or cultivate a fan audience because the larger literary marketplace has embraced their SF-inflected works.

Lethem's appreciation for – and intimate knowledge of – science fiction is evident not only in his "Squandered Promise" essay (which features a sharp, concise summary of trends in the genre since the New Wave) but also in several other nonfiction pieces he has written over the years, most of which were gathered in his 2011 book *The Ecstasy of Influence*. Significantly, the section including his essays on SF also lumps in meditations on postmodernism and postmodern writers, suggesting that he sees no categorical division between Dick and J. G. Ballard on the one hand and Italo Calvino on the other. The essay on Dick in particular, entitled "Crazy Friend," is a virtual love poem to the author, whom Lethem discovered – along with New Wave SF more generally – while growing up in Brooklyn in the 1970s. "I scored used copies of *Ubik* and *A Maze of Death* and *The Three Stigmata of Palmer Eldritch*," he writes, and in reading them "made Dick my own, forging a relationship into which I'd pour vast personal capital over the decades that followed."[23] He could have added "professional capital" as well because, after becoming a celebrated writer in his own right, Lethem was instrumental in persuading the Library of America to devote three volumes to gathering thirteen of Dick's best novels (including those cited in the quotation given earlier), thus further cementing Dick's burgeoning mainstream reputation, and he also coedited, along with Pamela Jackson, a selection of Dick's voluminous personal journals. Moreover, several of Lethem's early works gave evidence of the late SF author's abiding influence, and of the legacy of a youthful immersion in the genre more generally, with his second novel, a postapocalypse tale entitled *Amnesia Moon* (1995), being rife with allusions to Dick's fiction.[24] Yet, bespeaking the transformation in the literary landscape, Lethem's novels were, from the very first, published by mainstream presses and marketed as serious fiction.

At the same time, his fiction has enjoyed a warm reception within the SF genre, being nominated for four Nebula Awards and ten Locus Awards, and winning one Locus Award (for his first novel, *Gun, with Occasional Music* [1994]) and one World Fantasy Award (for his 1996 collection *The Wall of the Sky, the Wall of the Eye*). But nothing proves the ongoing collapse of cutting-edge SF and postmodern writing more conclusively than the career of Lethem's contemporary, Michael Chabon. In 2008, a year that essentially reversed the results of Pynchon's loss of a Nebula to Arthur C. Clarke three decades earlier, Chabon's alternative-historical murder mystery, *The Yiddish Policeman's Union* (2007), swept the major prizes bestowed by SF writers and fans, winning a Hugo, a Nebula, and a Locus Award while beating out works by more established SF talents such as Ian McDonald, Charles Stross, and Joe Haldeman. The fact that an earlier novel of Chabon's had won a Pulitzer Prize didn't cause him to be exiled to the mainstream; instead, he was embraced by the SF community, probably because of his frequent and vociferous praise of the genre in high-profile venues and his obviously heart-felt pronouncements of how deeply his youthful SF reading had colored his literary sensibility. Underlining Lethem's judgment about the growing irrelevance of categories such as "SF" and "mainstream" in the current state of the marketplace, Chabon has asserted that, on the one hand, he "never abandoned his genre reading" even after receiving literary acclaim but also that, on the other hand, he never "wanted to be a fantasy and science fiction writer"; rather, he simply "wanted to be a writer," and genre materials were just one of several influences on which he continued to draw.[25]

The novel for which Chabon received his Pulitzer, *The Amazing Adventures of Kavalier & Clay*, gives further evidence of the implosion of traditional divisions of the literary terrain. A sprawling epic of midcentury America, the story tracks the career of the eponymous duo, comic book creators responsible for a hit 1940s superhero title featuring the exploits of the Escapist, loosely modeled on Harry Houdini. Joe Kavalier, who draws and inks the series, himself barely escaped Nazi-occupied Czechoslovakia, so the theme has historical resonance. Chabon also addresses long-standing accusations that comic books and other popular material – including pulp SF – constitute mere "escapist" reading, that their impulse to abandon mundane reality militates against their ability to be recognized as serious art. The novel stoutly contests this notion, although it does contrast the willingness of Sammy Clay, Joe's cousin and the series' writer, to settle for commercial hackwork – "highly conventional, severely formulaic ... miniature epics" – with the quasi-novelistic ambitions of Joe, who feels that "escape from reality ... – especially right after the war – [was] a worthy challenge," calling out for the production of works of fantasy "that only the most purblind of societies would have denied the status of art."[26] Chabon's notion that the "escapism" of popular culture offers a genuine aesthetic refuge, especially for those traumatized by violence and suffering, is echoed in Junot Díaz's own Pulitzer-winning novel, *The Brief Wondrous Life of Oscar Wao* (2007), where a readerly "commitment to the Genres" is seen as quite appropriate for a teenage Dominican immigrant who fled political repression in his native country.[27] Indeed, the narrator mounts a strong defense of science fiction in particular as the only form of writing capable of capturing the sense of cultural estrangement experienced by a displaced "Antillean (who more sci-fi than us?)" who has become "a smart bookish boy of color in a contemporary U.S. ghetto."[28]

This is clearly an autobiographical observation on the author's part, at least judging from Díaz's comments in interviews – where, like Chabon, he has detailed his lifelong fondness for genre writing. As a teenager "who was going through the pain, the dislocation, the sorrow, the confusion of being an immigrant," he has said, he found in science fiction "all of this extreme stuff ... that resonated with a lot of the ideas and experiences and the historical shadows that have been cast from the Dominican Republic."[29] For writers like Lethem, Chabon, and Díaz, all of whom were born in the midst of the New Wave's epochal renovation of pulp-era SF during the 1960s, the lingering stigma of "category" writing has never been a pressing concern or a significant roadblock to mainstream success and literary acclaim. Yet some writers of an older generation who have turned their attention toward the genre have continued to manifest a prickly defensiveness regarding the categorization of their work as science fiction, though this has not stopped them from publishing such crossover texts.

While he has not himself expressed such views publicly, Cormac McCarthy produced in his 2006 novel *The Road* – yet another Pulitzer winner – a book that is at once perhaps the bleakest postapocalypse tale ever written and one that persistently foils attempts to read it as SF. The disaster that assails the world is only briefly glimpsed in flashbacks and no effort is made to explain it; instead, the narrative follows a nameless man and his son as they struggle to survive in a gray wasteland bereft of animal life, rummaging for stores of food while evading the cannibal packs that roam like feral monsters through the ruins. Flirting with outright nihilism before reaching an ambivalently upbeat conclusion, *The Road* reads much more like a moral parable than a work of SF, yet clearly McCarthy has thought through the social ramifications of the disappearance of the food chain in the rigorous way typical of the genre. Much more overtly science fictional is Canadian author Margaret Atwood's *Oryx and Crake* (2003), also a tale of apocalypse, though the nature of the catastrophe in her novel – genetic engineering run amok – is painstakingly researched and meticulously explained. At the same time, a fairly traditional "two cultures" model dividing science from the humanities structures its overall worldview, with the narrator clearly on the side of the latter faction – which explains perhaps why Atwood has resisted the use of the term "science fiction" as a label for her work, because SF has traditionally straddled this divide. Despite the fact that *Oryx and Crake* received the Arthur C. Clarke Award for best novel in 2008, Atwood dismissed the genre as being about nothing but "rockets, chemicals and talking squids in outer space"[30] – though she has since moderated this position somewhat, deigning to accept the alternative classification of "speculative fiction" instead.[31]

As the examples of Lethem, Chabon, and Díaz show, however, such views are much less prevalent among younger authors, who seem more willing – even eager – to move beyond traditional literary boundaries. Such a move would appear to challenge the very possibility of slipstream writing because (as we have seen) the term originally emerged as a way to separate SF proper from some sort of sketchy, postmodern, hybrid version. Sterling himself, in a 1999 follow-up essay, has acknowledged that the term never really designated a cohesive genre, although he still seems to hold out hope that it retains some descriptive purchase on the state of contemporary literary production.[32] Likewise, James Patrick Kelly and John Kessel, in the introduction to their 2006 book *Feeling Very Strange: The Slipstream Anthology*, admit that Sterling's coinage of the moniker was an attempt to "form a canon out of mist and wishful thinking," yet they proceed to offer their own definition – work that "embraces cognitive dissonance" by flouting norms of realism while borrowing liberally from popular genre fiction – that extends many of Sterling's animating assumptions.[33] Their collection includes work by Lethem, Chabon, and George Saunders – work that is usually marketed as "serious" fiction despite its SF content – alongside stories by offbeat genre talents such as Carol Emshwiller, Kelly Link, and Karen Joy Fowler – the general effect being to blur, rather than underline, the division between them.

Curiously, this blurring – which has become endemic to the current literary scene – has only served to spawn a host of efforts to coin fresh terms to describe new kinds of cross-border fictions: "new wave fabulism," "interstitial fiction," "transrealism." This frenzy of taxonomy, as de Zwaan has observed, is highly ironic given that what most of these labels seek to designate is precisely the implosion of borders between domains of literary production and the dispersal of genre materials throughout the corpus of contemporary fiction – in other words, the ongoing breakdown of literary taxonomy itself.[34] As Gary K. Wolfe has shown, this breakdown is happening *within* traditional genre fiction as well, with today's SF mingling promiscuously with mysteries, horror stories, and other popular forms whose borders were sharply demarcated during the era of the category pulps in the

1920s. Wolfe calls this phenomenon the "evaporation" of genre as such – a word that captures, perhaps better than any other, the current state of literary affairs.[35] Slipstream initially may have been intended to evoke, as Atwood has observed, a narrative form that "mak[es] use of the air currents created by science fiction proper,"[36] but in an atmosphere where genre SF is in the process of becoming pure vapor, no solid body may exist any longer that can generate such a powerful wake. Instead, there is simply the mixing of fictive elements at an almost molecular level. This is not to say that traditional literary divisions, with their attendant stigmas, have entirely disappeared (as Atwood's infamous "squids in space" crack indicates), but merely that they continue to undergo a radical metamorphosis that threatens, over time, to continue to unmake boundaries that once seemed quite fixed.

NOTES

1 As Paweł Frelik has pointed out, the term "mainstream," widely deployed within the SF field, is "inherently imprecise" but generally tends to denote "all serious prose fiction outside the market [i.e., category] genres" ("Of Slipstream and Others: SF and Genre Boundary Discourses," *Science Fiction Studies* 38.1 (2011): 24). The fact that we have such a term at all is evidence of a perceived sense, within the SF community, of a wholesale segregation from the larger literary marketplace.

2 For an analysis of the class stratification of American popular fiction during the nineteenth century, see Michael Denning, *Mechanic Accents: Dime Novels and Working-Class Culture in America*, 2nd ed. (New York: Verso, 1998); for a discussion of the emergence of pulp SF out of this matrix, see Mike Ashley, *The Time Machines: The Story of the Science-Fiction Pulp Magazines from the Beginning to 1950* (Liverpool: Liverpool University Press, 2000), 1–44.

3 Brian Stableford, *Scientific Romance in Britain 1890–1950* (London: Fourth Estate, 1985), 125.

4 On the Wells-James feud, see Leon Edel and Gordon Norton Ray, eds., *Henry James and H. G. Wells: A Record of Their Friendship, Their Debate on the Art of Fiction and Their Quarrel* (Urbana: University of Illinois Press, 1958). On the SF pulps as a "ghetto" quarantined from the concerns of highbrow readers, see James E. Gunn, *Inside Science Fiction*, 2nd ed. (Lanham, MD: Scarecrow Press, 2006), especially chapters 2 and 3.

5 For a discussion of Bradbury's crossover appeal in the context of evolving literary institutions during the period, see Evan Brier, *A Novel Marketplace: Mass Culture, the Book Trade, and Postwar American Fiction* (Philadelphia: University of Pennsylvania Press, 2010), 45–73.

6 For a fuller discussion of these postwar trends, see my essays "Fiction, 1950–1963," in Mark Bould, Andrew M. Butler, Adam Roberts, and Sherryl Vint, eds., *The Routledge Companion to Science Fiction* (New York: Routledge, 2009), 80–9, and "The New Wave," in David Seed, ed., *A Companion to Science Fiction* (Malden, MA: Blackwell, 2005), 202–16.

7 Bruce Sterling, "Slipstream," *Science Fiction Eye* 1.5 (1989): 77.

8 Ibid., 78.

9 Ibid., 80.
10 Frelik, "Of Slipstream and Others," 33.
11 Ibid., 27.
12 Sterling, "Slipstream," 78.
13 Victoria de Zwaan, "Slipstream," in Mark Bould, Andrew M. Butler, Adam Roberts, and Sherryl Vint, eds., *The Routledge Companion to Science Fiction* (New York: Routledge, 2009), 500–4.
14 Sterling, "Slipstream," 80.
15 Doug Davis, "Understanding Slipstream Fiction," *A Virtual Introduction to Science Fiction*, ed. Lars Schmeink, accessed December 7, 2013. http://virtual-sf.com/wp-content/uploads/2012/04/Davis.pdf.
16 See Tom LeClair and Larry McCaffery, "Interview with Joseph McElroy," in Tom LeClair and Larry McCaffery, eds., *Anything Can Happen: Interviews with Contemporary American Novelists* (Urbana: University of Illinois Press, 1983), 235–51. For a discussion of the novel as science fiction, see Salvatore Proietti, "Joseph McElroy's Cyborg Plus," *Electronic Book Review* (August 18, 2004), online, accessed December 7, 2013. http://www.electronicbookreview.com/thread/criticalecologies/seeing.
17 Ishmael Reed, *Mumbo Jumbo* (New York: Scribner, 1996), 18.
18 Thomas Pynchon, *Gravity's Rainbow* (New York: Penguin, 1995), 296.
19 Ibid., 674.
20 Brian McHale, *Constructing Postmodernism* (New York: Routledge, 1992), 228–9.
21 On the convergence of postmodernism and cyberpunk, see Larry McCaffery, ed., *Storming the Reality Studio: A Casebook of Cyberpunk and Postmodern Fiction* (Durham, NC: Duke University Press, 1992). For a discussion of Acker's novel in relation to slipstream discourses, see Victoria de Zwaan, "Rethinking the Slipstream: Kathy Acker Reads *Neuromancer*," *Science Fiction Studies* 24.3 (1997): 459–70.
22 Jonathan Lethem, "The Squandered Promise of Science Fiction," *The Hipster Book Club* (December 22, 2008), accessed December 8, 2013. http://hipster-bookclub.livejournal.com/1147850.html.
23 Jonathan Lethem, "Crazy Friend," in *The Ecstasy of Influence: Nonfictions, Etc.* (New York: Doubleday, 2011), 39–67.
24 See Umberto Rossi, "From Dick to Lethem: The Dickian Legacy, Postmodernism, and Avant-Pop in Jonathan Lethem's *Amnesia Moon*," *Science Fiction Studies* 29.1 (2002): 15–33.
25 "Michael Chabon Attacks Prejudice Against Science Fiction," *Wired* (March 7, 2012), accessed December 9, 2013. http://www.wired.com/underwire/2012/03/michael-chabon-geeks-guide-galaxy/.
26 Michael Chabon, *The Amazing Adventures of Kavalier & Clay* (New York: Random House, 2000), 486, 575.
27 Junot Díaz, *The Brief Wondrous Life of Oscar Wao* (New York: Riverhead, 2007), 20.
28 Ibid., 21–2.
29 "Junot Díaz Aims to Fulfill His Dream of Publishing Sci-Fi Novel With *Monstro*," *Wired* (December 3, 2012), accessed December 10, 2013. http://www.wired.com/underwire/2012/10/geeks-guide-junot-diaz/3/.

30 See David Barnett, "Science Fiction: The Genre That Dare Not Speak Its Name," *The Guardian* (January 28, 2009), accessed December 10, 2013. http://www. theguardian.com/books/booksblog/2009/jan/28/science-fiction-genre.

31 See her collection of essays *In Other Worlds: SF and the Human Imagination* (New York: Doubleday, 2011).

32 See Bruce Sterling, "Slipstream 2," *Science Fiction Studies* 38.1 (2011): 6–10.

33 James Patrick Kelly and John Kessel, "Introduction," *Feeling Very Strange: The Slipstream Anthology* (San Francisco, CA: Tachyon, 2006), vii, xii.

34 Victoria de Zwaan, "Slipstream," in Rob Latham, ed., *The Oxford Handbook of Science Fiction* (New York: Oxford University Press, 2014), 115–26.

35 See Gary K. Wolfe, *Evaporating Genres: Essays on Fantastic Literature* (Middletown, CT: Wesleyan University Press, 2011), especially chapter 2.

36 Atwood, *In Other Worlds*, 7.

8

SHERRYL VINT

Hollywood Science Fiction

Although there is more to science fiction (SF) cinema than Hollywood, there is no question that Hollywood dominates the medium, and not always to the genre's benefit. Hollywood is often believed to reduce the genre to juvenile space adventures of 1940s serials or more recent effects-driven block-busters, leading some familiar with print SF to dismiss media SF altogether. Yet there is more to Hollywood SF than this stereotype allows. This chapter will outline the major themes and trends in Hollywood film and television from its earliest days to the present, arguing that even in this most com-mercial form the genre gives us a language to conceptualize and interrogate problems of technologized modernity, from the social impact of science and technology on human life, to the struggle to create just communities, to the changing conception of what it means to be human.

Providing an overview of Hollywood SF is troubled by problems of defi-nition: as the critical tradition repeats *ad infinitum*, there is no consensus on how to define SF. Further, the term Hollywood does not encompass all filmed SF produced in the United States, but identifies a subset created within specific structures of production and distribution. Finally, what "counts" as "American" is not always clear in an industry in which key players move internationally and financing is often obtained from many sources. Thus it is crucial when reading this chapter to keep in mind that it does not describe the entire American tradition of filmed SF, much less SF cinema overall.

Special Effects

In *Screening Space* (1987), Vivian Sobchack argues SF film can be recognized by its use of several recurrent icons such as spaceships, artificial beings, and representations of otherwise inaccessible spaces, such as the inside of the body in *Fantastic Voyage* (Fleischer 1966), or the computer in *Tron* (Lisberger 1982). Yet SF is unlike other film genres, she continues, because "there is no *consistent* cluster of meanings provoked by the image,"[1] but rather meanings change "from film to film and from decade to decade."² SF film is defined by the types, not fixed meanings, of its icons, its distinctive worlds at one remove from our own.

Mass media SF is an example of what Tom Gunning calls "the cinema of attraction,"³ in which spectator interest is compelled by the power of making something visible, rather than by narrative. Sobchack contends that the distinctive aesthetic of SF film is "the cinematic realization of an *imaginary action* occurring in what seems to be documented *real space*,"⁴ emphasizing how SF films are "documentary in flavor and style"⁵ despite being set in radically different worlds. Film has always relied on techniques and themes central to SF, such as skepticism about urbanization and industrial production evident in Charlie Chaplin's *Modern Times* (1936) as much as in Fritz Lang's *Metropolis* (1927). Early films focused on the camera's power to estrange and remake the world it filmed. For example, American Mutoscope's short *The Sausage Machine* (1897) literalizes urban legend by showing dogs, fed into one end of a machine, emerge as sausages at its other. The Edison Company made this more science fictional, reversing the process – dog to sausage, sausage to dog – in *Dog Factory* (1904). Creators of such early U.S. cinema would go on to found Hollywood studios, and many early films embraced SF in narrative as well as technique, from *Twenty Thousand Leagues Under the Sea* (Paton 1905), the first adaptation of Verne's novel, to Edison's adaptation of *Frankenstein* (1910). The Selig Polyscope Corporation, whose founder would establish the first permanent film studio on the West Coast, produced the first *Dr. Jekyll and Mr. Hyde* (1908). Visual effects convey ideas as well as wonder, such as the interrogation of labor in *Liquid Electricity* (Blackton 1907), whose spray jolts its user into superfast motion, and *Work Made Easy* (Blackton 1907), featuring a machine that controls magnetic forces to enable non-manual labor. Many early shorts featured variations of animated dolls, influenced by Hoffman's "The Sandman" (1815), including *The Inventor's Secret* (1911), directed by a young D. W. Griffith, who would go on to make Hollywood history with *Birth of a Nation* (1915).

Hollywood SF continues to be central to new special effects that change cinema overall. Stuart Paton's *20,000 Leagues Under the Sea* (1916), featuring the first footage shot under water, is one of the earliest examples of this relationship. Gareth Stewart argues that movies about the future are simultaneously about the future *of* movies, always both reflecting and interrogating the technology that makes them possible.⁶ This tendency can be seen across the century of Hollywood SF: in Ray Harryhausen's work, such as *20 Million Miles to Earth* (Juran 1957); in Stanley Kubrick's innovations in *2001: A Space Odyssey* (1968); in George Lucas's invention of Industrial

Light and Magic to make *Star Wars* (1977); in the first use of CGI within the diegesis in *The Abyss* (Cameron 1989); in the bullet-time techniques invented for *The Matrix* (Wachowskis 1999); in the interpolated rotoscoping in *A Scanner Darkly* (Linklater 2006); and in the new 3-D technologies developed for *Avatar* (Cameron 2009). New audio effects have been developed for SF, such as Louis and Bebe Barron's groundbreaking compositions in *Forbidden Planet* (Wilcox 1956), or the haunting bars of "alien" music composed in *Close Encounters of the Third Kind* (Spielberg 1977). Sobchack contends that low-budget films, which cannot achieve estrangement at the level of visual detail, "try to locate their 'science fiction-ness' in the spoken word," from the mashup slang of *A Clockwork Orange* (Kubrick 1972) to the absurd, ritually intoned, "the gun is good, but the penis is evil" in *Zardoz*.[7]

Despite this emphasis on effects, Hollywood SF is a narrative genre. *Just Imagine* (Butler 1930) was Hollywood's answer to *Metropolis*, a vision of New York in 1980 complete with flying transport, food pills, test-tube babies, and skyscrapers. The film was an aesthetic and financial failure, its attempt to link the appeal of SF with popular musicals a disaster, and its hackneyed melodramatic plot representative of the most banal qualities of print SF. The film's high cost made studios leery of further SF production, and studios tended to limit SF-oriented film production for the next two decades to mad scientists, funded by but often not set in the United States, usually adapted from print sources, such as *The Mysterious Island* (1929), *Island of Lost Souls* (1932), *The Invisible Man* (1933), *Mad Love* (1933), *The Invisible Ray* (1936), and *The Gladiator* (1938); adventure serials for children, such as *The Phantom Empire* (1935), *Undersea Kingdom* (1936), *Flash Gordon* (1936), *Dick Tracy* (1937), *Buck Rogers* (1939), and *The Phantom Creeps* (1939); and effects-driven disaster films such as *Deluge* (1933), *Men Must Fight* (1933), an anti-pacifist film that features an air raid on New York by Eurasia, and *S.O.S Tidal Wave* (1939). The mad scientist films were largely indistinguishable from contemporary horror, and it would not be until the 1950s, according to Sobchack, that specifically science fictional *creatures*, instead of horror *monsters*, would emerge to interrogate "science as a *social force*."[8]

Mad scientists and serials continued into the 1940s as the only kind of SF on cinema screens, which seems to have reached something of a nadir in a decade that includes *Abbott and Costello Meet Frankenstein* (1948), many returns of The Wolfman, the Invisible Man, the Frankenstein family, and the like, and another attempt at a musical, an adaptation of *A Connecticut Yankee in King Arthur's Court* (1949) featuring Bing Crosby. Serials added a number of superheroes including *Batman* (1943), *Captain America* (1943), and *Superman* (1948), and featured alien invasion in *The Purple Monster Strikes* (1945), about a Martian who infiltrates a rocket program. Changes to Hollywood's conditions of production in the 1950s created more opportunities for SF, chiefly as a result of new competition from television, which changed how, and how often, Americans went to the cinema. Serials gradually died out and their cliffhanger adventures became the television exploits of *Captain Video and His Video Rangers* (1949–55), *Tom Corbett, Space Cadet* (1950–5), *Space Patrol* (1950–5), and *Rocky Jones, Space Ranger* (1954), all of whom instruct their young audiences in civic virtue – and proper consumption of sponsors' products – while saving the universe from malfeasance. The end of the decade saw the debut of Rod Serling's *The Twilight Zone* (1959–64), which showcased SF's capacity critically to interrogate given ideologies and challenge the status quo. *The Twilight Zone* showed that SF could be an adult genre, and revealed its capacity to present material that advertising-dependent network executives were wary of permitting into their "mainstream" shows.

The Imagination of Disaster

The challenge television presented to Hollywood's bottom line resulted in more pronounced bifurcation between Poverty Row productions, based on economies of scale, and main studio releases, increasingly oriented toward spectacles that would enable the big screen to distinguish itself from the small, prompting studios to look more favorably on SF. Contemporary Cold War culture, with its looming threat of nuclear annihilation, fears of communist invasion, and emphasis on the space race, created a perfect storm of conditions for the wealth of SF films released in the 1950s. The plethora of atomic monsters lurching across SF screens was so substantial that John Baxter dubbed this period "Springtime for Caliban,"[9] referring to films such as *The Beast from 20,000 Fathoms* (Lourié 1953), *Them!* (Douglas 1954), and *The Deadly Mantis* (Juran 1957): all, of course, influenced by the Japanese *Gojira* (Honda 1954), re-edited for release in the United States. The different American experience of the atomic bomb meant that its creatures lacked the ambiguity of Gojira, who is both destroyer of Tokyo and defender of the Japanese people. Susan Sontag sees in the American versions of these films what she calls "the imagination of disaster," that is, fantasy participation in "the destruction of humanity itself,"[10] buttressed by an anemic morality in which the scientist heroes share the same narrow emphasis on technologized instrumentality that characterizes the dehumanized invaders. Such films, she contends, are an inadequate response that normalizes the "psychologically unbearable"[11] violence inherent in our technologies.

Nuclear anxiety informs 1950s SF beyond creatures features, evident in the tense psychological drama *Five* (Obeler 1951) about survivors' struggles to reinvent civilization after a nuclear war. Nuclear anxiety also underlies Roger Corman's first SF film, *The Day the World Ended* (1956), and *The World, the Flesh and the Devil* (MacDougall 1959). The latter begins as the story of a lone black man, Ralph, who is suddenly granted access to a forbidden world of white privilege as the only survivor of global disaster. Ralph flirts with interracial romance when he discovers a surviving white woman, Sarah, and then retreats into a banal and unconvincing conclusion of camaraderie after an interval of violent struggle between Ralph and a surviving white man, Benson. Among the film's most memorable sequences is the ersatz relationship Ralph establishes with two white manikins, Betsy and Snodgrass, when he believes that he is the lone survivor on an earth otherwise empty of human life. His banter seeps into expressing the hostility born of years of systemic discrimination, until one day he throws Snodgrass off the balcony.

Poverty Row productions tended to emphasize horror and sex, in releases such as *Cat-Women of the Moon* (Hilton 1953), *Donovan's Brain* (Feist 1953), *Robot Monster* (Tucker 1953), *The Astounding She-Monster* (Ashcroft 1957), *Attack of the 50 Foot Woman* (Juran 1958), *The Wasp Woman* (Corman and Hill 1959) and *The Incredible Shrinking Man* (Arnold 1957). *Forbidden Planet* (Wilcox 1956) both indulged and warned against sexuality in its provocative images of a scantily clad Altaira and its dangerous "monsters from the id,"[12] a phrase Margaret Tarrant applies to the repressed sexual tension symbolized by all giant creature films.

Alien invasions proliferated, from the dire warning that Earth must reconcile itself to international cooperation or face extinction delivered in *The Day the Earth Stood Still* (Wise 1951) to the anxious invocation to "keep watching the skies" at the end of *The Thing from Another World* (Nyby and Hawkes 1951). *Invasion of the Body Snatchers* (Siegel 1956), the first of four adaptations of Jack Finney's novel, struck such a nerve with its vision of Americans replaced by cold and sinister pod people that this B-film became a genre classic. Often read as symbolizing fears of communist takeover, it is equally an indictment of the conformity of U.S. culture seeking to purge reds, homosexuals, and other suspect difference. The greater cynicism of the 1970s is reflected in Philip Kaufman's 1978 remake that refuses the solace of our hero surviving to resist this tide of acquiescence to people who, as Miles says in Siegel's film, "have allowed their humanity to drain away ... slowly instead of all at once." Films from the 1950s would define expectations for SF in decades to come. *Earth vs. the Flying Saucers* (Sears 1956) is recycled decades later as the jingoistic *Independence Day* (Emmerich 1996), a celebration of American exceptionalism that "earnestly girds family drama onto political crisis,"[13] and as *Mars Attacks!* (Burton 1996), which punctures the bombast of Emmerich's film, whose "global inclusiveness is as fake as [its] misogyny is real."[14] In *Mars Attacks!* all white, patriarchal figures die, and the sole character played straight in a film marked by hyperbole is African American, foregrounding "black working-class agency" as "a symbol of social significance."[15]

Such repetitions and rewritings, believed to ensure box office success, have defined Hollywood since at least the 1980s, following *Star Wars* (Lucas 1977), a film significant for establishing the importance of revenues from ancillary products. Although that film's dual emphasis on effects and franchise inspired much derivative and banal Hollywood SF, some films so produced still convey compelling ideas, such as the *Planet of the Apes* franchise that reoriented the original anti-nuclear-war film into a cycle that commented on civil rights and black power struggles in the early 1970s, and has been reinvented again to comment on relationships to other species and dangers of biomedicine in *Rise of the Planet of the Apes* (Wyatt 2011). Launching their own franchises, both Ridley Scott's *Alien* (1979) and James Cameron's *Terminator* (1984) were important films as well. *Alien* breaks with established SF tradition by making a woman the surviving representative of humanity, while *Terminator* not only articulated anxieties about automation and network computing, but also shifted the perception of women's physical power, working against the grain of the idealization of the white male hero in the dominant "muscular cinema" of the period.[16]

New Hollywood and SF

Before we reach blockbuster hegemony, we pass through the 1960s and 1970s, one of the most interesting periods of Hollywood SF. By the end of the 1960s, the studio system was falling apart because of competition from television and the 1948 *United States v. Paramount* decision that ended the studios' control over distribution. Eventually most studios were sold and boards of directors, whose chief objective was the bottom line, replaced control by movie moguls. Yet for a brief period many things were possible in Hollywood as studios began buying and distributing films made by independents, financiers were less risk-adverse because the system was not working anyway, and the restrictive Hayes code was replaced by MPAA ratings, which allowed more mature treatment of troubling themes. Significant social upheaval marks this period, embodied in student and other activism against the occupation of Vietnam and the draft; feminist and gay liberation; African-American, Chicano, and American Indian civil rights movements;

and a generalized refusal by the younger generation to invest further in values of economic achievement so central to American culture.

Hollywood made films that spoke to this ethos, some of them SF, including John Frankenheimer's *The Manchurian Candidate* (1962), about a spin-doctored political candidate brainwashed by communists, and *Seconds* (1966), about a successful middle-aged man who trades his wealth for the freedom of a bohemian lifestyle he ultimately finds equally empty; the bitter and influential *Planet of the Apes* (Schaffner 1968); the genre-changing *2001: A Space Odyssey* (Kubrick 1968), whose stunning and sublime special effects perhaps obscured its disconcerting message that our species needs to evolve beyond the stagnated human stage to survive; *Wild in the Streets* (Shear 1968), a tale of a rock star who rises to political power that is equally contemptuous of the manipulations of the media-driven political system and of the promise that enfranchising youth might produce something new; and *Gas-s-s-s! or It Became Necessary to Destroy the World in Order to Save It* (Corman 1970), a biting comedy about a mysterious gas that kills anyone over the age of twenty-five, whose title evokes the controversial statement published in the *New York Times* about the U.S. military's decision to bomb the Vietnamese village of Bến Tre. The same irreverent tone marks Kubrick's more aesthetically accomplished *Dr. Strangelove, or: How I Learned to Stop Worrying and Love the Bomb* (1964). More earnest expressions of nuclear anxiety appeared in *Panic in the Year Zero* (1962), *Fail Safe* (1964), and the series of nuclear devices pursued by James Bond in films such as *Doctor No* (Young 1962), *Goldfinger* (Hamilton 1964), and *Thunderball* (Young 1965), anticipating how SF themes and scenarios would increasingly become central to all action cinema.

Before *Star Wars* irrevocably shifted SF cinema to the blockbuster, 1970s SF film engaged with contemporary political issues. *Silent Running* (Trumbull 1972) and *Soylent Green* (Fleischer 1973) examine overpopulation and environmental destruction, and the latter seems influenced by the New Wave *Alphaville* (Godard 1965) in its depiction of women as interchangeable "furniture" attached to luxury apartments, reminiscent of Godard's branded seductresses, although the U.S. film is more interested in manly heroics than poetic subversions of techno-modernity. Technology is suspect in 1970s films, used to exploit and destroy humans in *The Crazies* (Romero 1973), about a chemical weapon accidently released within the United States; *Westworld* (Crichton 1973) and *Futureworld* (Heffron 1976), about the hidden dangers of technologies designed for amusement; *The Terminal Man* (Hodges 1974), whose treatment for violent seizures inadvertently creates a link between violence and pleasure centers of the brain; the blaxploitation *Dr. Black and Mr. Hyde* (1976), in which a therapy for liver degeneration turns its black inventor into a white monster who preys on his community; *Demon Seed* (Cammell 1977), whose AI takes a woman hostage and reproduces itself as a baby via her body; and *The Boys from Brazil* (Schaffner 1978), about cloning used to create an army of Hitlers. Political and military institutions are trusted as little as technology, from nature harnessed to plant bombs in *The Day of the Dolphins* (Nichols 1973), to the faked moon landing of *Capricorn One* (Hyams 1977), to the harsh view of corporate greed manifested as physical violence in *Death Race 2000* (Bartel 1975) and *Rollerball* (Jewison 1975), to the totalitarian repressions of *THX 1138* (Lucas 1978) and *Logan's Run* (Anderson 1976).

Star Wars and *Close Encounters of the Third Kind* were not only the most lucrative SF films but also among the top-grossing of all films of this decade. Their influence on SF that followed cannot be denied, but two other films, *The Spook Who Sat by the Door* (Dixon 1973) and *The Stepford Wives* (Forbes 1974), were better attuned to their contemporary context. The former celebrates revolutionary violence in its story of Dan Freeman, recruited into the CIA to meet minority quotas, who uses his Agency training to launch a black revolutionary movement. TransAmerica attempted to pull its United Artists logo from the picture and, although it did well at the box office, it was quickly taken out of circulation "because of the fear it would incite crime and violence."[17] *The Stepford Wives* is a chilling tale of backlash against feminism in its sinister picture of independent and career-minded women whose husbands replace them with saccharine, compliant, pastel-clad robots who aimlessly stroll the supermarket aisles beaming empty smiles in the film's final shots. The popularity of *Star Wars* may be explained in part by its refusal to engage with such disturbing visions or with "the moral vagaries of Vietnam, the ethical vagaries of Watergate, the anti-heroes of Hollywood films from earlier in the decade,"[18] offering instead a comforting return to simpler morality – though *Return of the Jedi* does psychically replay America's defeat in Vietnam, transplanted here to the Ewoks' forest moon of Endor and recast as a victory for liberal democratic values. Similarly, *Close Encounters of the Third Kind* resembles the anxious invasion films of the 1950s in structure, but its tone suggests wonder and possibility rather than threat.

Blockbusters and Franchise Fictions

The most important SF television of the 1960s was undoubtedly *Star Trek*, although it was not widely influential at the time; by the end of the 1970s, the series returned to the big screen with *Star Trek: The Motion Picture* (Wise 1979), and since then we have never been without a *Star Trek*, the

1980s films leading to television's *Star Trek: The Next Generation* (1987–94), whose cast took over the film franchise, spawning three more series that continued on television through 2005, followed by a reboot of the franchise in J. J. Abrams's *Star Trek* (2009). 1970s SF television tried to work this magic in reverse, adapting a number of successful films into series – *The Invisible Man* (1976–6); *Logan's Run* (1977–9); *Planet of the Apes* (1974); *Battlestar Galactica* (1978–9), a clear imitation of *Star Wars*; *Buck Rogers* (1979–81) – but none lasted more than a season or two. More successful were two series about cyborgs, soon to become a staple of 1980s cinema, *The Six Million Dollar Man* (1974–8) and its spin-off *The Bionic Woman* (1976–8): two of the most critically discussed films of the 1980s, *Blade Runner* (Scott 1982) and *Terminator*, express anxiety about the erosion of difference between humans and machines. From another point of view, John Carpenter's paranoid masterpiece *The Thing* (1982) visualizes fears of an unstable America no longer certain who is friend or foe, a motif Sobchack describes as "Aliens R. US,"[19] evident in the psychedelic devolution of *Altered States* (Russell 1980); the critique of racism in *The Brother from Another Planet* (Sayles 1984), *Enemy Mine* (Petersen 1985), and *Alien Nation* (Baker 1988); the friendly aliens needing assistance from grieving families in *E.T.* (Spielberg 1982) and *Starman* (Carpenter 1984); and the personified software agents in *Tron* (Lisberger 1982).

As Reagan's television campaign assured voters that it was "morning in America" and a new era of security and prosperity was soon to emerge from the combined forces of economic deregulation and military technology, SF cinema offered a more pessimistic view of dark urban futures of stark poverty and the criminalization of dissent, such as *Escape from New York* (Carpenter 1981), with its vision of Manhattan as an urban prison; *Repo Man*, whose poor are abandoned like so much trash on the streets; *The Running Man* (Glaser 1987), in which executions have become televised entertainment; and *RoboCop* (Verhoeven 1987), that delegates city governance to Omni Consumer Products and its automated, military police force. Although the titular Robocop is able to overcome his programming and value human life over profit, technology was overwhelming against us in 1980s films from an AI's decision to start a nuclear war in *WarGames* (Badham 1983), to the subliminal advertising supporting alien invasion in John Carpenter's biting anti-Reagan satire *They Live* (1988). The popular *Back to the Future* films, which began in 1985, were more aligned to the nostalgic optimism cultivated by the Reagan administration. Although Spielberg's hugely success *E.T.* did make the military the antagonist, its thematic emphasis on innocence and the private family makes it complicit in Reagan-era wistfulness. In his discussion of the film, Robin Wood distinguishes between qualities of openness and regeneration he calls child-like, and a regressive sentimentalism he labels childish, critiquing the film as achieving only the latter.[20]

The contrast between *Repo Man* and *Red Dawn* (Milius), both released in 1984, epitomizes this polarized America: one castigates the suicidal ethos of a nation that sacrifices its working classes to profit and global domination, while the other validates Reagan's justification of interventions in Latin America by demonstrating that if the United States did not fight communism abroad it would be condemned to do so at home, a theme shared by the television miniseries *Amerika* (1987), set in a United States occupied by the Soviet Union. For the most part, however, television of the 1980s expressed liberal viewpoints, such as *Star Trek: The Next Generation*; *Alien Nation* (1989–90); and *Quantum Leap* (1989–93), about a physicist moving through time, driven by "an unknown force to change history for the better." The innovative *Max Headroom* (1987), adapted from a British film, critiqued corporations and technology run amuck, and was ahead of its time thematically but its VR character now has a dated look. It likely would have run for more seasons had it been introduced a couple of years later when specialty cable channels such as SciFi (now Syfy), launched in 1992, emerged.

Superman (Donner 1978) returned to the cinema in the late 1970s, followed by a number of sequels in the 1980s, and the decade ended with the release of *Batman* (Burton 1989). Superhero franchises are now a significant part of Hollywood SF.[21] The current Marvel sequence of single-character and Avengers-ensemble films is the most successful example to date of transmedia storytelling, which promises to shape SF in the twenty-first century, poised to exploit the political economy of integration in which studios are owned by massive media corporations with other holdings in video games, comic books, music, and more. Superhero and video game adaptation became increasingly important to Hollywood SF during the 1990s, and the number of titles that might be considered SF increased massively. It thus becomes more difficult to generalize about Hollywood SF from the 1990s given the number and diversity of titles released.

Men in Black (Sonnenfeld 1997), a light-hearted action film that became a franchise, used the homology between extraterrestrial-alien and immigrant-alien to scrutinize systemic racism, territory frequently explored in the most influential television series of the decade, *The X-Files* (1992–2002). Not only did the film cast Will Smith – who was for SF of the 1990s what Charlton Heston was to the 1970s, or Arnold Schwarzenegger to the 1980s – but it made visible Nama's argument that "blackness and race are often present in SF films as narrative subtext or implicit allegorical subject."[22] When

Smith's character is asked to complete a marksmanship course with several white candidates, he remains calm as others wildly fire. He shoots just one target, a white girl with blonde braids, ignoring the bug-eyed monsters leering from others. He carefully explains his assessment: a creature hanging from a street lamp is just working out; another who appears to be snarling is merely ill; but the white girl, "middle of the ghetto, bunch of monsters, this time of night with quantum physics books? She about to start some shit." Although played for humor, this scene points to the role of projection in viewing marginalized populations as always already a threat. *I, Robot* (Proyas 2004) would similarly explore how casting Smith disrupts an easy mapping of racial difference onto aliens or artificial beings, revealing how often SF codes humanity as white.

Gattaca (Niccol 1997) explores questions of discrimination through genomic profiling, positing a future in which destiny is coded in one's genes and celebrating Vincent, who achieves his dream of going into space through perseverance, despite the limitations of his body. While not capitulating to genetic determinism, the film takes on a disturbing cast in Vincent's foil, Jerome, a man whose genetic profile entitles him to any career he chooses but whose paraplegic body marks him as useless: Vincent's apotheosis is intercut with Jerome's suicide, a sacrifice he makes to ensure that the substitution of their genetic profiles will never be revealed.

Kubrick's *2001* signaled a shift in SF film from thinking about the threat of technology toward thinking about how it might change humanity, a motif that found its fullest expression in cyberpunk cinema in the 1990s, also deeply influenced by Japanese anime widely circulating in the United States by then. Such films, many adapted from print, interrogate the fusion of humans with technology and include *Lawnmower Man* (Leonard 1992); *Johnny Mnemonic,* (Longo 1997); *Twelve Monkeys* (Gilliam 1995), inspired by Chris Marker's avant-garde SF short *La Jeteée* (1962); *Total Recall* (Verhoeven 1990); *Dark City* (Proyax 1998); *The Thirteenth Floor* (1999); and, of course, *The Matrix* (1999), whose innovative special effects transformed cinema and earned it a place in the National Film Registry, despite its rather hackneyed plot of a white hero saving the masses through Christ-like self-sacrifice (the same conclusion as *The Omega Man* [1971]). *The Matrix* struck a chord with contemporary culture, primed to embrace the slickness of its style, its sublime action sequences imported from Hong Kong, and its ecumenical citations from philosophy and religion, most prominently Jean Baudrillard's *Simulations* (1983), which appears in the diegesis. If Neo's rage against the machine ultimately did not add up to comprehensive revolutionary action, it nonetheless spoke powerfully to a widely shared sentiment of being ground under by the economy of flexible labor.

1990s television ventured into cyberspace with the short-lived *VR-5* (1995), but this decade was dominated by *The X-Files* and various Roddenberry series, including the darker, non–Star Trek *Earth: Final Conflict* (1997–2002). Other notable television series include *Babylon 5* (1994–8), an ambitious reinvention of space opera that anticipates the long narrative arcs that would become dominant in twenty-first-century television, and *Stargate SG-1* (1997–2007), a simplistic military adventure series, based on Emmerich's 1994 film, that not only became the longest-running SF television series, but also spawned two more series and several made-for-TV films. The phenomenal success of this banal series points to the ubiquity of SF imagery in contemporary culture, influenced by the success of the gaming industry and its dominant first-person-shooter format. Television into the 2000s includes many speculative series, now a staple of the small screen, albeit many of them closer to fantasy than SF, as well as a number of SyFy original series.

Conclusions: Twenty-First-Century SF

The wide appeal of SF in recent culture is a result of the ubiquity of technology in everyday life, gaming, links between SF and the blockbuster, the role of SF in generating new effects in an industry that privileges spectacle, and contemporary events from 9/11 and the erosions of civil liberties, to climate crises exacerbated by political corruption epitomized by FEMA failures, to the 2008 economic collapse. *Battlestar Galactica* (2003–9) was invited to the UN in 2009 as part of a panel on contemporary issues of human rights, children in war, and reconciliation of religious difference. *Lost* (2004–10) embodied 9/11 trauma at public and personal levels, achieving an audience far beyond genre fans. The apocalyptic dominates the recent television landscape, from *Jeremiah* (2002–4); to *Dark Angel* (2000–2); to *Falling Skies* (2011–); to *Revolution* (2012–), which daringly imagines patriots as its antagonists as it works through the trauma of the United States' *response* to 9/11; to *Under the Dome* (2013–), a massive *summer* hit, potentially changing industry patterns; to *Defiance* (2013–), launched simultaneously as show and game, exemplifying the economic possibilities of transmedia storytelling.

Recent film production also shows SF's wide appeal, from the cycles of superhero and blockbuster sequels such as the *Transformers* franchise or merged *Alien vs. Predator* films, to the return of the disaster film in *The Day After Tomorrow* (2004), *The Road* (Hillcoat 2009), and the epidemic of zombies, reinvented as medical infection, everywhere in contemporary culture from the comedy *Zombieland* (Fleischer 2009) to the earnest melodrama *World War Z* (Forster 2013). Such films articulate anxieties about neoliberalism, in which masses of people no longer needed by the economy exist as so much surplus life threatening to overwhelm us all. The ongoing sense of cultural crisis, beyond which life cannot continue as before, explains why SF appears so widely in contemporary Hollywood, from meditative independent films such as *Primer* (Carruth 2004) and *Another Earth* (Cahill 2011), to human relationships explored through SF imagery in *Eternal Sunshine of the Spotless Mind* (Gondry 2004) and *Inception* (Nolan 2010), to literalized metaphors of economic exploitation in *Repo Men* (Sapochnik 2010) and *Source Code* (Jones 2011). Hollywood SF has become an industry dominant in the twenty-first century, exported around the globe – and if too much of this seems mindless special effects, we should remember that, despite its facile resolutions, blockbuster SF speaks to the vicissitudes of our turbulent, science fictional times.

NOTES

1 Vivian Sobchack, *Screening Space: The American Science Fiction Film*, 2nd ed. (New Brunswick, NJ: Rutgers University Press, 1987), 68.
2 Ibid., 75.
3 Tom Gunning, "The Cinema of Attraction: Early Film, Its Spectator and the Avant-Garde," *Wide Angle* 8.3–4 (1986): 63–70.
4 Sobchack, *Screening Space*, 140.
5 Ibid., 88.
6 Gareth Stewart, "The 'Videology' of Science Fiction," in George Slusser and Eric Rabkin, eds., *Shadows of the Magic Lamp: Fantasy and Science Fiction in Film* (Carbondale: Southern Illinois University Press, 1985), 159–207.
7 Sobchack, *Screening Space*, 158.
8 Ibid., 50.
9 John Baxter, *Science Fiction in the Cinema* (New York: Paperback Library, 1970), 100.
10 Susan Sontag, "The Imagination of Disaster," in Heather Masri, ed., *Science Fiction: Stories and Contexts* (1965; Boston, MA: St. Martin's, 2008), 1005.
11 Ibid., 1014.
12 Margaret Tarrant, "Monsters from the Id," in Barry Keith Grant, ed., *Film Genre Reader II* (Austin: University of Texas Press, 1995), 330–49.
13 Debra White-Stanley and Caryl Flinn, "Movies and Homeland Insecurity," in Chris Holmlund, ed., *American Cinema of the 1990s* (New Brunswick, NJ: Rutgers University Press, 2008), 163.
14 Ibid.
15 Adilifu Nama, *Black Space: Imagining Race in Science Fiction Film* (Austin: University of Texas Press, 2008), 150.
16 Yvonne Tasker, *Spectacular Bodies: Gender, Genre and the Action Cinema* (New York: Routledge, 1993), 1.
17 Frances Gateward, "Movies and Legacies of War and Corruption," in Lester D. Friedman, ed., *American Cinema of the 1970s* (New Brunswick, NJ: Rutgers University Press, 2007), 110.

18 Paula J. Massood, "Movies and a Nation in Transformation," in Lester D. Friedman, ed., *American Cinema of the 1970s* (New Brunswick, NJ: Rutgers University Press, 2007), 185.
19 Sobchack, *Screening Space*, 293.
20 Robin Wood, *Hollywood from Vietnam to Reagan* (New York: Columbia University Press, 1986).
21 For more on the importance of the superhero in recent American SF, consult Chapter 9, "U.S. Superpower and Superpowered Americans in Science Fiction and Comic Books," as well as Chapter 3, "American Science Fiction after 9/11."
22 Nama, *Black Space*, 2.

9

MATTHEW J. COSTELLO

U.S. Superpower and Superpowered Americans in Science Fiction and Comic Books

In the February 1941 issue of *Life* magazine, editor Henry Luce declared the twentieth century the American Century. Advocating direct U.S. intervention in World War II, Luce argued the United States had become "the most powerful and the most vital nation in the world," but that Americans were uneasy with global power and reluctant to wield it. They had thus "failed to play their part as a world power." The solution, Luce claimed, was "to accept wholeheartedly our duty and our opportunity as the most powerful and vital nation in the world and in consequence to exert upon the world the full impact of our influence, for such purposes as we see fit and by such means as we see fit."[1] That same February, ten months before the attack on Pearl Harbor and America's entry into the war, the first issue of *Captain America* comics by Joe Simon and Jack Kirby appeared on newsstands with the iconic image of the Sentinel of Liberty socking Hitler on the jaw. Luce and Simon and Kirby recognized that America had become the most powerful nation in the world and assumed this brought responsibilities that conflicted with Americans' fear of international involvements, a persistent refrain since George Washington had warned of the consequences of entangling "our peace and prosperity in the toils of European Ambition, Rivalship, Interest, Humour or Caprice."[2] Simon and Kirby's *Captain America*, like tales of the superhero in general, was constructing a vision of an America coming to terms with wielding its recently acquired global power.

At the start of the twentieth century America had become one of the richest nations in the world and was increasingly involved in international trade. Having acquired colonies during the Spanish-American War, the United States intervened in Asia and Central America politically and militarily. The United States was becoming a global power, but Americans maintained an isolationist ethos justified by Washington's address. From the Great War to the Second World War Americans would need to learn a new ethos; during World War II and the Cold War, they would need to be mobilized behind national security crusades. As they became aware of the reality of America's rise to globalism and the consequences – both at home and abroad – of foreign intervention, Americans would reflect on the economic and moral costs of empire. The superhero narrative is one venue through which Americans construct that global role.

America's role as a global superpower in the twentieth century was fostered, reflected, and challenged by the superhero narrative in science fiction and comics. The emergence of a literate urban population and new methods of cultural dissemination – pulp magazines, four-color printing, motion pictures, and radio – created the demand, and the rise of American power provided the context in which the American heroic tradition and narratives influenced by British colonial adventures would define America's encounter with the world. First educating Americans about global responsibilities, then celebrating national crusades in World War II and the Cold War, and then reflecting on the costs of empire – superhero narratives helped construct Americans' vision of their nation's power and global role.

Superheroes have had a mixed reception in the world of science fiction. Scholes and Rabkin devote merely two pages to a discussion of comic book superheroes, identifying Superman as "the most influential science fiction comic strip of all time,"³ while Lester del Rey dismisses Superman as "pseudo science fiction."⁴ More recent work seems to suggest greater acceptance as Brooks Landon includes Moore and Gibbons' *Watchmen* in his recommended reading list and Corey Creekmur advocates for a more scholarly treatment of superheroes in a review in *Science Fiction Studies*.⁵ Whether in comic books, novels, film, or television, the figure of the superhero has frequently drawn on science fiction terminology, talents, and tropes. Narrative trends in superhero comics, like twentieth-century American science fiction more broadly, have been closely tied to America's rise to globalism, and are an important venue in which Americans construct their sense of themselves as a global nation. Comics-style superbeings have been frequent characters in science fiction, among them A. E. van Vogt's Slan, Gully Foyle in Alfred Bester's *The Stars My Destination*, Zenna Henderson's People, and even *Star Wars*'s Jedi Knights or *Star Trek*'s Spock and Q. The ties between superheroes and science fiction can also be seen in the number of creators who have crossed fields, from Jerry Siegel, Mort Weisinger, and Jules Schwartz – all early science fiction fans – to mid-century creators Edmond Hamilton, Bester, and Harlan Ellison, to the more recent multimedia creators J. Michael Straczynski and Joss Whedon.

Learning to Be a Global Power: Imperialism, the Great War, and Depression

The first modern American superhero emerged on the eve of the Great War. Edgar Rice Burroughs's *A Princess of Mars* was first serialized in 1912, introducing John Carter. Carter is fundamentally American, a Civil War hero and entrepreneur; he acquires great powers when transported to the lighter gravity of Mars, where he redeems the Martian community from its racial conflicts and near destruction. Carter uses his power and virtue to unite Red and Green Martians, ending centuries of war, prevents the annihilation of the Martian race, and wins the heart of Princess Dejah Thoris. The allegory of American global involvement, using its virtue to bring peace to warring peoples, is an unsubtle reversal of Washington's warning that global involvement would undermine U.S. virtue.

A *Princess of Mars* contains several elements common to an American heroic narrative. Crossing boundaries between civilization and wilderness to gain wisdom and power to redeem an innocent, Edenic community has been a central American heroic motif. Lawrence and Jewitt identify it as a monomyth of the American superhero.[6] Slotkin similarly sees the melding of wilderness and civilization as the source material for the development of American national identity.[7]

The early American superheroes in comic strips and pulp magazines cross national and cultural boundaries to bring America to the world and the world to America. The global wilderness possesses secrets that Americans can exploit. Often American heroes partner with aliens from whom they draw wisdom: The Lone Ranger brings justice to the savage West with the aid and wisdom of the native Tonto; The Green Hornet brings justice to a savage urban America with the aid and wisdom of Kato. The Shadow learned his power to cloud men's minds in Asia. These boundary crossings – with images drawn from British colonial literature and Orientalist stereotypes – bring America into contact with the world, but in a manner consistent with earlier American heroic narratives.

As John Carter brings American virtues to Mars, later heroes will bring them to the world. Often cast as the first true superhero, Lester Dent's Doc Savage was bred and trained to be the perfect human specimen, physically strong, nearly indestructible, and supremely intelligent. Doc dedicates his life and fortune to bring justice to the world, which he did for 188 issues of his eponymous pulp magazine between 1933 and 1949. In comic strips Alex Raymond's Flash Gordon (introduced in 1934) similarly brings American values to the planet Mongo, using his powers to defeat the evil threat of Ming the Merciless. Buck Rogers, a WWI veteran from Pennsylvania, published in various forms from 1928 onward, traveled to the future to use American values to stop global war.

America's pragmatic, rational individualism also helped create a future in which American virtues could spread farther. New wonders could be seen daily as automobiles and airplanes replaced buggies and balloons and radio provided immediate access to the wider world and new forms of entertainment. These technologies promised a fantastic future for Americans with ever widening possibilities, creating an environment for the development of "scientifiction" in the 1920s. The ideology of Hugo Gernsback in *Amazing Stories* – that all social problems could be solved eventually by the appropriate application of science – is mirrored in the generally beneficial application of power by costumed crime fighters. Meanwhile, the availability of SF pulps in the 1920s and 1930s provided a ready outlet for the creation of superhero narratives. Doc Smith's Lensmen (serialized in *Astounding* magazine beginning with *Galactic Patrol* in 1937), with their super-powerful alien technology and American virtue, resolved millennia-old galactic disputes. Philip Wylie's 1930 novel *Gladiator* casts the superpowered hero as an alienated, unhappy, brutal person. Hugo Danner is the son of a chemist who experimented on his son *in utero* to create a superior human being, endowed with super strength, invulnerability, and great intelligence. Hugo is an outsider, unable to fit in with humans. He becomes increasingly antisocial and must suppress his murderous impulses. Only during the Great War, where his brutality is seen as an asset, does Hugo find release. Alone, Hugo lacks the social connections and upbringing to make him a vessel of American virtue, leaving him capable only of destruction and violence. Where Doc Savage represents beneficial American power bringing justice to the world, Hugo Danner represents anomie and destruction. Still, this tale, like other super crime fighter narratives, brings America into contact with a broader world, envisioning American power as essential to securing global order. By creating a superhero with no social connections, lacking American virtues, and wielding only force, Wylie suggests that when Americans come to the world they must bring more than power; they must bring virtue.

In less than a decade, influenced by Wylie's novel, two teenagers from Cleveland would nurture their superhero in the womb of American values, crossing science fictional boundaries to create the most famous American superhero. Like his predecessors, Superman is the product of a boundary crossing, from the planet Krypton to America. Melding middle-American values with superpowers in the alien orphan raised by Kansas farmers creates the ideal entity to symbolize America's rise to global power. Introduced in 1938 in *Action Comics* #1, Superman is at first more rogue vigilante than the superhero he would become; few remember that he is *causing*, not preventing, the famous car crash on the magazine's cover. His adventures during his first few years see him battling gangsters and corrupt politicians in a populist crusade.[8]

Superman's success led to a proliferation of superheroes. Between 1938 and 1941 hundreds of comic book superheroes were created. In the pages of *Astounding Science-Fiction* psychic supermen such as A. E. van Vogt's Slan triumphed over oppression, and Isaac Asimov imagined super social scientists (armed with psychic powers) guiding a galactic empire through its decline in his Foundation stories. Brian Atterbery sees the superman as so prevalent in the science fiction of this era that he treats it as a hackneyed formula.[9] The many readers of these stories knew that super-powerful heroes were necessary to save the comic book and science fictional worlds they inhabited, just as only American power and virtue could solve the problems of the real world.

Early comic book heroes were products of science and of magic and myth. While Superman was an alien, and Captain America and the Flash were products of chemistry, the original Green Lantern got his powers from a mystical Tibetan lamp, Captain Marvel was empowered by a wizard, Hawkman the reincarnation of an ancient Egyptian priest, and Wonder Woman a creature out of Greek myth. Like their pulp predecessors, these heroes needed to cross into the mystical wilderness, to meld with it, to gain their powers. In turn, they entered the global arena, using their new powers and American virtues to bring justice to all.

Constructing a Triumphant Nationalism: World War II and the Cold War

World War II offered a clear global crusade for these American heroes to champion. Captain America, Uncle Sam, Wonder Woman, the Patriot, the Shield, and others all battled the evil Axis. Superheroes moved from educating Americans about global commitments to trumpeting America's arrival to power. In a famous Superman comic strip published in *Look* magazine in 1940, Superman flies to Berlin and Moscow, capturing both Hitler and Stalin to be tried by the League of Nations. Captain America smashing Hitler and beating stereotypically stentorian German or buck-toothed, bespectacled Japanese soldiers demonstrated how superior Americans had to be to these would be global conquerors. American superpower could, would, and as importantly *should* triumph over these morally and physically degenerate global threats.

The end of World War II left America in a dominant global position, producing more than 60 percent of global wealth, with a huge military and a monopoly on the most awesome weapon of destruction ever created. Rich and powerful beyond human dreams Americans now assumed a global role to protect the world from the evils of communism. This would mean a peacetime draft, global intelligence networks, and military interventions in alien places such as Guatemala, the Congo, and Vietnam. Raised on Doc Savage and the Shadow, Americans knew only American virtue could redeem the global wilderness. During the war, Superman and Captain America taught them that American power would triumph. Now, the superhero would help construct the nationalist project of Cold War America.

Superhero growth slowed considerably during the war; Wonder Woman was the last major new character introduced during this first, triumphal phase of heroes (traditionally designated the "Golden Age" by fans).[10] Superheroes continued to dominate the medium for the next few years, but after the war the decline in readership became apparent. By 1951 only National's Superman, Batman, and Wonder Woman remained in print. While they fell from favor in comic books, superheroes continued to educate Americans through other media. In 1946 *The Adventures of Superman* radio broadcast added the phrase "The American Way" to his role as champion of truth and justice, transforming the hero's character and ideology and contributing to the construction of the social consensus that many see as characterizing the 1950s.[11] Mark Waid argues that in support of America's rise to globalism, the comic book Superman "gradually curbed his rebel ways to become more of a super lawman – a global Boy Scout."[12] Superman's successful migration to television led to a brief superhero revival as Timely tried to create a new superhero, Marvel Boy, and resurrected its three main heroes – the Human Torch, Submariner, and Captain America – for brief runs. Retaining a triumphalist vision of America, these heroes engaged in a global, nationalist crusade, but this time as anticommunists. Captain America was subtitled "Commie Smasher" and fought Soviet agents and Korean soldiers. Marvel Boy helped avert a global and interplanetary war instigated by a character oddly similar to Joseph Stalin in 1951. Captain America's creators, Joe Simon and Jack Kirby, introduced nationalist anticommunists the Fighting American in 1954 and Private Strong in 1959 for Prize comics.

More commonly, the comic book superheroes that survived into the 1950s were less realistic, involving more fantasy and humor, less magic and more science.[13] Superman battled several alien supermen, mad scientists, and super apes; he was first exposed to kryptonite and met his scientifically created inverse, Bizarro. Even Batman traveled through time and across dimensions meeting Batmen from the future, from other planets, and even a diminutive imitator from another dimension, the Batmite. In 1956 National editor Julius Schwartz, a founding member of the Futurians and active science fiction fan, sought to resurrect the superhero. Beginning with the Flash and Green Lantern, Schwartz would revive National's stable of heroes, giving birth to what fans call the "Silver Age" of comics.[14]

These new heroes were empowered by scientific rather than mystical boundary crossings. The new Green Lantern's powers come not from a

Tibetan relic, but from a power battery provided by an intergalactic police force; Hawkman is now empowered by Nth metal from the planet Thanagar. Some new heroes are aliens (Martian Manhunter); others are earthlings who are aliens elsewhere (Adam Strange, who zeta beams to the planet Rann). Representing the power of American technology and the promise of scientific advances, these new heroes face alien invasions, supervillains empowered by advanced technology, and other science fictional-based threats.

Timely Comics (now called Atlas) had been publishing science fiction-themed monster comics in the late 1950s. Never one to avoid a trend, publisher Martin Goodman told his editor-writer Stan Lee to copy National's successful super-group book, *The Justice League of America*. Lee and artist Jack Kirby created *The Fantastic Four*, and started a new version of superhero storytelling that combined super-antiheroes and soap opera set in the context of contemporary New York. This proved a successful formula and led to the prominence of what was soon to be known as Marvel comics. In the early 1960s, Marvel comics were commentaries on Cold War politics, reflecting a vision of American global dominance. The Fantastic Four gain their powers while beating the commies in the space race. Munitions inventor Tony Stark, injured in a bomb blast in Vietnam, creates a suit of armor to become Iron Man, a rabid pro-military anticommunist. Bruce Banner is testing a new atomic bomb for the U.S. military when exposed to gamma rays that turn him into the Incredible Hulk. Neither the Hulk nor Iron Man question Cold War policy as a quarter of the stories between 1964 and 1966 feature them fighting communists. The fear of atomic war looms, though; created under the mushroom cloud of nuclear war, Marvel heroes' origins derive mostly from radiation, whether direct exposure (the Fantastic Four and Hulk), indirect exposure through radioactive waste (Daredevil) spiders (Spider-Man), or through a general increase in radiation in the atmosphere due to testing of nuclear weapons (X-Men).

Marvel heroes are often antiheroes, outsiders. The Hulk and the Thing both gain strength but become ugly monsters that are shunned, as are the mutant X-Men. Spider-Man is hunted as a criminal, and Captain America is a man out of time, resurrected in the 1960s with the values of the 1940s. The outsider antihero has its twins in the science fiction of the early to mid-1960s. Heinlein's Valentine Michael Smith (*Stranger in a Strange Land*) and Herbert's Paul Atreides (*Dune*) cross boundaries of race and ideology to acquire new wisdom and powers, not to support established power, but to challenge it. Similarly, Marvel superheroes are firmly anticommunist, but are victims of nuclear technologies and skirt moral boundaries. At their inception, then, they are a nascent questioning of the triumphal American global role, pointing to a concern with the costs of empire.

From Vietnam to the War on Terror

By 1964 the triumphalist culture of postwar America was coming undone. This year – in which the long postwar baby boom came to an end, inflation began to creep into the economy, and formal American combat troops first took the field in Vietnam – found Americans' trust in government starting to decline, a trend that would escalate over the next decades, reaching its nadir in 1991, rising and then falling again to an all-time low in 2014.[15] The social unity seen as necessary to confront the communists was waning with American influence. Comic book superheroes in the second half of the decade confronted political issues that revealed not unity and moral certainty but division and moral ambiguity. The youth revolt would appear in a variety of stories, with Captain America and Spider-Man confronting campus protests, and the Teen Titans meeting counterculture-themed villains such as the Mad Mod and Captain Rumble. Even if not directly confronting political issues, superheroes came to challenge social order. In late 1967, when Frank Robbins took over as writer, Batman comics began offering stories with increasingly deadly villains and an outsider hero. The stories became darker and increasingly gothic after Neal Adams became artist in 1969.

Rather than celebrating the emergence of America as a global power, superheroes were now confronting the costs of empire at home and abroad. American military dominance seemed to be vanishing, and American virtue was unclear. Soviet technological advances meant that the nuclear monopoly of the 1950s had become nuclear parity, and the dominant American policy of Massive Retaliation was replaced by Mutually Assured Destruction. By 1968 there were more than 500,000 American troops fighting in Vietnam, yet victory was elusive. This conflict – cast as part of the anticommunist crusade – was increasingly difficult to justify. Both Iron Man and Captain America go to Vietnam, but have trouble defining the enemy and asserting the morality of U.S. action. Americans also faced economic decline. The U.S. share of global production fell from more than 60 percent in 1940, to nearly 40 percent in 1960, and to 25 percent in 1980.[16] Richard Nixon acknowledged America's declining economic fortunes in August 1971 when he removed the major pillars of the postwar financial order – letting the value of the dollar float, closing the gold window, imposing a "surcharge" on imports and wage and price controls. The series of government scandals from Watergate to Abscam, and revelations of covert operations in the Third World added a moral dimension to economic and political decline. Throughout the 1970s, the so-called Bronze Age, the superhero would be used to challenge American virtue, asking if the imperial United States lived its values. The answer would invariably be no.

Dennis O'Neil and Neal Adams's seventeen issues of *Green Lantern/Green Arrow* were a watershed in the treatment of social issues in superhero comics. Formerly a copy of Batman, Green Arrow had grown a beard and abandoned the Arrow Cave and Arrow Car to champion the underclass. Green Lantern, the galactic policeman and agent of order, would join him on a trek through America where they encountered racism, militarism, and government oppression. Green Arrow's sidekick, Speedy (essentially a bow-totting Robin), would become a heroin addict, representing a generation of children neglected by their parents. Captain America would, in an extended allegory by Steve Engelhart and Sal Buscema, confront Watergate, a scandal so disillusioning that Captain America resigned his costume and fought as "Nomad: The Man without a Country" for nearly a year. American power and virtue were in question, and not only Captain America, Green Lantern, and Green Arrow, but most superheroes could do little but stumble along, fighting both supervillains and the social malaise of the epoch.[17]

The Reagan administration deployed a reinvigorated Cold War language in the 1980s, but it did not command the same power as in the 1950s. American wealth and military might were no longer a basis of global hegemony. The Soviet Union, likewise, had exhausted its political power and was now seen as a decadent, overly bureaucratized behemoth heading for inevitable collapse. Superheroes neither celebrated America's global triumph nor challenged its moral virtue, but came to behave in a morally questionable fashion. Neither paragons of virtue nor inner-directed moral individuals, heroes became darker and more brutal, represented by the "grim and gritty" tone of Miller and Jansen's *Daredevil*, Todd McFarlane's *Spawn*, and the popularity of vicious antiheroes such as the Punisher and Wolverine.

High Cold War rhetoric might have been again in vogue, but the triumphalist vision of American dominance was not. Scholars explored the possibility of world order in an era of American decline in such works as Robert Keohane's *After Hegemony* and Paul Kennedy's best-selling *Rise and Decline of the Great Powers*. A brief surge in the American economy in the mid-1980s could not alter the secular trend of relative decay. In this potentially postimperial era, the superhero was neither triumphalist nor index of virtue, but increasingly scrutinized as a type, challenged and problematized as American power was challenged and problematized; "deconstructing" the superhero became a proxy for challenging American power.

Three seminal texts of the period "deconstruct" the superhero in a specifically global context, tying the disarray of the superhero world to America's imperial decline. Moore and Gibbon's *Watchmen* incorporated the recently acquired stable of superheroes from financially troubled Charlton into the DC (formerly National) universe. *Watchmen* posits a dark alternative history where the United States wins in Vietnam, Richard Nixon serves five terms as president, and an imminent nuclear confrontation between the United States and the USSR requires superheroes to construct a fiction of alien invasion that kills millions to avert nuclear war. The superheroes are not virtuous, but brutal vigilantes, some using their powers as government agents to commit horrible crimes, others unconcerned with humanity, and still others whose hubris is so great they decide the fates of millions. Miller and Jansen's *The Dark Knight Returns* envisions a global nuclear confrontation that nearly destroys even Superman; the triumphalist hero becoming the victim of imperial decline, while only the gritty vigilante outsider, Batman, portrayed as a brutal psychotic, can hold off chaos. The postmodern fugue of Chaykin's *American Flagg!* envisions a world fifty years in the future where the United States and the USSR have removed their governments from the Earth and joined forces to create a new imperial order. *Flagg!* depicts a world of rampant consumerism, government mind control, and corporate power, the only hero a venal, over-sexed former video star turned mall cop. Americans perceived the virtue and power of their nation in decline and the global order it had provided collapsing; the superhero could no longer serve as an index of triumph and virtue and became itself a subject of ironic exploration.

One might have expected the end of the Cold War to be greeted with a renewed celebration of American power. While a short-lived euphoria did accompany the fall of the Berlin Wall, the costs of American empire continued to temper that enthusiasm. The U.S. economy was anemic, bled of resources in part by military spending that equaled that of the rest of the world. The global interventions of the Cold War had undermined American faith in the virtue of the American progressive global mission. Superhero comics increasingly emphasized betrayals, echoing a concern that the American dream was, in fact, being betrayed. This all-pervasive pessimism has led to the contemporary era of comics production commonly being designated the "Dark Age" by collectors and fans. In lengthy story arcs in the early 1990s, Batman's back is broken, leaving him crippled; Superman and Green Arrow die; and Green Lantern Hal Jordan is possessed by an evil force and brutally destroys the Green Lantern Corps. Captain America is killed by the very serum that gave him his powers, and Iron Man betrays the superhero group the Avengers to its time-traveling villain, Kang the Conqueror. As declining American power and virtue seemed unable to fulfill its promise to bring order to the world, so the superheroes were unable to maintain their promise to bring order and justice to their universe. As the Americans perceived their national ideals betrayed, so were the superheroes betrayed by their powers.

The twenty-first century opened with the United States still the dominant, if no longer hegemonic state. The new Bush administration seemed more concerned with domestic economic affairs than international relations. This changed on September 11, 2001, when passenger airplanes became guided missiles and more than three thousand Americans were killed. The attacks of 9/11 brought an immediate outpouring of support from the global community; for the first time NATO evoked its mutual defense clause, with Europe rising to defend the United States. Blood donations soared and relief agencies and telethons received record donations. Comic book companies published special books of superhero art to raise funds for relief. The superhero films that became popular in the first decades of the twenty-first century construct a virtuous and necessary role for American power in an age of global terrorism. In Christopher Nolan's *Dark Knight* trilogy (2005, 2008, 2012), Bruce Wayne crosses cultural and moral boundaries to acquire the ability, will, and virtue necessary to redeem Gotham City from the terrorism of the League of Assassins, including the construction of a citywide total surveillance network. Joe Johnston's *Captain America: The First Avenger* (2011) recasts World War II as a battle between American virtue and a terroristic Nazi organization called HYDRA. In Joss Whedon's *The Avengers* (2012) a disparate group of superheroes must learn that they are one community before they can defend the Earth from alien invasion.

In comic books, the superhero narrative challenged the war on terror almost from its inception. Several stories between 2002 and 2004 indicted American global adventures during the Cold War as the source of anti-American terrorism, or identified the U.S. government as complicit in the attacks. Many deploy a common narrative of an attack on an apparently innocent civilian U.S. population, a failure of domestic authority to meet the threat, and the need for superheroes to intervene. In these stories, the heroic myth defined by Lawrence and Jewitt is twisted. Frequently the U.S. government, not some foreign terrorist, is behind the attack on American citizens. In "The Harvest," (2003) a Superman story in *Action Comics*, U.S. President Lex Luthor is in league with an anti-American terrorist. In the Avengers "Red Zone" (2003), the U.S. government has been infiltrated by the uber-Nazi Red Skull, who launches a biological attack at Mount Rushmore. In other stories the attacked civilian community is shown not to be innocent; in *Captain America*'s "Enemy" (2002), the town that suffers the terrorist attack is revealed to manufacture cluster bombs, and the terrorist attacks against America are equated with the U.S. firebombing of Dresden in WWII. Superhero films also moved to question the virtue behind the war on terror. In *Captain America: The Winter Soldier* (2014), Captain America discovers that the national security organization he has been working for is in fact indistinguishable from the neofascist organization HYDRA they have been fighting.[18] The American heroic narrative is subverted in these tales, at a moment when one would expect that narrative to have renewed power.

In Marvel's *Civil War* (2006–7) the rash actions of young superheroes cause an attack on a civilian population killing more than six hundred people, beginning a year-long allegory of the USA Patriot Act. The superhero community is divided over government registration, with Captain America leading the anti-registration forces and Iron Man leading the pro-registration coalition. On the brink of victory, Captain America surrenders, realizing that heroes fighting heroes is no battle for justice. This story is followed by *Secret Invasion* (2008), in which shape-shifting aliens invade the Earth, and the identity of heroes is unclear. At DC, a series of crossovers from *Identity Crisis* (2004) to *Final Crisis* (2008) raises the issue of the hubris of the superhero; given their power and moral clarity, should they be able to serve as judge and jury? The heroes psychically interfere with both villains and other heroes in *Identity Crisis*, while the hubris of the Guardians of the Universe threatens the welfare of the universe and the Green Lantern Corps in *Blackest Night* (2009–10); in *Infinite Crisis* (2005–6) the original 1940s Superman returns not as a hero but as supervillain, attempting to destroy a cosmic order he now believes has become hopelessly corrupt. In less mainstream comics, such as Robert Kirkman's *Invincible* or Mark Waid's *Irredeemable*, the superpowered hero becomes a threat to society. Even DC Comics has posited Superman as villain in its popular *Injustice* comics and video game line. Garth Ennis's *The Boys* assumes superheroes are without restraint, necessitating a clandestine organization whose job is to rein them in. American power, even when cast as a justified reaction to a devastating attack, is no longer constructed as virtuous and heroic. Instead, in the first decade after the American Century, American superhero narratives cast America as culpable in these attacks and portray such displays of power as hubristic and threatening.

The American superhero has been intimately tied to the growth and decline of American power over the past century. Costumed crime fighters and science fiction adventurers crossed the boundaries that separated the United States from the world in the 1920s and 1930s to educate Americans about the exercise of global power. During the 1940s and 1950s, superheroes in comic books, radio, and television helped construct the triumphalist American national project first to confront the Axis and then to fight the Cold War. As the costs of that project came home to Americans, superheroes were used first as an index of American moral behavior, and later a proxy for American decline through their deconstruction. In the twenty-first century, superheroes have been used to construct a nuanced vision of American global power, at some times challenging U.S. policy in the War on Terror and at others helping to construct a vision of the American community in an age of globalism. While the American Century may be over, the American superhero still helps Americans contemplate and construct their place in the world.

NOTES

1 Henry Luce, "The American Century," *Life Magazine* 10.7 (February 1941), accessed May 12, 2014, http://www.informationclearinghouse.info/article6139.htm.
2 George Washington, "Farewell Address," in *Writings* (New York: Library of America, 1997/1796), 962–77 (975).
3 Robert Scholes and Eric S. Rabkin, *Science Fiction: History, Science and Vision* (London: Oxford University Press, 1977), 108.
4 Lester Del Rey, *The Worlds of Science Fiction, 1926–1976* (New York: Garland Publishing, 1980), 306.
5 Brooks Landon, *Science Fiction after 1900: From the Steam Man to the Stars* (New York: Twayne Publishers, 1997); Corey K. Creekmur, "Superheroes and Science Fiction: Who Watches Comic Books?" *Science Fiction Studies* 31.2 (2004): 283–90.
6 While they suggest this is superheroic, in many ways it is merely a heroic myth – they identify it not only with masked crime fighters from the Lone Ranger to Superman, but also with Owen Wister's *Virginian*, *Star Trek*, and many other sources that are not necessarily superheroic. See John Lawrence Shelton and Thomas Jewitt, *The Myth of the American Superhero* (New York: Eerdman's, 2002).
7 Richard Slotkin, *Regeneration through Violence: The Myth of the American Frontier, 1600–1800* (Norman: University of Oklahoma Press, 1973).
8 Umberto Eco and Natalie Chilton, trans., "The Myth of Superman," *Diacritics* 2.1 (Spring 1972): 14–22.
9 Brian Atterbery, "The Magazine Era: 1926–1960," in Edward James and Farah Mendlesohn, eds., *The Cambridge Guide to Science Fiction* (London: Cambridge University Press, 2003), 32–47.
10 Gerard Jones, *Men of Tomorrow: Geeks, Gangsters and the Birth of the Comic Book* (New York: Basic Books, 2004), 224.
11 Wendy Wall, *Inventing the "American Way": The Politics of Consensus from the New Deal to the Civil Rights Movement* (London: Oxford University Press, 2009), 163–5.
12 Mark Waid, "Introduction," in *Superman in the Fifties* (New York: DC Comics, 2002), 5–9.
13 The more childish stories may have been influenced by the self-censoring Comics Code, established in 1954 in the wake of anti-comics protests and Senate hearings. Directed mainly at horror and crime comics, the Code restricted violent images and prohibited horror comics and any challenge to established authority.
14 Schwartz used his connections to science fiction fandom to build his staff, including long-time fan Mort Weisinger as editor and Edmund Hamilton as writer of Superman in the late 1950s.

15 See Pew Research, "Trust in Government 1958–2010," Pew Research (April 18, 2010), http://www.people-press.org/2010/04/18/section-1-trust-in-government-1958–2010/. Jeffrey Jones, "Americans' Trust in Executive and Legislative Branches Down," *Gallup Politics* (September 15, 2014), http://www.gallup.com/poll/175790/americans-trust-executive-legislative-branches-down.aspx.

16 Estimates for 1945 are taken from William H. Branson, Herbert Giersch, and Peter G. Peterson, "Trends in United States International Trade and Investment since World War II," in Martin Feldstein, ed., *The American Economy in Transition* (Chicago, IL: University of Chicago Press, 1980), 183–274 (183); other data are from the World Bank.

17 Matthew Pustz, "'Paralysis and Stagnation and Drift': America's Malaise as Demonstrated in Comic Books of the 1970s," in Matthew Pustz, ed., *Comic Books and American Cultural History: An Anthology* (New York: Continuum Press, 2012), 136–51.

18 For more examples, see David Higgins's contribution to this volume, "American Science Fiction after 9/11."

10

PATRICK JAGODA

Digital Games and Science Fiction

This chapter explores the relationship between American science fiction and digital games – an umbrella term that will include video, computer, mobile, and transmedia games while excluding card, board, and tabletop games. The analysis that follows takes three approaches to the intersection of science fiction and game studies: genre theory, cultural studies and historical contextualization, and a materialism that emphasizes the ways that digital games enable players to access and imagine the historical present.

Literary Versus Ludic Genres

The relationship between science fiction and digital games brings up several complexities inherent to the concept of genre. For several decades, defining genre has been a central undertaking in the study of both science fiction literature and film. While many scholars have attempted provisional definitions, careful analyses of science fiction texts suggest the impossibility of any total classification; however we define science fiction as a "genre," though, it is clear that the meaning of genre in digital games means something fundamentally different than it does in literature or even film. Genre in these latter cases often becomes aligned with narrative structures, central themes, and overarching styles (whether textual or visual) as, for instance, in the western, the mystery, or the romantic comedy. Genre in games, on the other hand, is often defined by core mechanics and available modes of play or, in broad terms, the nature of the game's interactivity.[1] As Thomas H. Apperley contends, "*Interactivity* – the way in which the game is played, rather than watched – is a nonrepresentational feature common to all video games."[2] In computer, video, and mobile games, after all, players do not simply read or watch a linear narrative but instead participate interactively in the construction of an avatar, the exploration of a world, and the completion of objectives. These qualities became central through exchanges in the late 1990s and early 2000s during which scholars such as Espen Aarseth, Markku

Eskelinen, Gonzalo Frasca, and Jesper Juul argued for the importance of medium specificity in the study of games and the establishment of a field of "ludology" that would take game mechanics and rules as its core elements of study. In discussions of genre, these writers treated narrative and audio-visual interfaces in games as secondary to procedural and action-oriented capacities. As Mark J. P. Wolf observes, "Just as different forms of dance (foxtrot, waltz, ballet, jazz) are defined by how the dancers move rather than how they look, an examination of the variety and range of video games reveals the inadequacy of classification by iconography of even narrative-based games."[3] Thus, even though a game may contain a fantasy world or a gangster narrative, its genre aligns, in large part, with its interaction type, yielding categories such as "first-person shooters," "real-time strategy games," and "construction and management games."

Despite ludology's insistence on the centrality of player actions, narrative and iconography are not irrelevant to digital game genres. In a variety of ways, games often seek to adapt science fiction texts. Across ludic genres, they may include science fiction visual themes (e.g., *Space Invaders* or *Asteroids*), complex stories (e.g., *Mass Effect* or *Bioshock*), and worlds conceived in other media (e.g., *Star Wars: Knights of the Old Republic* or *Enter The Matrix*). Such games suggest a correspondence with science fiction literature and film. As Henry Jenkins notes, "When game designers draw story elements from existing film or literary genres, they are most apt to tap those genres – fantasy, adventure, science fiction, horror, war – which are most invested in world-making and spatial storytelling."[4] In its propensity toward what Darko Suvin calls "cognitive estrangement,"[5] science fiction frequently devotes more detail to the realization of a world than to the description of character psychology or to the development of a plot. In commenting on the internal consistency of narrative worlds in science fiction literature, Steven Kagle makes an explicit connection to games: "Like the best of games, the best science-fiction works are usually those in which either arbitrary rules of play or arbitrary laws of science and human behavior are kept to a minimum."[6] Science fiction literature is often rule-bound and treats readers as players who can learn the fundamental elements of a fictional world and play along. In establishing the immersiveness of their worlds, games specifically generate what play theorist Johan Huizinga calls the "magic circle," the boundary separating the space-time of games from everyday life.[7]

Though the interest in worlds suggests similarities between linear science fiction narratives and games, the adaptation process – or the incorporation of science fictional modes of awareness into digital games – also involves substantial variations. Games, even when they retain narratives, often undergo structural metamorphoses. Namely, interactive stories are frequently nonlinear, multilinear, enactive, or emergent. As Jenkins again observes, "Game designers don't simply tell stories; they design worlds and sculpt spaces."[8] Moreover, the *experience* of playing through a science fiction game departs from reading a science fiction narrative. Kevin Veale contends, "Videogames bring science fiction into the affective present, for they offer players a direct feeling of responsibility for how the problems of alternative worlds are negotiated." The feeling of experiential immediacy and interactive immersiveness, in turn, offers "a different way of engaging with the speculative questions and issues presented by science fiction texts."[9] A video game such as Jonathan Blow's platformer *Braid* (2008), for example, explores the science fictional premise of worlds in which time operates differently than in our physical reality. It does so through mechanics that allow the player to solve puzzles by reversing time, slowing down or speeding up temporal flow, synchronizing or suspending different time streams, calling on a shadow self that exists at a slight delay, and dropping a ring that slows objects based on their proximity to its center. This game, thus, raises speculative questions through the immediate player experience of agential actions and interactive processes rather than the exposition of a science fiction novel (such as Lightman's *Einstein's Dreams*, one of the literary inspirations of *Braid*) that describes alternative temporal worlds.

A Brief History of Science Fiction Games

Histories of the science fiction genre often turn back to the nineteenth-century works of authors such as Mary Shelley, Edgar Allan Poe, Jules Verne, and H. G. Wells, as well as other precursors in early non-realism, utopian literature, and modernist writing. Carl Freedman dates modern science fiction, including the term itself, to "the American pulp tradition established in 1926 when Hugo Gernsback founded *Amazing Stories*."[10] In film, Sobchack has dated the emergence of American science fiction film, as a consistent and major cinematic genre, which was frequently dystopian and anxiety-laden, to the post-Hiroshima era. Science fiction digital games have an even later genesis. It is significant, however, that the science fiction game occupied a privileged place alongside the emergence of computer games *as such* in the 1960s.

Steve "Slug" Russell, the creator of *Spacewar!* (1962), which is widely considered to be the first computer game, set his original interactive hack in outer space. Russell was an enthusiastic reader of science fiction paperbacks, including Lester Dent's *Doc Savage* pulps.[11] His first digital game, created for the PDP-1 computer, was a multiplayer competition in which users maneuvered two spaceships ("the needle" or "the wedge") to avoid the gravity well of a star, managed finite missiles and fuel, and tried to shoot each other down. Though Russell had hoped to maintain realism through the game's mechanics with unpredictable torpedo trajectories, he ultimately introduced fiction into this aspect of the game, creating dependably direct torpedoes that violated the rules of physics. Russell's space battle would influence numerous significant game experiments in the 1960s and the emerging video game industry in the 1970s.

There are many reasons that, during the first decades of digital games, science fiction became a core generic influence. Though the genre's broader popularity across media in the United States is relevant, specific institutional and cultural factors were also at play. Following World War II, computers came to shape the ideological commitments, geopolitical strategies, and military systems that made up America's central role in the Cold War. As Paul N. Edwards contends, "Of all the technologies built to fight the Cold War, digital computers have become its most ubiquitous, and perhaps its most important, legacy."[12] In the 1960s and 1970s, access to computers and nascent networks was limited to government research labs as well as universities such as the University of Utah, Stanford University, and MIT (where Russell created *Spacewar!*). Thus, far from the widespread computing of the early twenty-first century, early game production and play were limited largely to a homogenous population of white, male engineers at a few facilities in the United States where such work was even feasible. As Anna Anthropy writes, "When computers were first installed in college campuses and laboratories, only engineers had the access to the machines, the comparative leisure time, and the technical knowledge to teach those computers to play games. It is not surprising that the game they made looked like their own experiences: physics simulations, space-adventures drawn from the science fiction they enjoyed."[13] Partial computer access thus arguably restricted the early cultural imaginary, including dominant genres, of digital games in the United States.

Along with the orientation of early game creation toward engineers and computer programmers (instead of designers and artists), digital games were also shaped by an American Cold War research agenda that privileged space travel, weapons development, and computing. This point is important because the United States was the source of digital games and (along with Japan) led the development of this form for several decades. It is perhaps unsurprising, then, that scientific and technological themes were so prominent in early games. Arguably, technoscientific change has always been a key subject of science fiction, dating back to the evolutionary and anthropological theories that influenced late nineteenth-century novels such as H. G. Wells's *The Time Machine* (1895), *The Island of Doctor Moreau*

(1896), and *The War of the Worlds* (1899), as well as the work of Verne, London, and Doyle. Cold War culture, however, made technoscience an even more central dimension of American culture and geopolitical power. During the early 1970s, early arcade games took on technological themes, especially space travel. Both the first coin-operated game (*Galaxy Game*, 1971) and the first commercially available arcade game (*Computer Space*, 1971) imitated or extended aspects of Russell's *Spacewar!* Though the first computer game was developed in a university setting, the first consumer video game console – the Magnavox Odyssey (1972) created for play on a television set – came from Ralph Baer, an engineer working at defense contractor Sander Associates that created circuits and other parts for the American military and space programs. During its commercial run in the early to mid-1970s, the Odyssey console included the science fiction cartridge *Interplanetary Voyage* (1973).[14]

Science fiction games became a mainstay, if not *the* dominant genre, in an American landscape made up of computer, video, and arcade games, taking a position alongside sports (*Pong*, 1972), maze (*Gotcha*, 1973), and racing (*Gran Trak 10*, 1974) games in the early 1970s. This genre again took center stage, however, in the late 1970s. Part of this resurgence was connected to the overwhelming cinematic success of George Lucas's *Star Wars* (1977) and its sequels. Arcade developer Cinematronics, which specialized in vector display games, released a series of successful science fiction games during this period, including *Space Wars* (1977), *Star Castle* (1980), and *Cosmic Chasm* (1982). Some of the biggest arcade hits of the time also developed around similar themes. Taito's game *Space Invaders* (1978) was inspired by both Wells's *The War of the Worlds* and Lucas's *Star Wars*. The game, which grossed more than a billion dollars in arcade business alone, features a cannon-like avatar that defends a position against an extraterrestrial invasion.[15] Another hit game, *Asteroids* (1979), features a triangular ship that destroys flying asteroids and UFO enemies. That same year, *Galaxian* (1979) proved a success with only minor variations on *Space Invader*'s theme of destroying a swarm of alien invaders.[16]

Though there are a host of cultural reasons for the genre's popularity in early digital games, there are arguably also technological reasons for the prominence of science fiction among games of this period. Eugene Jarvis, creator of the arcade shooter *Defender* (1980), has observed that science fiction space battles were so common in the games of the late 1970s and early 1980s because the abstraction of outer space "covered up the inadequacies of [existing console] hardware." Given limited RAM and other hardware constraints (unique to particular platforms), programmers had to be creative in their designs. Though the graphics of a game like *Defender* remained minimalist and abstract, the innovative mechanics of the game enabled complex interactions and different types of play. As Steven Kent explains, "*Defender* had an elaborate control panel with a joystick for controlling altitude and five buttons for firing weapons, dropping smart bombs, accelerating, changing directions, and jumping into hyperspace."[17]

Science fiction themes were so prominent in digital games of the late 1970s (for both cultural and technological reasons) that Toru Iwatani, the creator of *Pac-Man* (1980), even noted that he came to the idea for his innovative hit arcade game by searching for alternatives to the genre. In 1979, he saw "many games associated with killing creatures from outer space" but few games organized around negotiating mazes.[18] Though *Pac-Man's* success led to another transformation of the game market and its dominant genres, the early 1980s continued to bring innovative and successful science fiction games. For example, several games created for the Atari VCS home console, which launched in 1977, drew on science fiction. One game that departed from the standard space war premise was *Missile Command* (1980). This game simulates a Cold War scenario in which a nuclear aggressor is invading six cities (originally the Soviet Union targeting the six major cities on the American West Coast). The player must use a limited number of missiles launched from three antimissile silos to defend these cities. In the fashion of arcade games, the game encourages the achievement of a high score but resists total victory. *Missile Command* ends, in an apocalyptic fashion, with a white atomic explosion and a screen that reads "The End" in place of the standard "Game Over." Among the many noteworthy aspects of this game is its self-reflexive dimension – its use of technoscientific fictional tropes in a digital game. As David Sudnow writes, in his remarkable experiential video game memoir *Pilgrim in the Microworld*: "I'm not big on war, wasn't even allowed a cap gun as a kid, and *Missile Command* models the calculated insanity of the worst imaginable twentieth-century scenario. How powerful and eerie that the computerized arena seduces us to transcend the nightmare it presents."[19]

Along with this explicit Cold War simulation, Atari released numerous other science fiction games for the VCS. The outer space shooter *Yar's Revenge* (1981) became the best-selling original cartridge for the VCS console. This game was not only a success in its own right but also inspired spinoffs across media. As Ian Bogost and Nick Montfort observe, "In *Yar's Revenge*, the unique nature of the game elements, the possibility for one's ship to both fire and eat away at a shield, and the unusual shape of the ship also offered hooks to which other fictional media could attach."[20] These media included the comic *Yar's Revenge: The Qotile Ultimatum*. In

1982, Atari also released *Star Wars: The Empire Strikes Back* (1982), which became "the first video game of any sort that was based on any *Star Wars* movie."[21] The same year saw the publication of *E.T. The Extra-Terrestrial* (1982), a massive commercial failure that is notorious for being one of the most poorly designed games in the medium's history and one perceptual factor in (or at least symptom of) the game industry crash of 1983.

Since the resurgence of the game industry in the mid-1980s, science fiction games have continued to enjoy widespread success. Though the relevant games released since this period are too numerous to review here, even in a cursory fashion by decade, it is important to note that a greater number of these games have moved from earlier arcade-style "shoot 'em ups" to numerous genres of interactivity. Certainly 2-D science fiction shooters have continued with games such as *Star Soldier* (1986) and *Mars Matrix* (2000) and have also been supplemented with 3-D shooters such as *Star Fox* (1993) and *Star Wars: Rogue Squadron* (1998). Alongside shooters, however, science fiction has played a central role in other ludic genres. Clyde Wilcox and Kevin Wilcox observe, "In many respects the market for computer games resembles the market for fiction: science fiction consists of genres like hard science extrapolation, space wars, social science extrapolation, utopias, and dystopias."[22] While fiction genres have inspired a number of ludic genres, science fiction narratives, visual styles, and themes also map onto interactive genres that are unique to digital games.

While a complete survey of ludic genres that have incorporated science fiction elements is impossible here, a few categories that have been key since the mid-1980s are worth noting. These have included platforming games such as *Metroid* (1986), *Mega Man* (1987), and *Out of This World* (1991); both turn-based and real-time strategy games, including *Spaceward Ho!* (1990), *X-COM: UFO Defense* (1993), and *Starcraft* (1998); space exploration simulations such as *Nomad* (1993) and *X: Beyond the Frontier* (1999); survival horror games such as *Dead Space* (2008); a range of action-adventure and narrative-oriented role-playing games such as *Mass Effect* (2007), *Fallout 3* (2008), and *To the Moon* (2011); and game-like visual novels including *Bionic Heart* (2009) and *Analogue: A Hate Story* (2012). Since the release of *Wolfenstein 3D* (1992) and *Doom* (1993), first-person shooters have also become an immensely popular genre, often making use of science fiction environments. Of 499 first-person shooter games surveyed in 2011, Michael Hitchens found that 113 had science fiction settings and another 74 had related near-future settings.[23] This action genre, which requires fast-paced hand-eye coordination, has yielded such critically acclaimed science fiction games as *Half-Life 2* (2005) and *Bioshock Infinite* (2013), and first-person games without shooter components, including the dystopian parkour game *Mirror's Edge* (2008) and games with speculative mechanics such as *Portal* (2007).

Beginning around the turn of the twenty-first century, several new digital game genres emerged with novel platforms, technologies, and modes of production, extending the scope of science fiction games. Massively Multiplayer Online Role Playing Games (MMORPG) have expanded multiplayer interactions and world making into huge virtual online environments, including fictional planets, galaxies, and cyberpunk cities. MMORPGs have most often drawn from fantasy source material. Nevertheless, science fiction instances with thousands of players such as *Anarchy Online* (2001), *EVE Online* (2003), and *Love* (2010) have experimented with utopian societies and collective forms of organization. Another experimental genre that emerged during this period is the Alternate Reality Game (ARG), which tells a transmedia story that includes online components while stretching out into offline environments. These games, which have been especially popular in the United States, require players to adopt key roles in a narrative that they discover or help produce with the designers. Key ARGs have included the future murder mystery *The Beast* (2001), the AI-oriented game *I Love Bees* (2004), and the dystopian *Year Zero* (2007). During these years, mobile games also gained popularity in the United States, especially with the proliferation of smartphones and tablets. Mobile devices have encouraged the production of adaptations of earlier science fiction game genres as well as innovative designs, such as *Near Orbit Vanguard Alliance (N.O.V.A)* (2009), *The Silent Age* (2012), and *Waking Mars* (2012). Finally, since about 2007, emergent categories of "independent games," "artgames," and "DIY game making" have opened up still other avenues that run alongside and intersect with mainstream commercial production. These movements have yielded science fiction games across numerous genres of interactivity, including *Braid* (2008), *Saira* (2009), *The Swapper* (2013), and *Irrational Exuberance* (2013). Most of the games I have mentioned in this brief historical survey can be understood as belonging to multiple ludic and narrative genres, altering the in-process genre of science fiction games in a variety of ways.

Game Materiality, Speculative Processes, and Historicity

Though establishing a chronology of and context for science fiction games helps us see patterns since the 1960s, the history *of* games is not identical with their historicity – that is, *the experience of history as such* that is grounded in digital game technologies and their formal expressions in the late twentieth and early twenty-first centuries. Elsewhere, I have argued that a sense of computer and video games as a unique art form requires a more intimate understanding of the new sensorium that they open up – that is, the specific experience of spatiality, temporality, speed, graphics, audio, and procedural activity that they make available.[24] Given the expression of cognitive estrangement through often-experimental mechanics in science fiction games, this genre becomes crucial in helping us make sense of the historicity of digital games. It is worth emphasizing that the emergence of digital games during the Cold War – and their co-development with the short American Century that began in the mid-twentieth century – is important to making sense of their historical legacy and their affective relationship to the present. The American scientific apparatus and military-industrial complex assembled to fight World War II produced numerous technologies that altered the latter half of the twentieth century, including the atom bomb and the programmable computer. In the final months of the war, U.S. Director of the Office of Scientific Research and Development Vannevar Bush took an active part in reorienting postwar scientific efforts toward a new technological horizon in which he presciently imagined specialized computing unfolding into ubiquitous digital media.[25] Bush, who wanted to neutralize the destructive developments of the early Cold War, saw new media as moving science toward the creation of connections among people. Despite these intentions, computers have been used for a variety of purposes since that time – to coordinate air strikes and defenses, to organize civil infrastructures, to manage new modes of labor, and to enable emergent forms of art and entertainment. Thus, digital games, arguably the most popular of the expressive media made possible by computers, belong to overlapping militaristic, commercial, and artistic histories.

To analyze how science fiction digital games have represented and channeled the post-1960 world, a careful study of the effects of mechanics and interactive systems on historical consciousness and imaginative capacities becomes essential. How, in other words, do the medium-specific aspects of science fiction games foreground the historicity of technologies, cultural beliefs, emotions, affects, bodies, and social ways of being in our time? Moreover, how do these games encourage different types of speculation that complicate or multiply how the present might be understood and engaged? Though an extended answer to these questions is not possible here, three brief examples may be suggestive.

The first-person science fiction shooter *BioShock* (2007) is set in a dystopian underwater city called Rapture that is governed by a version of Ayn Rand's Objectivist philosophy. *BioShock* experiments with many aspects of science fiction's historical materialism. At a narrative level, it extends a central feature of science fiction: what Samuel R. Delany calls the genre's "*thingyness*" that involves the "the practically incantatory task of naming nonexistent objects"[26] Instead of making character dialogue or even the description of imaginary objects central, the game teaches players about its world through interactions with things – audio recordings, posters, and architecture. Even more profoundly, the game foregrounds the mechanics and activity that is common to the genre, including melee and gun-based combat, management of limited resources, and exploration. Through its high-speed gameplay and a self-reflexive relation to its predetermined "on rails" path, *BioShock* highlights the centrality of action, and indeed the impossibility of inaction, in digital games. In an iconic twist, the player learns that the protagonist, Jack, has been programmed to obey commands that are accompanied by the phrase "Would you kindly?" These words are uttered repeatedly throughout the game by Frank Fontaine – the player's purported guide who proves, in the end, to be the very antagonist that is controlling Jack and driving him to violence, while also directing the player toward tasks that are necessary for progressing. Through this mechanism, *BioShock* allegorizes the possibilities and limits of agency in digital games. Through the character of Andrew Ryan, a business magnate who resembles the protagonist of *Citizen Kane* and envisions Rapture as a technoscientific utopia, the game also criticizes a particularly American mode of agency that privileges entrepreneurial success and capitalist progress.

While a science fiction novel may describe a world and imagine character interiority, a science fiction game generates a world for navigation, invites participatory role playing, and requires actions in pursuit of objectives. *BioShock* and its sequels use science fiction narratives organized around themes such as genetic enhancement and quantum theory, as well as moral choices built into the narrative, to defamiliarize and question the imperative to progress that is at the heart of first-person shooter games. In a broader sense, the game also foregrounds the centrality of action and activity as key human modes in the early twenty-first century. Despite its critical medium-specific dimensions, *BioShock* participates in the very hyperactivity and information overload, which it identifies as aspects of our time, through progress-oriented achievements and a hypermediated head up display (HUD) interface.

A second game, *Spore* (2008), is a different kind of science fiction experience that privileges life simulation and system building. This game experiments with numerous ludic genres. The player oversees the evolution of a species from a single-celled organism to an interstellar culture. Each evolutionary stage is captured with a different game genre including 2-D action ("cell stage"), 3-D adventure and life simulation ("creature stage"), real-time strategy ("tribal stage" and "civilization stage"), and exploration ("space stage"). *Spore* draws from many scientific fields, including evolutionary and systems theory. Even as it often reverts to anthropomorphic representations, *Spore* attempts to speculate about radically nonhuman forms. Technologically, the game makes players aware of their relationship to computation through an implicit interaction among developer design, player choices in creature composition, and responsive computer code. *Spore* relies on procedural animation that produces moving graphics of user-created creatures in real time. This in-process collaboration raises questions about the feedback loops between human players and nonhuman software that has become nearly ubiquitous (at least in the first world) since the late twentieth century. Though the game remains speculative along a number of fronts, it also foregrounds (though not always critically) the centrality of technology in nation building and imperial projects, as the player "progresses" between evolutionary stages. Istvan Csicsery-Ronay Jr. has argued that science fiction as a genre is indebted to the mediation enabled by the form of the novel and the technological expansion that characterizes imperialism.[27] Similarly, several game genres, especially simulation and real-time strategy games, betray empiricist foundations in attempts to reproduce the world through interactive models. The science fiction game extends the imperial roots of the science fiction novel through a material reliance on computation and digital media, which support contemporary forms of imperialism and postindustrialism, including those that are specific to the American Century. An analysis of *Spore* raises the crucial issue of how digital technologies constitute historical consciousness in the present.

One final game, the puzzle-platformer *Swapper* (2013), demonstrates the importance of innovative mechanics to the science fiction imaginary of games. This game is set on a nearly abandoned space station where experiments about a series of seemingly interconnected and conscious rock samples have been unfolding. The game's visual interface (detailed but largely empty spaces, dark lighting, and life-like figures based on clay models) and sound design (melancholy melodies, arrhythmic soundscapes, and ominous, nonhuman sound effects) contribute to a meditative world that involves the player's participation from the start. Though *Swapper* features an immersive deep-space narrative and futuristic world, the core of its speculation takes place through the gameplay itself. In order to solve spatial puzzles, players access a cloning device that enables them to reproduce their avatar up to four times. Additionally, players are able to transfer their consciousness to any of the clones. The game uses procedures, decisions, and activity to raise complex ethical and metaphysical questions about the nature of consciousness. It is never certain, for instance, whether a "swap" of consciousness negates the initial being or transfers it to another material form. It is also unclear whether each discarded clone constitutes the murder of a sentient life form or only of a mechanical copy. The game does not describe this uncertainty but makes the player complicit, through the necessary use of the swapping mechanic, with a troubling form of scientific experimentation. Through its mechanics and immersive audiovisual assets, *Swapper* identifies actions and interactive processes as key components of ethical thought in the present.

Conclusion: Science Fiction Across Media

Digital games alter the nature of cognitive estrangement, speculative thought, and world building that have been central qualities of science fiction literature. They do so through the introduction of gameplay mechanics, procedural capacities, navigable worlds, and multimedia interactions. Games have also, reciprocally, affected older forms such as the novel and cinema. Science fiction novels such as *Ender's Game* (1985), *Snow Crash* (1992), *Daemon* (2006), *Halting State* (2007), and *Ready Player One* (2011) explore the cultural and technological underpinnings of digital games while also drawing from their aesthetics. Science fiction films such as *WarGames* (1983), *eXistenZ* (1999), and *Gamer* (2009) similarly examine ludic scenarios and employ digital game aesthetics. In a different sense, films such as *Avatar* (2009) and *Prometheus* (2012) feature long sequences that privilege the exploratory aesthetics of game-like virtual worlds over the narrative drive of many science fiction action films; recent military SF films like *Doom* (2005) and *Battle: Los Angeles* (2011) adopt the story logic, pacing, and visual look of military SF gaming, while recent time-travel films like *Source Code* (2011) and *Edge of Tomorrow* (2014) draw on the by-now familiar game mechanic of "saving" and "reloading" for their narrative structure. Though the ongoing study of science fiction games must attend to medium-specific features, the broader media ecology within which all science fiction works appear will also prove important. *The Matrix* has already offered a strong example of a science fiction world that, far from being self-contained, stretches across feature films, animated shorts, comics, video games, and an online virtual world.[28] Such distributed works, which are especially prominent in the United States, invite comparative transmedia analyses. Thus, science fiction increasingly takes on new properties of extensibility that invite not only sequels of novels or films but also the production of open-ended worlds that include both old and new media elements that are narrative and ludic, prescribed and participatory, experienced individually and networked for collective play. The rapid expansion of digital media – and its sundry art forms of which digital games remain the most popular in our time – opens up many unexplored realms for science fiction studies.

NOTES

1 It is worth noting that film theory also complicates the relationship between film and narrative, most notably through Tom Gunning's concept of "the cinema of attractions" in "The Cinema of Attractions: Early Film, Its Spectator and the Avant-Garde" in Thomas Elsaesser and Adam Barker, eds., *Early Film* (British Film Institute, 1989).

2 Thomas Apperley, "Genre and Game Studies: Toward a Critical Approach to Video Game Genres," *Simulation & Gaming* 37.1 (2006): 7.

3 Mark J. P. Wolf, *The Medium of the Video Game* (Austin: University of Texas Press, 2002).

4 Henry Jenkins, "Game Design as Narrative Architecture," in Noah Wardrip-Fruin and Pat Harrigan, eds., *First Person: New Media as Story, Performance, and Game* (Cambridge, MA: MIT Press, 2004).

5 Darko Suvin, *Metamorphoses of Science Fiction: On the Poetics and History of a Literary Genre* (New Haven, CT: Yale University Press, 1979), 7–8.

6 Steven Kagle, "Science Fiction as Simulation Game," in Thomas D. Clareson, ed., *Many Futures, Many Worlds: Theme and Form in Science Fiction* (Kent, OH: Kent State University Press, 1977), 228.

7 Johan Huizinga, *Homo Ludens: A Study of the Play-Element in Culture* (New York: Roy, 1950).

8 Jenkins, "Game Design as Narrative Architecture."

9 Kevin Veale, "Making Science Fiction Personal – Videogames and Inter-Affective Storytelling," in Jordan J. Copeland, ed., *The Projected and the Prophetic: Humanity in Cyberculture, Cyberspace & Science Fiction* (2011). Accessed May 12, 2014. http://www.interdisciplinarypress.net/my-cart/ebooks/ethos-and-modern-life/the-projected-and-prophetic.

10 Carl Freedman, *Critical Theory and Science Fiction* (Hanover: Wesleyan University Press, 2000), 14.

11 Steven L. Kent, *The Ultimate History of Video Games* (New York: Random House International, 2002), 18–20.

12 Paul N. Edwards, *The Closed World: Computers and the Politics of Discourse in Cold War America* (Cambridge, MA: MIT Press, 1996), ix.

13 Anna Anthropy, *Rise of the Videogame Zinesters: How Freaks, Normals, Amateurs, Artists, Dreamers, Dropouts, Queers, Housewives, and People Like You Are Taking Back an Art Form* (New York: Seven Stories Press, 2012), 5–6.

14 Kent, *The Ultimate History of Video Games*, 21–31.

15 Steve Bloom, *Video Invaders* (New York: Arco Pub), 1982.

16 Kent, *The Ultimate History of Video Games*, 62–137.

17 Ibid., 145 and 147. Eugene Jarvis quoted on p. 145.

18 Ibid., Iwatani quoted on p. 141.

19 David Sudnow, *Pilgrim in the Microworld* (New York: Warner Books, 1983).

20 Nick Montfort and Ian Bogost, *Racing the Beam: The Atari Video Computer System* (Cambridge, MA: MIT Press, 2009), 94. The discussion of *Yar's Revenge* ranges from 81–97.

21 Ibid., 119.

22 Clyde Wilcox and Kevin Wilcox, "New Gateways to Adventure: The Creation and Marketing of Science Fiction Computer Games," in George E. Slusser, Gary

Westfahl, and Eric S. Rabkin, eds., *Science Fiction and Market Realities* (Athens: University of Georgia Press, 1996), 196.

23 Michael Hitchens, "A Survey of First-Person Shooters and Their Avatars," *Game Studies* 11.3 (2011), accessed May 12, 2014, http://gamestudies.org/1103/articles/michael_hitchens.

24 Patrick Jagoda, "Fabulously Procedural: *Braid*, Historical Processing, and the Videogame Sensorium," *American Literature* 85:4 (December 2013).

25 Vannevar Bush, "How We May Think," *Atlantic Monthly* 176.1 (July 1945): 101–8.

26 Samuel R. Delany, *The Jewel-Hinged Jaw: Notes on the Language of Science Fiction* (Middletown, CT: Wesleyan University Press, 2009), 23.

27 Istvan Csicsery-Ronay, "Science Fiction and Empire," *Science Fiction Studies* 30 (2003): 231.

28 For an extended discussion of *The Matrix* as part of "convergence culture," see Henry Jenkins, *Convergence Culture: Where Old and New Media Collide* (New York: New York University Press, 2006).

11

KAREN HELLEKSON

Fandom and Fan Culture

Fans are people who actively engage with something – a text, objects such as coins or stamps, favored sports teams – and *fandom* is the community that fans self-constitute around that text or object. Fans consume artworks, create their own, police community rules, and engage with each other in complicated, self-referential, multivocal discourse, the very expression of which generates the shared community. In order to best disseminate the artworks and texts associated with their fandom, fans have tended to be early adopters of technology, be it a hand-letter press, VHS tapes, Photoshop software, or the Internet. As such, fandoms have varied greatly in their practices and expressions in different times, places, and social contexts – but what they all have in common is the desire to share an often passionate, affective response to the item in question with like-minded others.

The study of fans and fan culture is inextricably linked with the genre of science fiction. Fans have always been engaging with texts, often in transformative ways by literally scribbling in the margins, rewriting scenes, and crafting new endings; however, the current model of participatory fandom evident in Western culture has been structured by the patterns of interaction created by the science fiction fandom that began in America in the mid-1930s before spreading out into other locations, genres, and media forms.

A History of Science Fiction Fandom

Early science fiction fandom grew out of clubs dedicated to SF and weird fiction pulp magazines that were launched in the late 1920s, such as *Startling Stories*, *Wonder Stories*, and *Weird Tales*. Clubs in Los Angeles, Philadelphia, and New York City were particularly active. New York groups included the Greater New York Science Fiction Club, the New York chapter of the national Science Fiction League (founded in 1934 by influential editor Hugo Gernsback), and the Brooklyn Science Fiction League.[1] These clubs formed, broke apart, often over political differences, and reformed.

In 1937 several New York organizations coalesced into the Futurians, SF's best-known fan club. Many of the club members were young – in their teens and twenties – and aspired to be writers or editors themselves. Members of this mostly male club included now-familiar names such as Isaac Asimov, Damon Knight, Sam Moskowitz, Frederik Pohl, Judith Merril, and Donald A. Wollheim, many of whom have written memoirs of their experiences in early fandom.[2]

These fans created two modes of expression that remain with SF fandom to this day: exchanging written texts (mostly nonfiction) and meeting up in person at a themed convention. These activities created a self-defined cohesive group organized around a common interest that we would now call a fandom. The texts that early fans exchanged comprised letter columns and fan magazines, catalyzed by Hugo Gernsback. Gernsback provided an opening for fan engagement not only by creating the national Science Fiction League, with its area chapters, but also by including letter columns in the pulp magazines he published. He printed letters of comment sent in by readers and included the writers' street addresses. This permitted readers to get in touch with one another directly, allowing them to correspond, then meet up and network. In the first issue of *Amazing Stories* (1926), Gernsback writes, "How good this magazine will be in the future is up to you. Read *Amazing Stories* – get your friends to read it and then write us what you think of it. We will welcome constructive criticism – for only in this way will we know how to satisfy you."[3] Fans took this invitation seriously; they also considered it a mark of distinction when Gernsback published their letters or otherwise responded to them. (A similar congenial interactivity between creators and fans on letters pages would later help drive Marvel Comics's explosive popularity in the 1960s.) Gernsback's willingness to engage in back-and-forth with the young fans of his "scientifiction" magazines was emulated by the fans themselves as they engaged each other.

From this it was a short step to creating texts to share among one another. The first SF fan magazine, *The Comet*, edited by Raymond A. Palmer, appeared in May 1930, published out of Chicago.[4] A slew of others followed. Most had very small readerships, correspondingly small print runs, and erratic publication frequency. Fans could subscribe, or they could donate a fan magazine to receive one in exchange. Several libraries today hold extensive fan magazine collections of these early SF and weird tales fan magazines in nonlending archives, including the University of California at Riverside, the University of Iowa, Syracuse University, and Liverpool University, available for scholars to visit and study.

Physically, fan mags – the word *fanzine* was not coined until 1940[5] – were stapled-together pieces of ordinary-sized letter paper, sometimes folded in half. Often one side would remain empty so it might be addressed and the postage stamp affixed. Sometimes covers were made of colored heavy paper, and covers often included artwork as well as the fan mag's title. The writer would prepare the magazine on a typewriter, then reproduce it. Early modes of reproduction included simple carbon paper, Ditto machine (spirit duplication), hectograph, and mimeograph. Photocopying came later. Artwork, if included, would be hand drawn and might be colored by hand, so each copy would be unique. Sometimes the writer would paste in a photograph, often of a fan being profiled. Fan mags' content primarily provided extensions of the now-familiar letters of comment. Editorials and reviews of current issues of SF magazines would often be included. Fiction rarely appeared, and if it did, was often about the fans themselves. In fact, as J. B. Speer notes, the early meaning of the term *fan fiction* did not mean "fiction written by fans," but "fiction written about fans."[6]

As Neil Patrick Hayden describes,[7] after fan magazines had been established, fans co-opted APAs (amateur press associations, from groups formed in the late 1870s by the owners of hand letter presses to disseminate their work) for the SF world. The Fantasy Amateur Press Association, or FAPA, was founded by SF/F fan and Futurian Donald A. Wollheim in 1937, who learned about APAs from weird tales writer H. P. Lovecraft. In this nifty mode of dissemination, which remains in use, fans would create a zine and then send a certain number of copies to a master editor, who would collate them and then mail the bundles to all the contributors.

Fans thus built their communities via the technologies then current: reproduction and postal mail. But they also met in person, as the vogue of fan clubs and SF leagues hints. The first World Science Fiction Convention, or Worldcon, was held in conjunction with the 1939 New York World's Fair over the Fourth of July weekend.[8] The World's Fair theme of "The World of Tomorrow" meshed nicely with science fictional interests. Worldcons have been held ever since, with a break during World War II. It is no coincidence that fandom became active during what is now known as the Golden Age of Science Fiction, which is usually dated from 1939 (the date of the first Worldcon) to 1946. Indeed, the activities of the fans – who were the writers, editors, and consumers of SF literature – ended up not just constituting a fandom but the genre of SF itself.

Fandom in the 1940s, 1950s, and early 1960s saw the codification of many of the firsts noted earlier. Some fans organized their lives around fandom, with marriages and children resulting; FIAWOL (fandom is a way of life) became a catch phrase. Fans kept up extensive correspondences, published fanzines, and organized and attended conventions. Filk, or SF-related, fan-created, and fan-sung songs, often with new lyrics to familiar tunes, became active in the early 1950s and remains popular today, with new genres such as Harry Potter – themed wizard rock (also known as "wrock"). Cosplay, or costume play, was enshrined at many conventions as part of a big stage show, where fans would model the costumes they created. SF magazines continued to publish new fiction, although the market contracted sharply in the 1950s as many magazines folded. Serializations of many novel-length SF texts by now-classic writers appeared, which would then go on to be published as stand-alone books. SF fandom was thus a fandom of literature, and it was being led by professional writers who were formerly among the first fans. This permitted, even encouraged, contact between writers and fans.

As David Hartwell outlines, fans continued to create a complex, often exclusionary vocabulary that cemented their role as insiders and tastemakers.[9] Fanzines, APAs, and in-person conventions all continued, with local conventions and Worldcons important nexuses of connection. Histories of SF fandom in the 1940s and 1950s by Harry Warner Jr., an active fan and letter writer, describe fannish activities from an anecdotal point of view and highlight the personalities that populated this era and the culture they constructed.[10] Extensive letter writing by prominent fans bridged distances between fans and forged friendships and alliances. Zines provided a forum for fan essays, analysis, and later fan fiction. Retrospective works about this era by active fans such as Warner and histories of fandom such as those that appear in the fanzine *Mimosa* demonstrate a kind of fannish self-analysis that remains important as fans create and contextualize their experiences.[11]

Science Fiction Media Fandom

The landscape of fannish activity changed in 1967. That year saw the publication of the first SF media zine, *Spockanalia*, which marked the rise of SF media fandom, as opposed to SF literature fandom. According to Joan Marie Verba, this *Star Trek* zine was created after fans saw the pilot of *Star Trek* at the 1966 Worldcon in Cleveland.[12] Naturally, a zine was the result. SF media fandom thus grew directly out of SF literature fandom, and its catalyst was *Star Trek*. These early *Star Trek* media fans also initiated what has since become a staple in fandom: the save-the-show campaign, run by fans to try to resurrect a canceled show. *Spockanalia* included an editorial that described a letter campaign to save the recently canceled program.

As Francesca Coppa explains, women – and they were mostly women, in contrast to the boys and men who comprised fandom in the mid-1930s – engaged in media fandom in a primarily transformative mode.[13] Not content to stick with letters of comment, essays, poems, and the occasional piece of fiction (which quickly morphed into entire zines dedicated to fan fiction), these *Star Trek* fans created vidding, a fannish art form pioneered by Kandy Fong, whose slide show, "What Do You Do With a Drunken Vulcan?," appeared in 1975.[14] Fong used *Star Trek* film snippets literally picked up from the cutting room floor and played a slide show of still images to a popular filk song, which fans received enthusiastically.

The genre evolved into videorecorded clips from the episode strung together, expertly edited on VHS tape, and timed to a specific song. In continuing with the fannish penchant of turning technologies to their own ends, be they letter presses or videotape, fan vidders have lately turned to digital technologies, which permits them not only to clip images and sync them to music, but also to alter the images. In fan vids, also known as songtapes, images are chosen to fit the song lyrics, but the very best vids use this to create a new story – a romance, perhaps, between two characters not engaged thus canonically, transforming the original text into an art form that tells a new story by rereading and reconstructing images from a fannish point of view.

In addition to vidding, early media fandom was associated with zine culture, as Camille Bacon-Smith's ethnographic report describes.[15] Zines, which previously had been mostly news, reviews, and analysis, now turned to fan fiction. The homoerotic genre of slash also gained prominence, so called because of the typographical slash used between character names to indicate a romantic relationship; Kirk/Spock slash remains the best-known example. Slash received quite a bit of critical attention, especially in the mid-1990s, not only because the communities that created it were interesting for scholars to study from an ethnographic point of view but also because of the recognition that slash dealt with rupture, rewriting, and the Other, thus placing slash, just like SF, in contrast to the mainstream.

The fannish zine culture has always relied on a gift economy, although this is now being called into question, as writers collected by Kristina Busse argue.[16] Fanzines have traditionally been sold for the cost of reproduction and postage, with any overage used to seed the next project or donated to a charity. Fans' fear of cease-and-desist orders from producers or adverse attention from writers or actors has resulted in a fannish convention of making no money from their projects, thus relegating fans to amateur status. Fans also attach disclaimers to their work to indicate that they understand they have no right to the characters or situations. So strong is this ethos that fan-created and fan-disseminated software created for arching fan fiction includes disclaimers on every page as a default setting. Fans perceive this fly-under-the-radar, make-no-money strategy as circumventing copyright law, although, as Rebecca Tushnet explains, fan artworks fall under fair use and parody (with the term used in its legal sense).[17]

Early fan studies academic scholarship published in the 1990s describes how media fans, in Henry Jenkins's term, poached the work of producers in order to create something of value, and the creation and exchange of these new artworks in turn constituted the fannish group.[18] This reading of fan activity – which valorized the work fans did to analyze texts and construct new meanings, and placed fan works in opposition to that of the producers who created the canonical text – remains current, although in 2013 Jenkins and colleagues updated the ideas of fan – producer networking and dialogue to reflect changes in the fan environment, notably Internet trends.[19] Spreadable media, in which fan networks take on the role of distribution of content, complicates the fan – producer power divide as fan activities force a change in traditional modes of corporate control. Instead of top-down decrees from The Powers That Be, fans desired actual dialogue with the producers.

Just as media conventions spun off from SF fandom, so did other specialty fan conventions. For example, MediaWest*Con is an important annual convention devoted to SF/media fandom, entirely run by fans and without guests. Another well-known convention, Vividcon, is dedicated to vidding. In addition, many local groups host fan conventions. In addition to fan-run conventions, for-profit organizations such as Creation Entertainment run them, and Comic-Con, formerly a haven for comic book fans, has expanded to become a giant media extravaganza, with producers and actors on hand to hawk the latest SF/F TV show or film. Filk, cosplay, zines, and fan-created artwork may all play important roles at these events. The convention model pioneered by early SF fans has thus been endlessly replicated and tweaked to reflect the specific interests of the fan group.

Fandom Moves Online

The move toward SF/F media fandom was one important step in the evolution of fan activity, as it broadened the base of potential fans by moving outside literature. Another was the mainstreaming of the Internet in the mid-1990s. With the advent of fannish presence online, fans no longer transmitted the norms of their culture in person. This created tension between fan communities as long-established conventions of fan behavior were questioned or simply ignored – if the fan even understood she was part of a larger community that had rules. Yet it was also easier to find like-minded people to share ideas and exchange artworks. Niche fandoms created and disseminated their own cultures, fractioning a formerly fairly cohesive fan practice.

As Kristina Busse and I have previously noted, the Internet permitted fans to engage with one another without geographic proximity.[20] Fans used – and continue to use – Usenet, Listserv mailing groups, discussion bulletin boards and forums, and fan-appropriated or fan-created blog platforms such as LiveJournal and Dreamwidth to engage with one another, to share reviews and creative artworks, and to act as de facto fiction or post archives. Sites such as Deviant Art and 4chan sprang up to share artwork. Fans have also pressed more recent media tools such as Twitter and Tumblr into service: Twitter may be used for short posts ostensibly written by a media character, or users may utilize it to construct a multivocal story. Tumblr permits aggregation of links and images of interest, with the goal of broad sharing.

Producers also create sites to encourage fan engagement. Early experiments included fan forums, some moderated and some not. The Bronze, a forum associated with *Buffy the Vampire Slayer*, was created by the producers of the show a few months after the show aired in 1997; when the forum moved in 2001 and changed its format, fans instead founded another site. Auteur J. Michael Straczynski made himself available to engage with fans on a *Babylon 5* site, an early example of producers talking to fans that Kurt Lancaster analyzes in detail.[21] And LucasFilm hosted an annual official *Star Wars* fan film award from 2002 to 2012. However, the contest had restrictive rules, and fan creators, who had to be amateurs, were required to choose from a specific palette of images, music, and sounds, which were provided. The relationship between producers and consumer-fans remains a fraught one even as the changing media landscape permits dialogue between the two stakeholders.

More recently, as Jonathan Gray notes, producers have begun creating media extensions of properties – spoilers, promos, DVD extras, games, contests – to generate excitement and involve fans, as well as to attempt to control the narrative about the text before it is even consumed.[22] In addition, fans' unpaid labor often directly benefits producers. For example, fans create and disseminate subtitled versions of films and TV programs, a practice known as fansubbing, thus greatly expanding the reach of the property at no cost to the producer and creating a market that the producer may wish to exploit later.[23] Producers' attempts to harness the unpaid labor of fans have caused significant controversy.

SF literature fandom still exists, of course. Yet it seems that media fandom has eclipsed it in terms of numbers of fans and diversity of activity. It is a truism that once a visual adaptation of a written text is released, fan activity escalates. For example, *Harry Potter* and *Lord of the Rings* fandom existed before the films were released, based on the books, but on a much smaller scale. Once the wildly popular film series began, fan activity exploded. Film and television fandoms – and, increasingly, anime and game fandoms – have gained prominence and membership, even as SF literature fans age.

Why Science Fiction?

Of course, not all fans center their activities around SF texts. Contemporary readers of Jane Austen's work would extend or rework her narratives. Sherlock Holmes was an early fandom; fans wrote and exchanged Holmes pastiches in what might be called the first fan fiction.[24] However, SF, supernatural, and so-called cult texts tend to draw active, vocal fans who work together to build a community around a source text. *Star Trek, Blake's 7, The X-Files, Xena: Warrior Princess, Buffy the Vampire Slayer, Battlestar Galactica, Twilight, Harry Potter, Doctor Who* – all these media sources have attracted particularly extensive fan activity as well as critical scrutiny from academics. Yet even texts like *The Man from U.N.C.L.E.* and *The Professionals* (1960s-era spy shows) and the Sherlock Holmes canon might be said to contain a kind of engagement with the technological that marks them as akin to SF, be it winning the day through cleverness and gadgetry or solving a crime by applying a rigorously scientific method.

Large fandoms tend to organize themselves around SF, fantasy, or supernatural texts. So-called cult texts rely on a perception that they work against the mainstream, one reason why SF/F is associated with cultish – that is to say extreme – behavior. Something about the fantastic in a text invites engagement, although notions vary of what that ineffable something is: the world-building? the characters? the situations? However, cult texts create a disrupted, nonrealistic world, where the Other, be it monster, alien, or angel, impinges on our construction of the real world, thus opening the everyday up to fabulous possibilities. This forces a questioning of the status quo and valorizes, even normalizes, those who struggle against it. However, as Sharon Marie Ross notes, the specific elements of a text that make it cult, and that thus invite affective engagement, may be less important than the act of creating a social audience.[25]

Fandom's three waves, as articulated by Jonathan Gray et al., have greatly broadened the definition of *fan*, and this is paralleled by changes in the culture industry.[26] The first wave of fandom celebrated fandom as cultural resistance. Epitomized by Jenkins's *Textual Poachers* (which in turn engaged theories by Fiske and De Certeau[27]), fans were seen as seizing the work of producers; fandom was a subculture of resistance to a dominant mass culture. The first wave of fandom pitted the producer against the consumer-fan; it also attempted to turn the "get a life!" pathologic mode of viewing fans to a more celebratory one while retaining the fan as the Other.[28] The second wave of fandom engaged new media and saw a proliferation of self-identified fan communities, often bound together by the Internet. Following Bourdieu, second-wave fandom analyzed fan practices in terms of hierarchies of taste. Sociological analyses also abounded, with scholars focusing on fan identity construction. During this wave, producers sought to more overtly engage fans, so the relationship became less confrontational. The fan remained the Other. Finally, third-wave fandom (the current cultural moment) has broadened the notion of what might be considered fannish to the everyday. Sports fans, comic book collectors, and Martha Stewart fans could be considered in much the same way that SF and media fans had been considered previously. The third wave sees the fan as Us. During this phase, producers engage regularly with fans, even attempting to co-opt their passion and labor by attempting to turn it to create buzz and build viewership. The primary importance of third-wave fandom is its broadening of the stakes from relatively small subcommunities (fandoms) to a larger field: everyday life.

Views of fandom have shifted in academic and popular discourse, first by valorizing fannish behavior, then by broadening fandoms' constituents, and finally by expanding fannish activity to the everyday, with lessons learned from the fannish experience used to explicate sociocultural practices more generally. Fandoms are creating new traditions that often do not fit the generalizations put forth about fan fiction and media fandom. Examples include *yaoi*/boys' love texts and artworks, soap opera scripts, anime fan fiction and costuming, and fantasies imagining fan relationships with musical artists. Moreover, the advent of the Internet means that community norms, formerly policed in person, are now policed within smaller, self-created communities that owe allegiance to no one but themselves, thus expanding the field of engagement. The seeds that SF fandom planted in the mid-1930s continue to bear fruit; the fannish experience that early SF fans pioneered lives on in a multitude of new formats, yet the affective engagement and constructed communities that fandoms are built on remain the bedrock of fan experience today.

NOTES

1   Dave Kyle, "The Science Fiction League," *Mimosa* 14 (1993): 17–24, http://www.jophan.org/mimosa/m14/kyle.htm.
2   Isaac Asimov, *In Memory Yet Green: The Autobiography of Isaac Asimov, 1920–1954* (New York: Doubleday, 1980); Damon Knight, *The Futurians: The Story of the Science Fiction "Family" of the '30s that Produced Today's Top SF Writers and Editors* (New York: John Day, 1977); Sam Moskowitz, *The Immortal Storm: A History of Science Fiction Fandom* (Atlanta, GA: Atlanta Science Fiction Organization Press, 1954); Frederik Pohl, *The Way the Future Was: A Memoir* (New York: Ballantine Books/Del Rey, 1978).
3   Hugo Gernsback, "A New Sort of Magazine" (editorial), *Amazing Stories* 1 (April 1926): 22.

4 N3F Editorial Cabal, "A Brief History of Science Fiction Fandom," *N3F*, April 1, 2003, http://n3f.org/2013/04/a-brief-history-of-science-fiction-fandom/; 'zineWiki, *Comet*, http://zinewiki.com. For more on the central importance of Gernsback in the development of both science fiction and science fiction fandom, see Chapter 1 of this volume, "The Mightiest Machine: The Development of American Science Fiction from the 1920s to the 1960s."

5 "Fanzine," *Science Fiction Citations* (2008), http://www.jessesword.com/sf/view/186.

6 J. B. Speer, *Fancyclopedia* 31.1 (1944) (fanzine). Speer's text is available online at the *Fancyclopedia 3* wiki (http://fancyclopedia.wikidot.com/).

7 Neil Patrick Hayden, "H. P. Lovecraft, Founding Father of SF Fandom," Tor.com, December 3, 2009, http://www.tor.com/blogs/2009/12/h-p-lovecraft-founding-father-of-sf-fandom.

8 Speer, *Fancyclopedia*.

9 David G. Hartwell, *Age of Wonders: Exploring the World of Science Fiction* (1985; New York: Tor, 1996).

10 Harry Warner Jr., *A Wealth of Fable*, 3 vols. (Fanhistorica Press, 1976–7) (fanzine), and *All Our Yesterdays* (Advent, 1969).

11 *Mimosa*, fanzine published 1982–2003, http://www.jophan.org/mimosa/.

12 Joan Marie Verba, *Boldly Writing: A Trekker Fan and Zine History, 1967–1987* (Minneapolis, MN: FTL Publications, 1996), http://www.ftlpublications.com/bwebook.pdf.

13 Francesca Coppa, "A Brief History of Media Fandom," in Karen Hellekson and Kristina Busse, eds., *Fan Fiction and Fan Communities in the Age of the Internet* (Jefferson, NC: McFarland, 1996), 41–59.

14 Francesca Coppa, "Women, *Star Trek*, and the Early Development of Fannish Vidding," *Transformative Works and Cultures* 1 (2008), doi:10.3983/twc.2008.0044.

15 Camille Bacon-Smith, *Enterprising Women: Television Fandom and the Creation of Popular Myth* (Philadelphia: University of Pennsylvania Press, 1992).

16 Kristina Busse, editor, special section, "In Focus: Fandom and Feminism: Gender and the Politics of Fan Production," *Cinema Journal* 48.4 (2009).

17 Rebecca Tushnet, "Legal Fictions: Copyright, Fan Fiction, and a New Common Law," *Loyola of Los Angeles Entertainment Law Journal* 17 (1997): 641–86, http://digitalcommons.lmu.edu/cgi/viewcontent.cgi?article=1347&context=elr.

18 Henry Jenkins, *Textual Poachers: Television Fans and Participatory Culture* (New York: Routledge, 1992).

19 Henry Jenkins, Sam Ford, and Joshua Green, *Spreadable Media: Creating Value and Meaning in a Networked Culture* (New York: New York University Press, 2013).

20 Hellekson and Busse, *Fan Fiction and Fan Communities*.

21 Kurt Lancaster, *Interacting with "Babylon 5": Fan Performances in a Media Universe* (Austin: University of Texas Press, 2001).

22 Jonathan Gray, *Show Sold Separately: Promos, Spoilers, and Other Media Paratexts* (New York: New York University Press, 2010).

23 Jorge Díaz Cintas and Pablo Muñoz Sánchez, "Fansubs: Audiovisual Translation in an Amateur Environment," *Journal of Specialised Translation* 6 (2006), http://www.jostrans.org/issue06/art_diaz_munoz.php.

24 Karen Hellekson and Kristina Busse, eds., *The Fan Fiction Studies Reader* (Iowa City: University of Iowa Press, 2014).

25 Sharon Marie Ross, *Beyond the Box: Television and the Internet* (Oxford: Blackwell, 2008).

26 Jonathan Gray, Cornel Sandvoss, and C. Lee Harrington, *Fandom: Identities and Communities in a Mediated World* (New York: New York University Press, 2007).

27 John Fiske, *Reading the Popular* (New York: Routledge, 1989); Michel De Certeau, *The Practice of Everyday Life* (Berkeley: University of California Press, 1984).

28 Joli Jenson, "Fandom as Pathology: The Consequence of Characterization," in Lisa A. Lewis, ed., *The Adoring Audience* (London: Routledge, 1992), 9–29.

PART III

Themes and Perspectives

12

JOHN RIEDER

American Frontiers

The frontier, as theme and setting, is important to American SF in at least three ways. The first involves the proximity of American SF and the Western in American popular culture. Much American SF reconstructs the nation's mythic pioneering past as a science fictional future, transferring both the symbolic and ideological values of the American frontier and the tropes of the American Western to outer space. A second version of the SF frontier, just as entangled with ideologies of progress and destiny as the first, is the vanguard constituted by technological innovation rather than geographical exploration and territorial expansion. Both of these versions of the frontier participate in the ideology of American exceptionalism, the representation of American political, military, and economic power as free from the corrupting burdens of history that turn it into domination and oppression elsewhere. A third version of the frontier envisions it not as an empty place waiting to be penetrated and settled by intrepid pioneers but as a meeting place between cultures or civilizations, a borderland or contact zone where there are always two sides to any story, and where exploring the radical differences between those two sides often becomes the heart of the adventure.

The most exhaustive historical account of the figure of the frontier in American political and ideological discourses is Richard Slotkin's trilogy, *Regeneration Through Violence: The Mythology of the American Frontier, 1600–1860* (1973), *The Fatal Environment: The Myth of the Frontier in the Age of Industrialization 1800–1890* (1985), and *Gunfighter Nation: The Myth of the Frontier in Twentieth-Century America* (1992). Slotkin traces the durable and adaptable Frontier Myth according to which "the conquest of the wilderness and the subjugation or displacement of the Native Americans who originally inhabited it have been the means to our achievement of a national identity, a democratic polity, an ever-expanding economy, and a phenomenally dynamic and 'progressive' civilization."[1] The "ideological underpinnings" of America's Frontier Myth are the quasi-natural laws of "capitalist competition, of supply and demand, of Social Darwinian 'survival of the fittest' as a rationale for social order, and of 'Manifest Destiny' that have been the building blocks of our dominant historiographical tradition and political ideology."[2]

In the late nineteenth century, when both the American Western and American SF were just beginning to take shape in popular culture, the Frontier Myth developed along two extremely influential paths, a "populist" version whose greatest exponent was historian Frederick Jackson Turner and a "progressive" one whose most influential spokesman was Theodore Roosevelt. Roosevelt's version was Social Darwinian and imperialist; Turner's was agrarian, decentralizing, more focused on the cumulative behavior of ordinary pioneering husbandmen than on the heroic deeds of explorers, hunters, and soldiers. But both versions firmly identified the frontier itself as the lynchpin for an exceptionalist account of American history that identified the rigors of the frontier as the catalyst of America's capacity for continual renewal and reinvention of itself. Not surprisingly, this highly charged figure held together ambivalent, even contradictory values, simultaneously celebrating progress and bathed in nostalgia, firmly ensconced within an evolutionary notion of historical stages of development based on an opposition of savagery and civilization and at the same time invoking a cyclical logic of redemptive return to the cleansing innocence of the wilderness.[3]

The Myth of the Frontier

This exceptionalist account of the American frontier, particularly in its progressive and imperialist Roosevelt version, exerted enormous influence on American popular cultural visions of the future from the 1893 World's Fair exposition in Chicago to the construction of Tomorrowland in 1950s Disneyland. Its influence has faded, however, as the frontier thesis of Turner has yielded to the New Western historiography that sees the American frontier experience not as what distinguishes and privileges America but as a typical instance of territorial expansion in capitalist settler colonies. Slotkin writes, for instance, that "The Myth of the Frontier is the American version of the larger myth-ideological system generated by the social conflicts that attended the 'modernization' of the Western nations, the emergence of capitalist economies and nation-states."[4] Patricia Limerick, the primary spokesperson for this school of thought, sees the American West as a scene of invasion, conquest, and expansion of the world market, typical of global imperialism.[5]

Although American exceptionalism is far from dead, this change in the dominant historiography can certainly be registered in the difference separating the planetary romances of Edgar Rice Burroughs in the 1910s or the space pioneers of Robert A. Heinlein's juvenile fiction in the 1950s from the settlers of Kim Stanley Robinson's Mars trilogy in the 1990s – or, one might equally say, the Wild West of Tom Mix or of John Ford's *Stagecoach* (1939) from that of Clint Eastwood's *Unforgiven* (1992). SF and the Western have in common their early development in the dime novel in America, a shared if not identical indebtedness to the historical novel, and a strong affinity to the medievalist and imperial adventure fantasies that enjoyed popularity during the Romance Revival of the late nineteenth century. Their most decisive common ground, however, is the crucial role the frontier setting plays in establishing their generic identities. In American SF, outer space has long served as the "final frontier" announced by Captain James Kirk in the credits sequence of *Star Trek* – "final" not because it is the last frontier, but because it promises an inexhaustible supply of them.

Transposing the tropes of the Western frontier to adventures in space is one of the major characteristics of pulp-era SF. Rugged heroes, dangerous wilderness, hostile natives, and alluring females in need of rescue abound (the last especially prominent in pulp magazine cover art). The first great practitioner of the outer space Western is Edgar Rice Burroughs in his Mars novels, beginning with "Under the Moons of Mars" in *All-Story* magazine in 1912 (published in book form as *The Princess of Mars* in 1917). Slotkin comments that Burroughs's John Carter is "the perfect embodiment of the virtues of the White race as represented in the Myth of the Frontier," his Green Martians "fit the general stereotype of Indians as elaborated in works like [Roosevelt's] *The Winning of the West*," and his Red Martian princess, Dejah Thoris, is the "perfect reconciliation of the contradictory values attached to women in the Frontier Myth. Her Indian qualities make her an appropriate object for the indulgence of erotic fantasies, while her aristocratic lineage and status as both virgin and Indian captive identify her as a 'redemptive' White woman and an appropriate mate for the White hero."[6] This sort of racial and gender coding can be exquisitely re-mixed in SF, as in Catherine Moore's "Shambleau" (1934), where the title character is initially presented as a sort of Indian squaw being rescued by the hero from a racially motivated lynch mob in a Martian frontier town, but turns out to be a seductive, vampiric Medusa. However, Edmond Hamilton's "A Conquest of Two Worlds" (1932) is a rarity in its explicitly critical allegory of the genocidal Indian Wars. Most pulp SF of the period simply repeats and exploits the racial stereotypes that justified American territorial expansion, as in the anti-Asiatic sentiments that fueled the popular comic series *Buck Rogers in the 25th Century A.D.* (1929–67) and *Flash Gordon* (1934–present) in their first decade.

The contradictory values associated with the frontier as both the vanguard of civilization's progress and the site of a recurrent, cleansing return to primal nature were certainly central to the project of space exploration that De Witt Douglas Kilgore calls "astrofuturism," one embraced heartily by John W. Campbell, the powerful editor of *Astounding* who is closely identified with the so-called Golden Age of American magazine SF, and probably best typified by the work of one of Campbell's star writers, Robert A. Heinlein.[7] In his loosely connected future history stories from 1940 on and in his highly successful juvenile novels of the 1950s, Heinlein elaborated a solar system turned into the Western frontier of exploration (*Rocket Ship Galileo*; *Have Space Suit, Will Travel*), settlement (*Farmer in the Sky*, *The Rolling Stones*), and rediscovery of the spirit of the American Revolution (*Between Planets*, *The Moon Is a Harsh Mistress*). Kilgore accounts for Heinlein's "tremendous popularity and success" by his robust, self-confident, and ultimately celebratory embodiment of the contradictions of the Frontier Myth: "He is by turns an autocrat and a democrat; a hysterical racist and a defender of polarity; the enunciator of an unexamined sexism and a defender of a certain, limited gender equality; an advocate of large-scale, centralized governmental systems and a libertarian exponent of the virtues of small business and decentralized government."[8]

It is not that the seamy underside of frontier history was absent from Heinlein's vision of the future. "Logic of Empire" (1941), for instance, depicts indentured servitude on Venus as de facto plantation slavery. But although Heinlein sees the slavery as the inevitable effect of a capitalist system, his analysis shoves aside issues of justice in favor of ones concerning efficiency and expertise: "In any expanding free-enterprise economy which does not have a money system designed to fit its requirements, the use of mother-country capital to develop the colony inevitably results in subsistence-level wages at home and slave labor in the colonies. The rich get richer and the poor get poorer, and all the good will in the world on the part of the so-called ruling classes won't change it, because the basic problem is one requiring scientific analysis and a mathematical mind."[9] Exactly what branch of science the speaker means, and what problems the math is to be applied to, Heinlein does not explain. Elsewhere, however, it seems that when clever management and bold entrepreneurship offer the proper stimulus to scientific genius, not even the law of gravity presents a serious barrier to the energies of technical innovation ("We Also Walk Dogs" [1941]). Yet such solutions are always the product of individual initiative, and the inequality of human abilities remains truly insoluble.

The power of the astrofuturist vision only picked up steam with the onset of the space race and John F. Kennedy's declaration that space exploration constituted the New Frontier of the 1960s, vaulting some SF writers like Heinlein, Isaac Asimov, and Britain's Arthur C. Clarke into a position of ideological centrality, or at least visibility, quite unlike the niche market days of the '30s and '40s. But the triumphalist energy of the Frontier Myth was also being challenged by the revisionary picture of American history and society spurred by the civil rights movement, the increasingly frightening possibility of nuclear self-destruction, and the stirrings of a countercultural rebellion against postwar consumerism and the suburban lifestyle. Perhaps the most acerbic satiric revision of the Frontier Myth in the 1960s comes in Philip K. Dick's various renderings, most notably in the devastating opening sequence of *The Three Stigmata of Palmer Eldritch* (1965), of outer space colonies as deserts of despair, peopled either by slaves or by dupes of corporate and governmental pro-emigration propaganda. Dick portrays nostalgia for the frontier and the hope of its renewal in outer space as pure illusions. The way government and business cynically and deceitfully promote emigration to the nightmarish outer worlds in Dick's fiction harkens back to and travesties pro-imperialist arguments that depicted colonial expansion as a way to relieve the tensions of class struggle in the industrial core. The exceptionalist function of the American Frontier Myth breaks down precisely by virtue of this insistence on connecting the frontier to the inequalities and interests of the metropolitan center. Rather than a rupture from the past and an opportunity for renewal, the frontier in Dick's fiction is the dumping ground of capitalist society's overflow, directed by its motives, determined by its pressures, and infected by its systematic injustice.

The Dark Frontier

From the 1960s on, the overlapping of SF and the Western continues unabated, but it largely follows the "new western history" in framing the Western Frontier "within larger narratives of economic and cultural transfer" that see the American frontier experience as "a brief moment in a process dominated by big institutions and capital."[10] This revisionary movement calls into question not just the regenerative capacity of the geographical frontier but also the progressive, utopian potential of technological innovation, a potential evoked over and over again in the 1920s and 1930s by the gleaming, streamlined future cityscapes of Frank R. Paul's cover illustrations for the Gernsback magazines. From Verne onward, the breakthrough invention has not only been a staple of SF narrative but has often opened up new geographical frontiers to the protagonist-inventor, as it does in E. E. Smith's prototypical space opera *The Skylark of Space* (1928). If the astrofuturist vision posited a complementary relationship between the frontier of geographical expansion (outer space) and the one constituted by technological innovation (rocketry), the coalescence of these two senses of the frontier was already thoroughly characteristic of imperialist ideology. It was this complementarity that made travel away from the metropole into the wilderness seem to late nineteenth-century travelers like a trip into the past; the technologically saturated city represented the future that would inevitably ensue once the savage locale was taken into the embrace of civilization. Imagining that the future of human society lay in outer space depended to a significant degree on this logic connecting technological progress with the destiny of civilization. But when the penetration of industrial technology into colonized territories was reconceived as simple Western domination rather than something rendered inevitable by "the survival of the fittest," the shapes of future possibility changed accordingly.

The darkening of the future that resulted appears quite clearly in that thread of American exceptionalism documented by H. Bruce Franklin in *War Stars: The Superweapon and the American Imagination* (1988). Franklin shows that from the Revolutionary period on Americans indulged the fantasy of developing a superweapon that would put an end to international war by concentrating global power exclusively in American hands. A typical example is Garrett Serviss's "sequel" to H. G. Wells's *War of the Worlds* (1898), *Edison's Conquest of Mars* (1899), where Thomas Edison's invention of a superweapon to retaliate against the Martian invasion also unites the globe under American leadership. Such fantasies never had wider popular circulation or a more science fictional flavor than in the immediate aftermath of the bombings of Hiroshima and Nagasaki. Patrick B. Sharp, in *Savage Perils*, has demonstrated the continuity between the Social Darwinian ideology of Roosevelt's imperialism and the postwar government propaganda concerning atomic warfare, and has also shown how this ideology was increasingly challenged by emerging information about the long-term effects of nuclear radiation, but even more decisively by the transformation of an imaginary Pax Americana enforced by America's monopoly on atomic weaponry into the policy of mutually assured destruction as nuclear arsenals proliferated in the USSR and other nations. In the course of this development, SF tales of post-nuclear apocalypse mutated from revamped frontier myths of social or racial renewal to "new western" visions of environmental devastation and social chaos. From the 1970s on, there is no question that the dominant vision of the post-nuclear future (e.g., in the 1975 film adaptation of Harlan Ellison's *A Boy and His Dog*, or the *Terminator* films of 1984, 1991, and 2003, or Cormac McCarthy's 2006 novel *The Road*) sees it as a wasteland that unfolds the essential savagery of what passes for civilization in the American present.

Nonetheless the outer space frontier continued to function as utopian counterpart to such dire scenarios, for instance in physicist Gerard O'Neill's proposals for self-sustaining, manmade space colonies.[11] In the context of the influential 1972 MIT study *The Limits to Growth*, which argued for the ecological non-sustainability of contemporary industrial society, O'Neill's "suburbs in space" present an interesting combination of contradictory impulses: on the one hand, the space colony is bound by the necessity of achieving an autonomous and stable environment, a condition of perfect balance between production and waste; and on the other, the very project of inhabiting space stations (or emigrating to other solar systems; the SF motif of the generation starship exhibits the same tensions) represents a fantasy of release from earthbound limits to growth, the ultimate denial of the finitude of planetary resources. Thus the self-contained space colony simultaneously embraces both the fundamental capitalist fantasy of endless economic expansion and the antithetical ideal of sustainability, at least as a technical problem if not as a social telos.

A related variant of the manmade frontier setting is the notion of terraforming, the project of remaking other planets into earthlike ones with breathable atmospheres, tillable soil, and so on. The idea of terraforming clearly melds technological and geographical frontiers into another "final," inexhaustible form. At the same time the project of terraforming exposes one of the implicit foundational assumptions of the ideology of progress, faith in the unlimited capacity of Western scientific rationality to impress its will upon natural things. The most influential fictional exploration of terraforming is Kim Stanley Robinson's Mars trilogy, *Red Mars* (1993), *Green Mars* (1994), and *Blue Mars* (1996), where it is both part of an exploration of revolutionary social possibilities and the occasion of a heated debate over the assumption that humanity has the right to make nature over in its own image. But the terraforming of Mars, which is successfully transformed into a humanly habitable planet over the course of a couple of centuries, is almost as much accidental as deliberate, with massive changes unleashed upon the surface during the first of three Martian revolutions as the unintended consequences of the revolutionists' sabotage of the capitalist-colonialist infrastructure. And as if to counterbalance the hyper-rational technical project of refashioning the Martian atmosphere and surface, Robinson's political plot stresses negotiation and compromise, marshaling "a cacophony of voices that never quite resolve into a single, harmonious choir," as Kilgore puts it, in what Carl Abbott calls "the unruly and morally complex processes of community making."[12]

A quite different take on terraforming coheres with meta-fictional self-consciousness about SF, the Western, and the frontier in Joss Whedon's short-lived television series *Firefly* (2002). The world of *Firefly* features hyper-urban SF landscapes in a politically and economically hegemonic core surrounded by the widely scattered "outer worlds," terraformed planets whose settlements are consistently rendered in the visual style of the American Western. The same SF-Western hybridity permeates every level of the production from the costumes to the theme song and credits. The result is to put the American Western past on the same level of fictionality as the SF future. If the terraformed frontier in *Firefly* is quite literally manufactured as a place to absorb the overflow, and serve the purposes, of the metropolitan center, the meta-generic implication is that the Wild West was always such a construction. The new Western history's subversion of the Frontier Myth reaches a kind of logical conclusion here in the utter divorce of the American Western setting from any claim to historical referentiality.

What most obviously disconnects the generic Western frontier settings of *Firefly* from historical reference is that the outer worlds are created out of empty, previously lifeless planets. Everything and everyone on them has emigrated from the core; they are nothing but an expression of the core's needs and desires. But of course the actual American frontier was always already inhabited. *Firefly*'s terraforming is a metaphor for a history that simply erases the indigenous nations of the North American continent from the record, repeating and consolidating in historiography the genocidal effects of European-American colonization and settlement. Thus *Firefly* also erases one of the crucial components of the Frontier Myth, what Slotkin calls the "savage war" by which the frontiersmen lay the foundations for civilization in the wilderness. But what appears as the reenactment of a kind of Hobbesian social contract from one perspective appears as invasion and conquest from another. The natural war of all against all in the frontier wilderness also takes place on the site of a civilization, a peaceful order that is only precipitated into warfare by the intrusion of those Leslie Marmon Silko's *Almanac of the Dead* (1991) calls the Destroyers. The possibility of understanding colonial emigration from the point of view of the colonized has been a staple of SF at least since its classic realization in H. G. Wells's *War of the Worlds*, and beyond Wells's reversal of perspectives lies the more intriguing and difficult project of encompassing both sides of the story of contact between radically different societies. From SF's earliest days, rendering the SF frontier as a contact zone where alien worlds, histories, species, and civilizations meet has comprised a bracing alternative to the Frontier Myth's tales of pioneers, progress, and destiny.

An early, great exploration of the complexities of contact is Jack London's "The Red One" (1918). "The Red One" is from one point of view a treasure hunt, and so, like many other frontier adventure stories, a fantastic representation of the colonial project of resource extraction. The treasure in this case, the Red One itself, is an enormous, ancient, extraterrestrial object that a scientist named Bassett finds half buried in the interior of Guadalcanal in the Solomon Islands. But the treasure Bassett seeks is the meaning of the Red One rather than its substance, and thus the story turns out to be about the acquisition of knowledge – that is, confronting "the Medusa, Truth" as the final lines of the story put it.[13] Bassett thinks the Red One is a message from a higher civilization that has been ironically and tragically wasted on the savage natives of the island, who worship the Red One as a god and offer human sacrifices before it. But London makes it clear that the natives' idolatry and Bassett's own projection of otherworldly, transcendent significance onto the Red One are fundamentally alike, and this projection of meaning onto the opaque, uncommunicative object mirrors the misrecognitions and mutual incomprehension of Bassett's and the natives' interactions with one another. More than mere incomprehension, however, what unfolds in the space of contact is the play of desire and repulsion as Bassett vacillates between an idealized sense of kinship with the race that made the Red One and his disavowal of the common humanity he shares with the natives. Thus "The Red One" exposes an epistemological dilemma endemic to the frontier setting, the symmetrical but opposite problems of whether the exotic other can be understood in terms that are not merely a projection of what one already knows, and the risk that the contact zone might impose a redefinition on oneself.

This dilemma pervades the project of resource extraction, as not only objects but also people may be transformed from worthlessness to wealth, or vice versa, simply by moving from one economic system to another. Lost race fiction often plays out the fantasy of discovering precious metals or gems in places where their abundance makes them commonplace and therefore worthless to the natives. The blockbuster film *Alien* (1979) presents a particularly horrific scenario of such a transvaluation of values at the point of resource extraction, as the mining vessel *Nostromo* takes on board an alien life form whose value to the corporate weapons division immediately renders the lives of all the human crew members expendable. *Avatar* (2009) plays out the opposite possibility (and the one far more typical of imperial adventure fiction) as the hero undergoes a redemptive transformation from predatory colonialist to royal native. The fantasy of indigenization, one common to settler colonial ideologies, often sets to work tensions between assimilation and contagion like those antithetically exposed in *Alien* and *Avatar*. Octavia Butler's great Xenogenesis trilogy (1987–9; renamed *Lilith's Brood* in 2000) remains unmatched for the scope and complexity with which it explores the inextricable intertwining of species predation, resource extraction, cultural assimilation, and miscegenation in the alien contact scenario. In Butler's trilogy, the planet Earth itself is either redeemed from humanity's self-destructive folly by its assimilation to a higher civilization, or turned into the ultimate mining site, depending on how you look at it.

The Dialectic of the Frontier

Exploring the dialectic of assimilation and estrangement in coming to terms with the radically other has proven to be one of the richest veins of the SF frontier. Two classic examples involve the issue of translation across an extraterrestrial divide. In James Blish's "Common Time" (1953), an interstellar traveler contacts a benevolent alien race in the Alpha Centauri system but cannot properly remember the experience when he returns because the person the aliens established contact with is simply not him anymore. He can no longer inhabit the place of that subject, no longer understand the language they shared with one another, although stray phrases from their conversations seem almost to pronounce themselves in his speech. In Ted Chiang's "Story of Your Life" (1998), the first-person narrator recounts her experience learning the language of an alien race that has visited earth. The aliens have no front-to-back body orientation; they see in all directions at once and move in any direction with equal readiness. This lack of directionality turns out to be homologous with their temporal consciousness, so that, as the translator acquires facility in their language and learns to think in it, she finds herself able to remember the future. This leads her to conceive of her speech and actions as performances rather than choices – "An utterance that was spontaneous and communicative in the context of human discourse became a ritual recitation when viewed by the light of Heptapod B"[14] – as, from the present moment of the storytelling, the night on which she conceives her daughter, she tells her daughter the story of her life in the future perfect tense. The protagonist's situation between alien communication and human interaction is analogous to that occupied by Bassett in "The Red One," but utterly divorced from Bassett's ideology of progress and motives of appropriation. Chiang's meditative, philosophical, intellectually challenging tale thus takes the plot of contact to a kind of diametrical opposite from the adventure motifs of the treasure hunt while magnificently realizing the potential of cognitive transformation.

Ursula K. Le Guin's *The Left Hand of Darkness* (1969) integrates the protagonist's transformation by alien contact into a fictional anthropological report detailing an interstellar metropolitan society's investigation of a culture on its frontier that is the remainder, they surmise, of a scientific experiment in genetic manipulation. Le Guin includes "native" folktales and myths along with investigators' reports on the customs of the frontier planet's inhabitants, highlighting not only their bizarre, hermaphroditic sexual anatomy but also the two quite different religions that predicate the major political and economic differences between the planet's dominant nations. Le Guin's strategy of approaching SF world construction with the tools of ethnography – a strategy robustly present in early imperial adventure, especially of the lost race variety[15] – reaches its fullest development in *Always Coming Home* (1985), in her portrait of the Kesh people, a far-future, quasi-primitive, nonindustrial, noncapitalist, matrilineal, and impressively stable and peaceful society. The one continuous narrative recounting a Kesh woman's entry into and escape from a monotheistic, patriarchal, and militaristic community that is in the throes of self-destruction comprises only about a quarter of the book. The rest is devoted to ethnographic descriptions of the Kesh's customs, rituals, and material culture, and presentation of a wide miscellany of their stories, oral histories, songs, and poems.

The distinctly North American Indian quality of Le Guin's Kesh is due, according to Le Guin, to the fact that "Native American texts ... served [her] as an unfailing inspiration" in constructing them.[16] In recent years Native American writers have themselves increasingly been adapting the resources of SF to an "indigenous futurism" that programmatically challenges the generic boundaries of SF, in no small part by calling into question what counts for science.[17] For these writers the American present is haunted and cursed by the legacy of the Frontier Myth – an ongoing presence epitomized, for instance, in the figure of General George Custer, who appears reincarnated as a corrupt government agent in Gerald Vizenor's "Custer on the Slipstream" (1978); as an evil, shapeshifting trickster in Stephen Graham Jones's *The Fast Red Road* (2000); and as the egomaniacal, incompetent victim of a rebellion of the horses at Custer's Last Stand in Archer Pechawis's short film/performance piece "Horse" (2001). In the hands of such artists, SF continues to reshape and realign the meaning of the American frontier as a meeting ground of our visions of the past and the future.

NOTES

1 Richard Slotkin, *Gunfighter Nation: The Myth of the Frontier in Twentieth-Century America* (Norman: University of Oklahoma Press, 1998), 10.
2 Richard Slotkin, *The Fatal Environment: The Myth of the Frontier in the Age of Industrialization 1800–1890* (New York: Atheneum, 1985), 15. On the Social Darwinian foundations of frontier ideology, see also Patrick B. Sharp, *Savage Perils: Racial Frontiers and Nuclear Apocalypse in American Culture* (Norman: University Oklahoma Press, 2007).

3 William H. Katerberg, *Future West: Utopia and Apocalypse in Frontier Science Fiction* (Lawrence: University Press of Kansas, 2008), 18–23; Slotkin, *Gunfighter Nation*, 22–4.
4 Slotkin, *Fatal Environment*, 33.
5 Katerberg, *Future West*, 26.
6 Slotkin, *Gunfighter Nation*, 202–7.
7 De Witt Douglas Kilgore, *Astrofuturism: Science, Race, and Visions of Utopia in Space* (Philadelphia: University of Pennsylvania Press, 2003), especially the chapter on Heinlein, 82–110.
8 Ibid., 88.
9 Robert A. Heinlein, *The Green Hills of Earth and the Menace from Earth* (Riverdale, NY: Baen, 2003), 281.
10 Carl Abbott, *Frontiers Past and Future: Science Fiction and the American West* (Lawrence: University Press of Kansas, 2006), 104, 96.
11 See Kilgore, *Astrofuturism*, 150–85.
12 Kilgore, *Astrofuturism*, 235; Abbott, *Frontiers Past and Future*, 114.
13 Jack London, *The Complete Short Stories*, edited by Earle Labor, Robert C. Leitz III, and I. Milo Shepard (Stanford University Press, 1993), 2318.
14 Ted Chiang, *Stories of Your Life and Others* (Easthampton, MA: Small Beer Press, 2002), 140.
15 John Rieder, *Colonialism and the Emergence of Science Fiction* (Middletown, CT: Wesleyan University Press, 2008), 52–60.
16 Quoted in Abbott, *Frontiers Past and Future*, 126.
17 Grace Dillon, *Walking the Clouds: An Anthology of Indigenous Science Fiction* (Tucson: University of Arizona Press, 2012).

13

PRISCILLA WALD

Science, Technology, and the Environment

On August 6, 1945, change radiated from Hiroshima, Japan, a major urban port city with military and industrial significance and a population of a quarter of a million. Survivors' descriptions of the first military use of an atomic weapon sound like something out of science fiction. Two miles from the blast site, Mr. Tanimoto, a minister, saw a sudden flash of light followed by an eerie silence, while a fisherman at a distance of six miles heard a deafening roar. Morning turned to night for the minister as a cloud of dust and debris engulfed the city, and a dazed population surveyed the devastated landscape. Shadows that had once been people and animals haunted the city, and the unprecedented heat had burned clothing patterns directly onto people's skin. In an effort to lift a wounded woman into a boat, Mr. Tanimoto gently took her hands only to watch in horror as "her skin sloughed off in huge, glovelike pieces." As he sought to move the "slimy living bodies" out of the way of further harm, he had to keep reminding himself that these were human beings.[1]

A new world order arose from the ashes of Hiroshima and, three days later, Nagasaki. Humankind had harnessed, in the words of President Harry S. Truman, "the basic forces of the universe," and now faced questions about its own nature and fate with new urgency.[2] For prize-winning *New York Times* military editor Hanson Baldwin, "another chapter in human history [had] opened," turning "the weird, the strange, the horrible [into] the trite and the obvious" and "Americans" into "a synonym for destruction."[3]

Amid official proclamations of victory, the most prescient journalists shared Baldwin's dismay. For broadcast journalist Edward R. Murrow, the haze from the cloud had obscured the future itself, putting the survival of humanity in question.[4] His colleague Norman Cousins, the editor-in-chief of the *Saturday Review of Literature*, described "a primitive fear ... of forces man can neither channel nor comprehend ... filling the mind with primordial apprehensions," and *A Christian Century* magazine editorial noted "a spell of dark foreboding [that had been cast] over the spirit of humanity."[5]

'he journalists' language – *primitive fear, primordial apprehension, spell of dark foreboding* – suggests an evolutionary unraveling: humanity traveling back in time to stand helpless and astonished before the forces it had unleashed. Human evolution had taken millennia; this new technology gave humankind the ability to destroy the world in hours.

It is not surprising that science fiction (SF) would proliferate as a mass genre, especially in the United States, in the years following World War II, when the weird and horrible had become the trite and obvious. Critic Darko Suvin distinguished the genre by its difference "from empirical times, places, and characters of 'mimetic' or 'naturalist' fiction" and its possibility "within the cognitive (cosmological and anthropological) norms of the author's epoch."[6] The rubble of Hiroshima and Nagasaki was not the only legacy of global conflagration. SF flourished as rapid scientific and technological innovations and geopolitical transformations cognitively reoriented the postwar world.

A decade past the end of the Second World War, space travel was within human reach, and televisions were commonplace in American homes. Worldwide decolonization had left people, in the words of political theorist Harold Isaac, "stumbling blindly around trying to discern the new images, the new shapes and perspectives these changes have brought, to adjust to the painful rearrangement of identities and relationships which the new circumstances compel."[7] Looking inward, scientists had identified the structure of DNA and created an immortal cell line composed of human cells. Life was yielding its secrets, as the mysteries of the human past unfolded into new possibilities for its future. In fewer than two decades, human beings would create new living organisms through molecular cloning (recombinant DNA). In such a science fictional atmosphere, the genre proliferated, as it explored, with equal measures of wonder and terror, the pressing question of what it meant to be human in a rapidly changing world.

The End of the World as We Know It

Facing uncertainties about even the most immediate future, political theorists as diverse as Hannah Arendt and Frantz Fanon reached for science fictional metaphors to convey the profoundly defamiliarizing experience of human beings deprived of their humanity. Surviving the Nazi camps, explained Arendt, did not mean consigning them to the past; rather, the experience left the survivor with an inability to "believe fully in his own past experiences" and therefore to make sense of the present or imagine a future. "It is as though he had a story to tell of another planet, for the status of the inmates in the world of the living, where nobody is supposed to know if they are alive or dead, is such that it is as though they had never been born."[8] The dehumanization that shocked Europeans and Americans was no surprise, chastened Fanon, for the colonized, "those hordes of vital statistics, those hysterical masses, those faces bereft of all humanity, those distended bodies" who were "like nothing on earth."[9] Crushing cultures and spirits, centuries of colonization were tantamount to a "bloodless genocide which consisted in the setting aside of fifteen thousand millions of men."[10] The project of decolonization required more than a new political system; it mandated an entirely new account of humankind: "a new history of Man"[11] that would depict the cultural practices of the colonized not as deviations from a norm or remnants of a human past but as vital expressions of the marvelous variety that constituted a fully developed humankind. A decolonized world would entail nothing less than "the replacing of a certain 'species' of man by another 'species' of man."[12]

"Species" was a word newly loaded with significance in the mid-twentieth century, following the genetic insights that had reinvigorated evolutionary theory. In 1937, Ukrainian-born fruit fly geneticist Theodosius Dobzhansky had mesmerized the audience of his Jessup lectures at Columbia University with his explanation of what would become known as the evolutionary (or modern) synthesis. Bringing the insights of the new subfield of population genetics to evolutionary theory, Dobzhansky explained the mechanism of the continuous, gradual change that had eluded Darwin in his theory of "natural selection." English biologist Julian Huxley named this new theory as he popularized it with the publication of his 1942 *Evolution: The Modern Synthesis*.

Although lacking the spectacularism of the bomb, these insights fundamentally recast the conception of humanity, and SF quickly registered their implications, especially the role of chance in evolution and the inevitability of change. The human species was contingent and evolving; it was not even necessarily at the top of the food chain, as dramatized by the monsters of the hybrid genre of SF/horror film, which proliferated in the 1950s. The alien vegetable antagonist of Christian Nyby and Howard Hawk's 1951 *The Thing from Another World*, for example, challenged human hubris in its advanced technology and, according to the misguided scientist Dr. Carrington, its superiority. The evolution of its brain "was not handicapped by emotional or sexual factors," he explains; rather, the seedpods discovered in the creature's arm attest to the "neat and unconfused reproductive technique of vegetation. No pain or pleasure as we know it. No emotions. No heart." He rapturously dubs the creature "our superior, our superior in every way." The creature is ultimately disturbing not because it lives on the blood of animals and is significantly stronger than human beings and nearly indestructible, but because it evidently has no more regard for its human prey than "we have toward a cabbage field."[13]

But, insisted Huxley, whatever chance events had led humanity to its present state, the species was now surely distinctive in its ability to reflect on, and thereby influence, the workings of evolution. SF writers needed no invitation to take up that charge; future societies were not new to fiction, but the new evolutionary emphasis inspired the SF imagination. While some writers imagined the changes in humanity itself – the result of alien visitation in British author Arthur C. Clarke's *Childhood's End* (1953) or the chance discovery of the innate capacity of "jaunting" (teleportation) in Alfred Bester's *The Stars My Destination* (1956) – many of their peers explored the theme through cosmic encounters with alternative life forms, as in Isaac Asimov's early Foundation novels (1951–3) or A. E. Van Vogt's aptly named *The Voyage of the Space Beagle* (1950), both based on stories from the 1940s.

Uniqueness came with its burdens. Consciousness of evolutionary processes, Huxley insisted, gave humanity a "responsibility and destiny – to be an agent for the rest of the world in the job of realizing its inherent potentialities as fully as possible."[14] Natural selection was a description, not a promise. Humankind having "by now become the trustee[s] of evolution," it fell to them to choose whether to be a constructive or destructive force in its processes.[15] SF rehearsed both. Moreover, these works registered the evolutionary lesson that the trusteeship included more than humanity's future. Evolution was a planetary, maybe even cosmic, process; the future of humanity, inextricably linked to that of all living organisms. In *The Day the Earth Stood Still* (1951), the alien Klaatu comes to Earth to warn humanity that an increasingly interconnected cosmos cannot risk the danger posed by human aggression; they will have to learn to live peacefully or the planet will be destroyed. As Fanon had averred, the revolutionary program had to be an evolutionary program, culminating in a "new species of Man."

Humanity's wartime bellicosity was not the only planetary threat. Some of the most violent technologies of war extended their destructive influence through peacetime applications. The incidental effects of toxins developed for wartime use, for example, led to the development of herbicides and pesticides; now, biologist Rachel Carson argued in her 1962 *Silent Spring*, poison was coursing through the veins of the entire planetary system. No cosmic alliance needed to destroy the planet if Earth's most advanced species was rapidly advancing toward its own extinction.

Carson drew on the conventions of fantasy and SF to convey what she believed her readership could not fully accept, beginning her exposé of the environmental toxicity of pesticides and herbicides with the cautionary tale of an enchanted landscape: "There once was a town in the heart of America where all life seemed to live in harmony with its surroundings" until "a strange blight crept over the area and everything began to change."[16] With the evident appearance of an "evil spell," people and animals began to suffer from "mysterious maladies," and "everywhere was a shadow of death." A "strange stillness" settled on the land – "It was a spring without voices."[17] The problems, of course, turn out to be "no witchcraft, no enemy action had silenced the rebirth of new life in this stricken world. The people had done it themselves."[18] With this grounding revelation, the fabulous once-upon-a-time past becomes the ominous future of science fiction: a "Fable for Tomorrow."

Slipping among genres, *Silent Spring* depicts a fundamentally unstable world that oscillates ambiguously between an unnoticed present and an imminent, if not inevitable, future. "This sudden silencing of the song of the birds," laments Carson, "this obliteration of the color and beauty and interest they lend to our world have come about swiftly, insidiously, and unnoticed by those whose communities are as yet unaffected."[19] Building on end of the world anxieties concerning atomic warfare, she calls "chemicals ... the sinister and little-recognized partners of radiation in changing the very nature of the world – the very nature of its life."[20] Science continually shades into permutations of SF, horror, and fantasy, as though the imagination is stretching to understand the dramatic metamorphoses of a cognitively estranged world. The "extraordinary properties" of chemicals "convert plants or animals into a sort of Medea's robe by making them actually poisonous." The "world of systemic insecticides" is, for Carson, "a weird world, surpassing the imaginings of the brothers Grimm – perhaps most closely akin to the cartoon world of Charles Addams. It is a world where the enchanted forest of the fairy tales has become the poisonous forest in which an insect that chews a leaf or sucks the sap of a plant is doomed. It is a world where a flea bites a dog, and dies because the dog's blood has been made poisonous, where an insect may die from vapors emanating from a plant it has never touched, where a bee may carry poisonous nectar back to its hive and presently produce poisonous honey."[21]

Permeating the fundamental substance of humanity – blood, bones, sinew – the chemicals are colonizing the future, seeping into genes and "mother's milk, and probably into the tissues of the unborn child": the circulatory systems of people and of the planet.[22] They "have the power to strike directly at the chromosomes," contaminating "our genetic heritage, a possession that has come down to us through some two billion years of evolution and selection of living protoplasm, a possession that is ours for the moment only, until we must pass it on to generations to come."[23] Failing to be the stewards of evolution for which Huxley and others advocated, humankind had instead become an evolutionary force, unleashing catalysts that could turn cell division "alien and destructive."[24]

The human threat to the environment resulted not only from what humanity was putting into circulation, but also from what it was taking out. In 1969, at the end of the decade that witnessed the publication of *Silent Spring* and the environmental movement it reinvigorated, a report from the United Nations Economic and Social Council added overconsumption of resources to pollution, warning that the exhaustion of resources was, "for the first time in the history of mankind, ... a crisis of world-wide proportions involving developed and developing countries alike" and endangering "the future of life on earth."[25]

Apocalyptic anxieties shaped the nascent mass genre of SF in the decades following the Second World War. Threats took the form of nuclear annihilation in such realistic SF novels and films as *On the Beach*; *Alas, Babylon*; *Fail Safe*; and *Red Alert* (along with its dark comedy film adaption, *Dr. Strangelove*), and the more fantastical *A Canticle for Liebowitz* and *Planet of the Apes*; disease epidemics, as in *Earth Abides*, *Some Will Not Die*, and *I Am Legend*; environmental devastation and exhaustion on Earth, as in *Do Androids Dream of Electric Sheep*, or elsewhere, as in the polluted Martian landscape of " – And the Moon Be Still as Bright" and "The Settlers," and, most commonly, of alien invasions, in works including *The Thing from Another World*, *Invasion from Mars*, *Earth vs. the Flying Saucers*, and *The Body Snatchers*. These apocalyptic threats were a prominent part of political debate or at least a cultural imaginary (Barney and Betty Hill inaugurated the alien abduction account in the early 1960s), but an undercurrent that runs through these works suggests the genre's response to a more amorphous set of concerns about the changing nature of humanity as a result of both geopolitical transformation and biological metamorphosis.

A subgenre of alien invasion stories depicts those changes not through a dramatic conflict, but as the gradual and barely perceptible assimilation of human bodies. In Robert Heinlein's 1951 *The Puppet Masters*, William Cameron Menzies' 1953 *Invasion from Mars*, Philip K. Dick's 1954 "The Father-Thing," and Jack Finney's 1954 *Collier's* serial and 1955 novel, *The Body Snatchers*, aliens preserve the bodies and even memories of their victims, but destroy the more intangible characteristics that distinguish individuals. Finney's pod people in particular became iconic following director Don Siegel's 1956 cinematic adaptation, *Invasion of the Body Snatchers*. In short order, "pod people" became a watchword for mindless conformity and lack of emotion, and the numerous novelistic and cinematic retellings attest to how fully the "pod people" captured not just a zeitgeist but also a fundamental continuing concern.

Critics have variously offered these consummate conformists as allegories for communists and McCarthy-era Americans, but the power of the story lies in its depiction of these antagonistic ideologies as similarly discouraging individual initiative and creativity. Siegel famously sidestepped the political issue when he told an interviewer, "Many of my associates are certainly pods.... They have no feelings. They exist, breathe, sleep. To be a pod means that you have no passion, no anger, the spark has left you."[26] Nostalgia for rapidly disappearing small-town life and the sense of community it ostensibly fosters is evident in protagonist Dr. Miles Bennell's musings on the new technology of dial phones, which, he quips, are "'marvelously efficient, saving you a full second or more every time you call, inhumanly perfect, and utterly brainless,'" but, he laments, "'none of them will ever remember where the doctor is at night, when a child is sick and needs him.'" The pods incarnate the doctor's concern that "we're refining all humanity out of our lives."[27]

The emotionless, ambitionless pods quickly allow the town to fall to ruin, a foretaste of impending catastrophe. Pod Zero, former botanist Bernard Budlong, explains to the protagonists that they have exhausted the resources on every planet they have colonized, and he forecasts a rate of acceleration resulting in a rapid takeover of the planet and subsequent depletion of its resources within roughly five years, following which the pods will drift to a new planet and begin the process anew. To the dismay of Miles and his girlfriend, Becky, he responds (fifteen years before the UN report on the environment) that, after all, human beings have been doing a pretty good job of exhausting those resources themselves. Contemporary humanity, it seems, is well on its way to realizing a pod society without an alien invasion.

The pods are not only analogues for the dehumanizing effects of an increasingly urban and technological society, of colonialism, and of the careless destruction of the planet; they are also, Budlong explains, "completely evolved life." Having "the ability to re-form and reconstitute themselves into perfect duplication, cell for living cell, of any life form they may encounter in whatever conditions that life has suited itself for," they represent a new challenge to the idea of the human.[28] Contemporaneous insights from genetics, behaviorism, and cybernetics inform Budlong's elucidation of the process by which the pods "snatch" bodies: "every cell ... emanates waves as individual as fingerprints"; the human body "contains a pattern" that "is the very foundation of cellular life," which can be taken, "during sleep ..., absorbed like static electricity, from one body to another."[29] The unpossessed in the story cling desperately to their humanity, and anxiety surrounding its loss is the clear theme of the novel. "Only when we have to fight to stay human," muses Miles's cinematic incarnation, "do we realize how precious it is."[30] Humanity emerges in the novel as something intangible and ultimately inalienable; as such, it seems to transcend biology itself as Miles and Becky scare off the pods and, with them, the evolutionary insights they suggest.

Cinematic versions of the film would end more ambiguously; the pods are a looming threat at the end of Siegel's film and apparently victorious at the conclusion of Philip Kaufman's magnificent 1978 remake. Yet even Kaufman's comically tenebrous version depicts humanity as worth fighting for. Evolution may be inevitable, but the loss of humanity was lamentable nonetheless. The protagonist of Richard Matheson's 1954 novella, *I Am Legend*, in which an apocalyptic virus turns human beings vampiric, may concede that to "the new people of the earth" – a group of partially cured hybrids – he "like the vampires, ... was anathema and black terror to be destroyed."[31] But no reader could find the inheritance salutary, and only the first of three cinematic versions of Matheson's novella ends as bleakly, with the rest yielding to Hollywood in their depiction of small bands of human survivors who may yet, with the help of the protagonist's cure, prevail against the evolutionary tide.

"What Is Human Now?"

Humankind reached a new level of evolutionary agency when scientists at Stanford University and the University of California at San Francisco announced, in the early 1970s, their successful transference of the DNA of one living organism into another of a different species. The laboratory creation of new living organisms had precedents in such proto-science fictional works as Mary Shelley's *Frankenstein*, Nathaniel Hawthorne's "Rappaccini's Daughter," and H. G. Wells's *The Island of Dr. Moreau*. The experiments in these works stemmed from the imagination of mad or deluded men of science and constituted unmitigated threats to humanity. Humankind, to the literary imaginations of previous centuries, was not intended to play God or mess with the province of Nature. And yet in 1973, science journals such as *Proceedings of the National Academy of Science* and the *Journal of Molecular Biology* heralded just such an achievement as a scientific breakthrough. The technique of molecular cloning, or recombinant DNA, turned SF into science. Fueling the emergence of biotechnology as big business within a decade, it also sparked a public narrative that, conversely, turned science back into SF.

News of these discoveries reached the public initially because of an unprecedented conference organized to address the possibility of the need for self-regulation regarding this research. Chastened by the devastation caused by the use of nuclear weapons during World War II, many researchers involved with the creation of recombinant DNA tempered their excitement with caution. Works such as *Silent Spring*, moreover, had publicized the need to balance long-term consequences against short-term gains. Stanford researcher Paul Berg had planned to introduce a carcinogenic monkey virus into a laboratory strain of the common E. coli bacterium, but the potential scenario of a highly contagious human cancer virus prompted him to postpone his experiment and organize the Asilomar Conference of 1975. Including journalists, lawyers, and ethicists as well as scientists, the conference led to a moratorium on the most dangerous research until the NIH could establish guidelines to ensure public safety.

Initial journalistic accounts of recombinant DNA and Asilomar echoed the scientists' concerns for the safety of the public. But what one writer dubbed "the science-fictional fantasy of genetic engineering" quickly metamorphosed into SF horror as pundits speculated on "these modern Frankenstein creations" that "scientists will literally be loosing ... on the world."[32] Journalists mined popular culture for prototypes as in a *Newsweek* piece entitled "Safe Houses for Strange Life." Comparing the hazards of "new and potentially dangerous forms of life created by 'genetic engineering'" with those "brought to earth from other planets," the article described plans for "regional labs" that could serve as "'safe houses' for both genetic and interstellar 'monsters.'"[33] Such creatures populated the pages of the mainstream media and the imagination of their readers, as science writers described the pros and cons of researchers having harnessed the processes of evolution and probed the most basic secrets of life.

The products of recombinant DNA experiments were not the only biotechnological monsters on the block. The first immortal human cell line was created in 1951 to little fanfare outside the scientific world, but when researchers discovered, more than a decade later, that the robustness of the cells had caused it to contaminate subsequent cell lines, destroying many years and millions of dollars worth of research, the HeLa cell line made its public debut. The idea of human cells reproducing in a laboratory was especially uncanny, and accounts in the mainstream media in the 1970s and 1980s conflated the donor, an African American woman, with the cells. Describing how "Mrs. Lacks' body grew wildly in Dr. Gey's culture test tubes," these accounts produced a science fictional narrative of immortality and conquest. The donor was "dead, but her cancer cells live on."[34] The HeLa cells were "surreptitiously ... taking over cultures and laboratories here and abroad" and could "'take over the world'" if "'allowed to grow uninhibited.'"[35] HeLa was "on the wanted list and the charge is interfering with the orderly progress of science," sparking "a laboratory manhunt to track down renegade HeLa cultures." The racism and sexism is evident in these accounts, which, through the conflation, transformed a demure woman and a significant scientific advance into "a monster in the Pyrex."[36]

As recombinant DNA research catapulted biotechnology into a multi-billion-dollar business, ethicists and science writers worried about the dangerous social consequences of commodifying living organisms. In her 1977 *Playing God*, for example, June Goodfield had brooded about the danger of patenting life forms. "We can no longer possess, in the legal sense, a slave or a wife, or any category of living things," she mused. "But if we now can *possess* a group of living molecules and be protected by patent, is it not possible that commercial companies could slowly 'climb' the evolutionary ladder with living organisms, whose rights and development they wish to have solely?"[37] Central to her concerns was "the fear that we are losing our respect for each other, and for what it means to be human."[38] She thereby heralded the terms that would emerge with increasing frequency in the coming years. Lawyers and ethicists, for example, famously summoned the specter of bioslavery to argue both sides of a landmark legal case, *Moore v. UCLA*, which concerned the patent on a cell line derived from a white man's cancerous spleen. While Moore's lawyers sermonized against "the slippery slope" of bioslavery if someone else held property rights in their client's cells, the defense declaimed the danger of that slope if the courts were to recognize ownership even in one's own body parts.

The danger of the chimeras, clones, and other actual and fantastic creatures of the biotechnological revolution came less from any actual harm they might do to the world in which they would circulate than from their embodied challenge to the definitions of life and the human and therefore to conventional categories on which social structures – and ideas about social justice – rested. Influential futurist Alvin Toffler, for example, decried the hidden dangers of biotechnology in the creation of "new life forms with genes drawn from humans," which, he cautioned, could blur "the common (mainly implicit) definition of 'humanness.' Murder can be redefined if the victim is regarded as 'not human.' Slave labor is not slavery if the slaves are 'not human.'" And, in reference to the legal case, "if we can sell parts of our cells ... why not the entire body? And if body parts can be sold separately, why not the whole – for 21st-century bioslavery."[39]

The slippery slope from ethical speculation about science to the science fictional scenario of bioslavery makes sense in the context of Hannah Arendt's observation, in *The Human Condition*, that the emerging mass market genre of science fiction served as an especially noteworthy "vehicle of mass sentiments and mass desires."[40] The scenario of genetically engineered human beings deprived of their humanity and mass produced as slaves found vivid expression in Ridley Scott's *Blade Runner*, his 1982 cinematic adaptation of Philip K. Dick's *Do Androids Dream of Electric Sheep* (1968). The influence of biotechnology is evident in the differences between Dick's androids and Scott's more developed and sympathetic Replicants. Both have been created to serve the human beings who are sufficiently healthy and wealthy to have vacated their environmentally devastated planet for dangerous Off-world colonies, but Scott puts considerably more emphasis on the humanity of his Replicants. The film follows the four surviving Replicants of a slave revolt, who have braved the hostile planet to confront their maker, corporate head Eldon Tyrell, to demand an extension of their built-in four-year life span. Tyrell designed this planned obsolescence to prevent the development of their emotions, hence their claims to the entitlements of humankind, thereby facilitating enslavement. *Blade Runner* dramatizes the anxieties about the "slippery slope" from creating and patenting life in a laboratory to owning a human being. The danger the film exposes, however, lies neither in the actual harm the Replicants might do to humankind, nor in how the circumstances of their creation might erode the conception of the human, but in the corporate indifference to all forms of life manifested by Tyrell, whose boast that the Replicants are "more human than human" turns out to be all too true.[41] The Replicants evince more humanity than anyone else in the film, affirming, as in *The Body Snatchers*, the intangibility and transcendence of the biology of "humanity."

Within the decade, the launching of the Human Genome Project (HGP) would challenge assumptions of that transcendence as it intensified debates about the biology of human behavior and the predictability of human destiny, individual and collective. "We used to think our fate was in the stars," James Watson told a *Time* magazine reporter in 1989, a year after the NIH and DOE announced funding for the Project. "Now we know, in large measure, our fate is in our genes."[42] The tagline of Andrew Niccol's 1997 film *Gattaca* succinctly summarized the opposing claim: "there is no gene for the human spirit."[43]

For Octavia Butler, the clash of perspectives made sense in the context of the dehumanizing strategies of the past, as she explored in her Xenogenesis trilogy (known more recently as *Lilith's Brood*) of the late 1980s. The trilogy stages the conceptual clash between the human survivors of a nuclear war that has made the planet uninhabitable and the aliens that save them. The Oankali are, in effect, biotechnicians and radical ecologists who cohabit in productive symbiosis with the living organisms that comprise their technology. They are also evolutionary biologists: gene traders who move through the cosmos interbreeding with other species. Joyfully embracing evolution and ecology as fundamental life principles, they have mastered genetic manipulation in ways that ensure healthy reproduction; they even harness cancer, which they consider a great gift of the human species, to help them learn more effectively how to foster cell growth. Placing the human beings they rescue in suspended animation, they spend two centuries working to make the Earth able once again to sustain life.

The trilogy begins with the awakening of the humans, who quickly come to view their saviors as captors, as their fundamental understanding of freedom and meaningful existence clash. The legacies of colonialism and racial slavery have left humanity with an understanding of exclusion from history as a form of what historian Orlando Patterson calls "social death," and that is how they experience the evolutionary jump on which the Oankali insist.[44] "Humanity," to them, requires free will, choice, and the free play of emotion; it depends as well on a distinctly human lineage that extends from prehistory into any foreseeable future. The Oankali know that the hardwired traits of hierarchy and aggression will always lead to the destruction of humankind, but the interbreeding that the Oankali offer as salvation appears to the humans as termination: evolution, for them, is tantamount to extinction. In each of the three novels – *Dawn* (1987), *Imago* (1988), and *Adulthood Rites* (1989) – a hybrid protagonist facilitates a compromise, and the trilogy ends without fully affirming either worldview.

If all human beings received equal treatment – for better or worse – at the hands (or tentacles) of the Oankali, however, biotechnology could not make the same promise. Biologist Lee M. Silver drew on the SF scenario of how the differential access to genetic enhancements created by economic inequities might over time result in divergent species in his 1997 *Remaking Eden: How Genetic Engineering and Cloning Will Transform the American Family*. Arguing that genetic engineering would be but the latest – if especially dramatic – of the advantages wealthy parents gave their children, hence fostering a gradual evolutionary divide, Silver imagines a cosmos, not unlike Butler's, in which "far-flung communities ... begin to lose contact with one another" and, ultimately, "cultural memory of their species origin on the third planet in a nondescript solar system lost among the billions in the Milky Way."[45] Against the backdrop of the Human Genome Project, dystopic works of SF warned of the consequences of the changes Silver imagined. Genetic engineering exacerbated social inequities in such works as *Gattaca* and Nancy Kress's *Beggars in Spain* (1993), and, more extremely, turned engineered human beings or proto-humans into organ storage units for the wealthy in Robin Cook's *Chromosome 6* (1997), Kazuo Ishiguro's *Never Let Me Go* (novel 2005, film 2010), and Michael Bay's *The Island* (2005). Even if the changes were the result of evolutionary forces beyond human control, as in the *X-Men* franchise, the television series *Heroes* (2006–10), and Greg

Bear's *Darwin's Radio* (1990) and *Darwin's Children* (2003), SF suggested humankind's anxieties about confronting its own heirs.

Silver ends his speculative account with evolved humans' "coming face to face with their creator. What do they see?" he asks. "Is it something that twentieth-century humans can't possibly fathom in their wildest imaginations? Or is it simply their *own* image in the mirror, as they reflect back to the beginning of time?"[46] It is, of course, not just the evolutionary mirror that SF holds up to humanity; the world Harold Isaacs describes – the new shapes and perspectives, the painful rearrangements – are social and geopolitical changes for which the evolutionary metamorphoses of SF are also analogues. The technologies of a globalizing world have fostered genetic reconfigurations with permanent evolutionary changes in a biological and geopolitical double helix that offers a blueprint for the future. SF records the hopes as well as the fears of that future, as humanity ponders its intangibles, and mutants conceived in the laboratories of the imagination become prototypes of transformation.

NOTES

1 John Hersey, *Hiroshima* (New York: Random House [1946] 1985), 60–1.
2 "Text of Statement by Truman, Stimson on Development of the Atomic Bomb," *New York Times* (August 7, 1945), 4.
3 Hanson W. Baldwin, "The Atomic Weapon," *New York Times* (August 7, 1945), 10.
4 Edward R. Murrow, radio broadcast, August 12, 1945, *In Search of Light: The Broadcasts of Edward R. Murrow, 1938–1961* (New York: Knopf, 1961), 102.
5 Norman Cousins, "Modern Man Is Obsolete," *Saturday Review* (August 18, 1945), 8, and "Man and the Atom," *Christian Century* (August 22, 1945), 951.
6 Darko Suvin, *Metamorphoses of Science Fiction: On the Poetics and History of a Literary Genre* (New Haven, CT: Yale University Press, 1979).
7 Harold R. Isaacs, "Color in World Affairs," *Foreign Affairs* 47.2 (January 1969): 235–50, 235.
8 Hannah Arendt, *The Origins of Totalitarianism* [1948] (New York: Harcourt Brace Jovanovich, 1979), 44.
9 Frantz Fanon, "Concerning Violence," *The Wretched of the Earth* [1961], trans. Constance Farrington (New York: Grove Press, 1963), 35–106, 42–3.
10 Fanon, "Conclusion," *Wretched*, 311–16, 315.
11 Ibid., 315.
12 Ibid., 35.
13 *The Thing from Another World*, dir. Christian Nyby (and Howard Hawks), 1951. DVD.
14 Julian Huxley, "Transhumanism," in *In New Bottles for New Wine* (London: Chatto and Windus, 1957), 13–17.
15 Julian Huxley, *Evolution: The Modern Synthesis* (London: George Allen and Unwin Ltd., 1942), 578.

16 Rachel Carson, *Silent Spring* [1962] (Boston, MA: Houghton Mifflin, 2002), 1–2. I am borrowing extensively in my discussion of Carson from my earlier discussion of this work in "Botanophobia: Fear of Plants in the Atomic Age," *Japanese Journal of American Studies* No. 24 (2013): 7–27.
17 Carson, *Silent Spring*, 2.
18 Ibid., 3.
19 Ibid., 103.
20 Ibid., 6.
21 Ibid., 32–3.
22 Ibid., 16.
23 Ibid., 216.
24 Ibid., 230.
25 "Crisis of Human Environment," United Nations Economic and Social Council, *Report of the Secretary General on Problems of the Human Environment*, 47th Session, Agenda Item 10, May 26, 1969, pp. 4–6.
26 Stuart M. Kaminsky, "Don Siegel on the Pod Society," in Al LaValley, ed., *Invasion of the Body Snatchers: Don Siegel, Director* (New Brunswick, NJ: Rutgers University Press, 1989), 153–7, 154.
27 Jack Finney, *The Body Snatchers* (New York: Dell, 1955), 49–50.
28 Ibid., 153.
29 Ibid., 155–6.
30 *Invasion of the Body Snatchers*, dir. Don Siegel (1956) ... DVD.
31 Richard Matheson, *I Am Legend* [1954] (New York: A Tom Doherty Associates Book, 1995), 169–70.
32 Peter Gwynne, "Genetic Watchdogs," *Newsweek* (July 4, 1976): 106.
33 Conway, "Safe Houses for Strange Life," *Newsweek* (June 28, 1976): 15.
34 Connie Lauerman, "She's Dead – but Her Cancer Cells Live On," *Chicago Tribune* (March 14, 1976): 18. I am drawing here on research for two prior essays I have written on this subject and am indebted especially to Michael Gold, *A Conspiracy of Cells: One Woman's Immortal Legacy and the Medical Scandal It Caused* (Albany: State University of New York Press, 1986) for his account of the scandal that led to the publicity and to Hannah Landecker, "Immortality, In Vitro: A History of the HeLa Cell Line," in Paul E. Brodwin, ed., *Biotechnology and Culture: Bodies, Anxieties, Ethics* (Bloomington: Indiana University Press, 2000), 53–72 and *Culturing Life: How Cells Became Technologies* (Cambridge, MA: Harvard University Press, 2007), for her analysis of the media narrative.
35 B. J. C., "HeLa (for Henrietta Lacks)," *Science* (June 21, 1974): 1268.
36 Michael Rogers, "The Double-Edged Helix," *Rolling Stone* (March 21, 1976): 48–51, 51.
37 June Goodfield, *Playing God* (New York: Harper Colophon, 1977), xiii.
38 Ibid., 71.
39 Alvin Toffler, "What Is Human Now?" *Christian Science Monitor* (June 4, 1987), 20.
40 Hannah Arendt, *The Human Condition* (Chicago: University of Chicago Press, 1958), 2.
41 *Blade Runner*, dir. Ridley Scott, 1982. DVD.
42 Quoted in Leon Jaroff, "The Gene Hunt," *Time* (March 10, 1989): 67.
43 *Gattaca*, dir. Andrew Niccol, 1997. DVD.

44 Orlando Patterson, *Slavery and Social Death: A Comparative Study* (Cambridge, MA: Harvard University Press, 1982).

45 Lee M. Silver, *Remaking Eden: How Genetic Engineering and Cloning Will Transform the American Family* (New York: Avon Books, 1997), 290.

46 Ibid., 293.

14

ROGER LUCKHURST

American Weird

In March 1923, proprietor Clark Hennesberger joined the burgeoning pulp magazine market in fantastic stories with *Weird Tales*, subtitled
"A Magazine of the Bizarre and Unusual." It was in the generic pulp format
pioneered by Frank Munsey in *Argosy*: 7 x 10 inches with about 128 pages
of rough, untrimmed pulp paper and bright, lurid covers. The first edition
included Anthony Rud's "Ooze," a breathless tale of a scientist's backwoods
experiment with protozoan matter that produces a giant amoeboid thing
that devours his family. The story was so unsure of its generic status that
it contained a metafictional reflection about "the pseudo-scientific story":
"In plain words, this means a yarn, based upon solid fact in the field of
astronomy, chemistry, anthropology or whatnot, which carries to a logical
conclusion unproved theories of men who devote their lives to searching out
further nadirs of fact."[1]

This definition was very close to the formulations being tried out by Hugo
Gernsback, who coined the term "scientifiction" in his new journal *Amazing
Stories* in 1926, although as the magazine became established, one contribu-
tor to the "Discussion" letters page commented: "Scientific fiction does not
have to come within the range of possibility, but it should be plausible and
not contrary to any known facts or natural laws. Purely fanciful stories might
be better ranked as romances or 'weird tales' (all very well in their place)
than as 'scientifiction.'"[2] Yet both Gernsback's *Amazing* and Hennesberger's
Weird Tales appealed to the same literary forebears: Poe, Verne, and Wells.
Gernsback reprinted and serialized their stories, while readers of *Weird
Tales* early on demanded "more pseudo-scientific stories and more H. G.
Wells stories," to which the editor responded that "the so-called 'pseudo-
scientific' tales have ever been popular with the readers of *Weird Tales*, and
is the intention of the editor to publish more and more of these."[3]

Even so, *Weird Tales*' first *succès de scandale* was C. M. Eddy's "The
Loved Dead," published in 1924, a sensational piece of necrophiliac
Gothic that caught the attention of moral campaigners always concerned

with the corrupting influence of sensation fiction on its presumed lowly readers. Here was a magazine that also promised on its front page "A Wealth of Startling Thrill-Tales" and willingly crossed into the territory of "weird menace" typical of the so-called shudder pulps, which happily mixed up hard-boiled detective fiction, way-out Westerns, and sadistic sexual torture.[4]

A typical early issue of *Weird Tales* veered between these modes, and this perhaps accounted for its insipid and unprofitable start. After thirteen issues a new editor was installed, and Farnsworth Wright was to develop a stable of writers that finally created a distinctive niche for the magazine. The most prominent figures included Robert E. Howard, H. P. Lovecraft, and Seabury Quinn. In the 1930s, his successor editor Dorothy McIlwraith brought youthful figures like Robert Bloch, Ray Bradbury, C. L. Moore, and Fritz Lieber into *Weird Tales*.

It was Lovecraft who concocted something distinct from the generic soup of the '20s pulps. In 1925, Lovecraft composed the long essay *Supernatural Horror in Literature*, in which he offered a crisp definition of the weird considered as "a literature of cosmic fear."[5] This reached beyond the standard narratives and tropes of the Gothic, Lovecraft explained:

> The true weird tale must have something more than secret murder, bloody bones, or a sheeted form clanking chains according to rule. A certain atmosphere of breathless and unexplainable dread of outer, unknown forces must be present; and there must be a hint, expressed with a seriousness and portentousness becoming its subject, of that most terrible conception of the human brain – a malign and particular suspension or defeat of those fixed laws of Nature which are our only safeguard against the assaults of chaos and the daemons of unplumbed space.[6]

Lovecraft went on to establish a literary lineage of the weird, beginning with the English and German Gothic romance. His Anglophilia determined that the "modern masters" of the weird form were Arthur Machen, Algernon Blackwood, and Lord Dunsany. While these figures wrote in the Gothic or fantasy tradition, the latter part of Lovecraft's definition tacked away from theological terrors and toward scientific naturalism more typical of Wells, in which horror derives not from religious fears but what Lovecraft elsewhere termed the "cosmic indifference" of a universe expanded inconceivably in time and space by scientific discovery in the nineteenth century, and which coldly dethroned anthropocentric conceptions of the world. Because Lovecraft insisted that the weird was an effect of "atmosphere," a "*vivid depiction of a certain type of human mood*," it is not tied to a fixed typology and continues to slip category, slithering between Gothic and science fictional forms.[7]

Lovecraft offered suggestive hints that there might be a distinctively American dispensation to the weird, too. He imagined the first white Puritan settlers in their fragile outposts surrounded by "the vast and gloomy virgin forests in whose perpetual twilight all terrors might lurk" and "the hordes of coppery Indians whose strange, saturnine visages and violent customs hinted strongly at traces of infernal origin."[8] These terrors produced the delirious oddity of Charles Brockden Brown's *Edgar Huntly, or Memoirs of a Sleep-Walker* (1799) – a text marked by an uncontrollable contamination of somnambulism amongst its characters and a pathological horror of the native American – and the guilty disorders that beset the texts of Nathaniel Hawthorne, the greatgrandson of Salem's only unrepentant witch-hanging judge. The other key contributors to this American weird tradition are Edgar Allan Poe – perhaps most symptomatically in the progressively unhinged and gnomically irresolute *The Narrative of Arthur Gordon Pym of Nantucket* (1838) – and the short stories of Ambrose Bierce. Bierce repeatedly uses the spaces of the frontier to evoke "some overpowering presence – some supernatural malevolence" in narratives soaked in the traumas of the Civil War, in which Bierce had fought in many key engagements.[9] The foundational violence and race terror that underlies the American Republic would suffuse Lovecraft's own writing too.[10]

Lovecraft's attempt to construct a tradition of fictions of cosmic fear unlocked something in his own writing, which had hitherto been produced for amateur journals circulated amongst members of the United Amateur Press Association. Although Farnsworth Wright famously often turned down or demanded rewrites from Lovecraft, *Weird Tales* published several of his key fictions, including "The Call of Cthulhu," "The Whisperer in Darkness," and "The Dunwich Horror" (he also sold stories to what were becoming quintessential American SF magazines, *Amazing Stories* and *Astounding Science Fiction*). "Cthulhu" was an accumulation of fragmentary and elliptical texts hinting at unprintable horrors, on the model of Arthur Machen's classic 1894 tale "The Great God Pan" (famously denounced when published as "a nightmare incoherence of sex").[11] It also consolidated Lovecraft's notion of the Old Ones, at once a mythography of imaginary gods on the model of Dunsany's *Gods of Pegana* (1905) and a scientized conception of glimpsed survivals of humanity's malignant predecessors (and superiors), owing much to the fabulous prehistory of *Homo sapiens* invented by occultist Helena Blavatsky in *The Secret Doctrine*, one of the founding texts of the Theosophical Society, and subsequently elaborated by mystics like Rudolf Steiner. Other writers in Lovecraft's circle, such as Robert Howard and Clark Ashton Smith, also developed weird and exotic mythographies. Howard was much better at injecting energy into his plotting; Smith's visual power at evoking the pulp sublime often surpassed Lovecraft.

Long tales like "The Dunwich Horror" brought these expansive horrors close to Lovecraft's beloved ancestral home on the northeast seaboard, lovingly realized through his antiquarian obsession with decaying Old Colonial outposts. Here the fusion of Puritan terror of devil worship lurking behind every door and the "cosmic" vision of malignant forces that can undermine human integrity is evoked in the hysterical prose that reaches its apotheosis halfway through the tale:

> The thing that lay half-bent on its side in a foetid pool of greenish-yellow ichor and tarry stickiness was almost nine feet tall.... Above the waist it was semi-anthropomorphic; though its chest ... had the leathery, reticulated hide of a crocodile or alligator.... Below the waist, though, it was the worst; for here all human resemblance left off and sheer phantasy began. The skin was thickly covered in black fur, and from the abdomen a score of long greenish-gray tentacles with red sucking mouths protruded limply. Their arrangement was odd, and seemed to follow the symmetries of some cosmic geometry unknown to earth or the solar system.[12]

This is the quintessentially Lovecraftian weird: it redoubles the horror at the impossible hybrid being by using a mannerist style that itself deliriously slips category. Although this passage might cry out for psychoanalysis, the weird is not "uncanny" in Freud's sense of a frightening return of what has been lost, repressed, or superseded: there is nothing familiar here *at all*, only a weird confusion that overruns every discriminating taxonomy. The predominant affect is disgust, which, as Kant argued in his *Critique of Judgment*, derails aesthetic value because "disgusting objects present themselves to the imagination with an inescapable immediacy that prevents the conversion of the disgusting into something discernibly artistic."[13] That this disgust is motored by Lovecraft's depressingly regurgitated "Nordic" racism against "Asiatic" immigration into America in the 1920s is made evident by one of his first *Weird Tales* contributions, "The Horror at Red Hook," where there is no sublimation of the explicit belief that horror derives from the chaos of races living in the Brooklyn slums around the harbor. The rhythm of the prose is also a hypnotic race hate mantra.

There is something very *wrong* with Lovecraft's writing. Infelicitous style, chronic overstatement, and blunt melodramatics are typical of pulp prose, but Lovecraft spectacularly breaks every writing rule. The sentences are choked with clumps of adjectival weeds, paragraphs clotted with repetition, and a perversion of the "show don't tell" injunction to read something like "show *and* tell *everything*, repeatedly, reiteratively, redundantly." Despite all this, these mannerisms fire fitfully to create rather brilliant moments: the weird crawls out of these sentences precisely because of their awkward style. Lovecraft wanted to shake the version of reality created by anthropocentric delusion; to do this required a breaking open of language and genre to get beyond the limits of realism. Lovecraft's horror fictions employ a language that continually stumbles against the trauma of an unrepresentable Thing, the shards of a busted pulp sublime falling back into the debris of his sentences.

It was the awkwardness of Lovecraft's prose and his adherence to the amateur ethos that seemingly destined him for obscurity upon his death in 1937. He had published only one limited edition book in his lifetime; the rest vanished in amateur and pulp ephemera. In 1936, Lovecraft's ally and epistolary friend Robert E. Howard, mainstay of *Weird Tales* for a decade, committed suicide. This dreamer of the Atlantean warrior King Kull and Conan the Barbarian proved unable to cope with his mother's death. Clark Ashton Smith largely stopped writing after 1936, too, and *Weird Tales* was sold in 1938 to a new owner with more concern about the profitable bottom line. Farnsworth Wright died in 1940. Weird fiction might have vanished at this point, an uneasy and interstitial form flowering in the crevices during the formation of modern popular genres but dying out once this niche habitat disappeared.

Lovecraft was rescued by his devoted followers, particularly August Derleth and Donald Wandrei. They failed to interest the commercial publishing industry in Lovecraft's fiction, so established Arkham House and published three volumes of the maestro's prose between 1939 and 1943. These volumes, which sold very modestly at first, prompted leading American literary critic Edmund Wilson to issue the damning judgment that "the only real horror of most of these fictions is the horror of bad taste and bad art."[14] Derleth began to elaborate what eventually became known as Lovecraft's "Cthulhu mythos," either by completing unfinished Lovecraft fragments or freely improvising in the approved ornate style. Collaboration and ghostwriting was something Lovecraft had practiced throughout his career, so this was a logical extension of amateur collective writing. But this modest start could never have anticipated the vast elaboration of the mythos that has occurred nor its steady suffusion into popular culture. In the 1960s, mass market paperback selections of Lovecraft's tales sold in their millions and film adaptations began – micro-budget horrors at first, but H. R. Giger's designs for *Alien* and horror cinema's recent obsession with the tentacular sublime are unthinkable without Lovecraft. One now needs an encyclopedia to navigate the thousands of stories across multiple platforms composed inside the Cthulhu mythos.[15] Stranger still, the Old Ones have been extensively incorporated into the subculture of American occult movements: one can now authentically worship Cthulhu and consult various different versions of Lovecraft's once entirely imaginary grimoire, *The Necronomicon*.[16]

For decades, the flame of weird fiction was carried by dedicated amateurs (such as the indefatigable Lovecraft editor and historian of the weird, S. T. Joshi), and otherwise largely ignored, even by emergent Gothic and science fiction criticism in the academy, whose early forms of formalist, structuralist, or political criticism were not very comfortable with the weird's slippery defiance of category and lowly pulp status. If these genres were "paraliterature," existing outside or below the threshold of canonical literary forms, the Weird was a para-para-literature.[17]

Then, in an online forum discussion in 2003, English science fiction and fantasy writer M. John Harrison wondered passingly if there was a sense of an emergent new form that might tentatively be termed "The New Weird" ("Who does it? What is it? Is it even anything?" he asked).[18] Harrison had been associated with New Wave SF, and had been first published alongside J. G. Ballard and Michael Moorcock in *New Worlds* magazine in the late 1960s. Harrison's subsequent career has been a merciless deconstruction of the genres of apocalypse, space opera, and heroic fantasy, and with the New Weird he seemed to want to name a new generation of writers intent on slipping the moorings of popular genre in the same *soixante-huitard* spirit of rebellion that fostered the New Wave. Harrison named fellow British writers China Miéville and Steph Swainston as exemplary figures of this new tendency. Other critics were at the same time speculating on notions of the "post-genre fantastic," which had given up observing any boundaries between SF, Gothic, and dark fantasy.[19] Miéville promptly wrote the manifesto, "Long Live the New Weird." "Genres … a bunch of fuzzy sets at the best of times, are suddenly fuzzier than ever," Miéville claimed. A political radical, he regarded the New Weird as both "a renunciation and a return" to the Old Weird.[20] He had no time for the contents of Lovecraft's "foul racist drivel" or its conservative panic narratives about boundary transgression.[21] Instead, he has consistently aimed to recalibrate the slipperiness of the weird to respond to "the freeing up, the radicalisation of the world. This is post-Seattle fiction," he pronounced, unashamedly tying the genre to a leftist attack on the absurdist world of contemporary "capitalist realism."[22] The New Weird therefore revalued this interstitial mode of writing, turning its lack of generic fixity into a potentially revolutionary virtue.

Although any claims to a movement were almost immediately disowned by Harrison, Miéville, and others in this English group (conforming to the logic of resisting the ossification that generic labels risk), there have been American anthologies, such as *The New Weird*, and a readjustment of the trajectory of American horror and fantasy fiction since the '70s to shift the place of writers who have consistently wanted to slip between different modes of the fantastic, writers like Peter Straub, Jeff VanderMeer, and

Gene Wolfe. In the way of these things, it took the arrival of the New Weird to allow a retrospective construction of a longer tradition: *The Weird: A Compendium of Strange and Dark Stories,* with 1,100 double-columned pages of more than one hundred selections, appeared toward the end of this revival in 2011.

Perhaps the weirdest part of this recovery of the once-forgotten or discarded Weird is the place Lovecraftian horror fiction holds in the philosophical movement of "object-oriented philosophy," in which Lovecraft's sketchy and mostly secondhand knowledge of Schopenhauer and Nietzsche is elevated into a rigorous worldview to rival and directly contest his immediate contemporary, phenomenologist Edmund Husserl.[23] "The weird is the discovery of an unhuman limit to thought, that is nevertheless foundational for thought," philosopher Eugene Thacker has argued, inserting Lovecraft without pausing to reflect very much on form or genre into a long Western philosophical tradition.[24] Always a favorite with avant-garde critical theorists – Lovecraft is a reference point in Gilles Deleuze and Felix Guattari's *A Thousand Plateaux* (1980) – Lovecraft is also the starting point for the delirious hybrid philosophy/fiction/conspiracy theory *Cyclonopedia* by Reza Negarestani. For paraphilosophers, the Weird, it seems, has become good to think with.

I have tried to write a relatively "straight" history of weird fiction, but it is also important to acknowledge how arbitrary and contingent this trajectory truly is. In a comment on the *Weird Compendium,* Miéville challenges the notion that there can be a weird canon: "This canon changes. Its edges are protean, its membranes as permeable and oozing as the breaching biology of Lovecraft's Dunwich Horror. We interpret it, of course: our minds are meaning factories. But the ground below them is hole-y. There are cracks and chaos."[25] In fact, one of the striking things about weird fiction is its immensely self-conscious "re-marking" of its own genre status, the anxious construction of its own textual forebears and literary contours in the very act of writing.[26] Bierce constantly hails Poe; Robert W. Chambers's sinister *The King in Yellow* (1895) – recently highlighted in the first season of HBO's *True Detective* (2014) – composes fragments of its fatal book from tiny echoes of Bierce; Lovecraft builds his fictions inside a matrix of intertextual resonances from Poe, Bierce, Chambers, Machen, Blackwood, Dunsany, and a host of others. The fabricated history of Lovecraft's *Necronomicon* and the profusion of invented books amongst his circle (Clark Ashton Smith's *Books of Eibon,* Robert Howard's *Unaussprechlichen Kulten* – "Unspeakable Cults") is a "pseudobiblia" that explicitly foregrounds an ongoing self-fashioning of authoritative lineages for the weird.[27] The New Weird amplifies this process, extending the range of reference further, sometimes making the revival appear to be little more than the reshuffling in a different pattern of a tissue of citations.

If the diaeresis in the ancient usage of *weïrd* ties the term to *weyard* or *wayward* (as the Oxford English Dictionary speculates), then perhaps there is something intrinsic to weird fiction that makes it deviate from easy definition, makes deviation from any essence actually central to it. That, perhaps, accounts for its oneirism, its fascination with evoking states of delirium – a term that itself derives from the verb *delire*, meaning to deviate from ploughing the straight furrow, to veer off course, only later coming to indicate departure from reason.

In a way, then, it would respect the object of inquiry to offer a broken-backed essay in which the cultural history of the first part is challenged by the more theoretical reflections of the second. Here, then, is a set of indications as to why the weird might defy the boundaries of the companionable, definitional essay.

The fearful/exhilarating affect of the weird nearly always seems to derive from the transgression of boundaries, menacing obtrusions of one category into another. The quintessential North American Weird story in this regard might be Algernon Blackwood's "The Wendigo" (1910), based on his experiences of the Canadian wilderness during a failed experiment as a settler-farmer in the 1890s before his return to England. There is nothing visibly horrifying here (as so often in Blackwood), only an intense psychological portrait of feeling menaced by forces beyond the range of human senses that perfectly fuses interior states of paranoia and mental distress with sublime exterior landscapes. The borderless ooze that squelched into the first issue of *Weird Tales* is similarly about things that breach borders, the body-horror that bursts the "skin-ego" and unbounds the self.[28] Fishy or tentacular slime that disgusts for its borderless invasiveness has been there since Coleridge's "Rime of the Ancient Mariner," and memorably heightens the weirdest moments in tales like Arthur Machen's "The Novel of the White Powder" or the pseudopodia that feature in "The Novel of the Black Seal" (both embedded tales in *The Three Impostors*), or in any number of William Hope Hodgson's stories of fungal men that erupt from the primal gloop of the Sargasso Sea in *The Boats of "Glen Carrig"* (1907) or that appear through transdimensional portals in *The House on the Borderland* (1908) or *Carnacki, The Ghost Finder* (1913). Lovecraft only consolidated the trope. A related weird device is an obsessive evocation of non-Euclidean geometry, a disturbing disruption of the space-time continuum that marks the intersection of impossible planes of existence. Lovecraft's descriptions of the contortions of space in the attic in "The Dreams in the Witch-House" has a direct descendant in the terrifying contorted and shifting corridors of

Mark Z. Danielewski's *House of Leaves* (2000). There has been a similar influence from the impossible geometries of Clark Ashton Smith's "The City of the Singing Flame" (first published in *Wonder Stories* in 1931) or Lovecraft's *At the Mountains of Madness* (rejected by *Weird Tales*, but eventually published in *Astounding Science Fiction*). This trope emerged from Victorian speculations on the Higher Mathematics: the fourth dimension was the decidedly weird and occult theory promulgated by the eccentric Charles Howard Hinton in the 1880s, one of the first writers to use the category of "scientific romance" to describe his tortured excursions into fiction.[29] The genre nurtures these impossible spatial forms, whilst also insistently pushing to the edges and limits of things – beyond explored territory in the Arctic, through portals in remote territories of the Australian outback, or beyond the limits of the known universe.

If these persistent devices constitute a generic "re-marking" of the weird, then what they point to is a foundational *transgression* of any boundaries that could contain weird fiction. The law of genre is to insist on purity, but the law behind the law of genre, Derrida proposes, is an inaugural *impurity* that always confounds boundary or enclosure. The weird is miscegenate, a lowly mongrel that tends to slither out of reach. It is hard to define a national tradition (is there an "American weird" after all?), precisely because influences are often pulled together from multiple canons. The weird might just as well contain Théophile Gautier, Franz Kafka, Gustav Meyrink, or Bruno Schulz as Herman Melville and Edgar Allan Poe. At the same time, it seems entirely plausible to extend the American weird to run from Charles Brockden Brown to the sinister comics of Charles Burns, such as *X'ed Out* (2009), where weird affect crawls out of the gutters of his spookily disconnected panels, or the multimedia art of David Lynch, one of the best contemporary artists to grasp weird affect in cinema, TV, music, painting, and even his strip cartoon, "The Angriest Dog in the World." For that matter the web of the weird might draw in popular recent television productions like *The X-Files* (1993–2002), *Fringe* (2008–2013), and the series *American Horror Story* (2011–); films like *The Blair Witch Project* (1999), *Hellboy* (2004), and *The Cabin in the Woods* (2012); prose fiction from genre-adjacent writers like Shirley Jackson and Philip K. Dick; occult, UFO, and alien-abduction subcultures; haunting video games like *Amnesia* (2010), *Limbo* (2010), and *The Stanley Parable* (2011); even many of the gross-out horror comics like *The Haunt of Fear* and *Tales from the Crypt* that caused a national moral panic in the 1950s, ultimately leading to Senate hearings and the institution of the Comics Code. As if reacting like a bewildered Lovecraft narrator, the weird seems to expand and contract strangely, leaving one unable to judge with any appropriate sense of scale.

Those spatial edges and limits that fascinate are often markedly colonial boundaries too: what lies "At the End of the Passage" in Kipling's short story, first published in 1890, about the suicidal loneliness of colonial officials at the very edge of the administered world, is a horror that slides weirdly beyond representation. The weird lies beyond the imperial limit in the colonial romances of Rudyard Kipling and Bertram Mitford; in Lovecraft, it shivers in the decayed Old Colonial shipping towns of America or haunts the expansionist ambitions of America's Manifest Destiny in the Pacific. A wandering writer like Lafcadio Hearn passed through the exotic terrains of these limit-spaces for America, producing *Stray Leaves from Strange Literature* (1884) and collecting supernatural and weird folklore from the Caribbean to Japan, teasing encounters with Chinese ghosts and the Martinician *zombi*. The overrun borders of the weird can induce panic, revulsion, and conservative reaction, but can also be sly revenges on the arrogance of the imperial domination of space. It is worthwhile speculating that just as the Old Weird peaked with imperialism at the end of the nineteenth century, the New Weird emerged in the era of globalization and borderless "Empire," to whisper dark fantasies of the underside of uneven development again. That would make the weird less a genre than a *mode*, far more expansive and supremely difficult to demarcate.[30]

If this claim seems absurd, perhaps that is also because the weird, ultimately, is a question of *taste*. The mannerisms of weird fiction provoke a strong set of discriminations and expulsions: it is "bad art" (for Edmund Wilson), bad science fiction (for critics like Darko Suvin, who demand quasi-scientific cognition from their SF), bad Gothic romance (for those who favor delicate indirection over gross-out body-horror). To start with *Weird Tales* is to imply that the genre is a low pulp form, perhaps one of the lowliest. That has left it critically unregarded, except to those who embrace what is sometimes called "trash aesthetics," where value is created precisely by resisting aesthetic norms of the beautiful.[31] Even here, though, weird fiction is difficult to pin down. The principal reference point for the ornate style, the outré content, and the delight in using the sublime to wreck the niceties of the beautiful, is surely the Decadent movement, stretching from Charles Baudelaire through J.-K. Huysmans to Oscar Wilde. Poet Arthur Symons defined the Decadent style as marked by "an intense self-consciousness, a restless curiosity in research, an over-subtilizing refinement upon refinement, a spiritual and moral perversity ... For its very disease of form, this literature is certainly typical of a civilization grown over-luxurious, over-inquiring, too languid for the relief of action."[32] Lovecraft certainly saw himself in this mode, living out his life as a Poverty Row Decadent. Of his models, Poe was an icon for Baudelaire and the French decadents, while English writers

like Arthur Machen and M. P. Shiel published works in the 1890s in the
Keynotes series, the epicenter of English Decadence. In this way, the weird
has to be regarded as simultaneously high *and* low, a kind of war on the
banality of middlebrow, mainstream literary culture. It is an acquired taste,
messy, mean, and miscegenate, but for that very reason the weird continues
to speak powerfully to our times.

NOTES

1 Anthony M Rud, "Ooze" (1923), reprinted in Peter Haining, ed., *Weird Tales*
(London: Xanadu, 1990), 248–63 (259).
2 Preston Slosson, "Discussions," *Amazing Stories* 3.3 (June 1928): 272.
3 "The Eyrie" (letters page), *Weird Tales* 7.6 (June 1926): 357.
4 See Robert Kenneth Jones, *The Shudder Pulps: A History of the Weird Menace
Magazines of the 1930s* (West Linn, OR: FAX Collectors' Editions, 1975),
and as evidence of genre hybridity see also Paul Green, *Encyclopedia of Weird
Westerns: Supernatural and Science Fiction Elements in Novels, Pulps, Comics,
Films, Television and Games* (Jefferson, NC: McFarland, 2009).
5 Lovecraft, *Supernatural Horror in Literature* (New York: Dover, 1973), 15.
6 Ibid., 15.
7 Lovecraft, "Notes on Writing Weird Fiction," http://www.hplovecraft.com/writ-
ings/texts/essays/nwwf.aspx.
8 Lovecraft, *Supernatural Horror*, 60.
9 Ambrose Bierce, "The Death of Halpin Frayser," *Complete Short Stories*, edited
by E. J. Hopkins (New York: Doubleday, 1970): 58–72 (61).
10 For a more transatlantic history, see S. T. Joshi, *The Weird Tale: Arthur Machen,
Algernon Blackwood, M. R. James, Ambrose Bierce, H. P. Lovecraft* (Austin:
University of Texas Press, 1990).
11 See Machen, "The Great God Pan," in Roger Luckhurst, ed., *Late Victorian
Gothic Tales* (Oxford: Oxford World's Classics, 2005).
12 Lovecraft, "The Dunwich Horror," in Roger Luckhurst, ed., *The Classic Horror
Stories* (Oxford: Oxford University Press, 2013), 97–8.
13 Immanuel Kant, *Critique of Judgment*, cited in Carol Korsmeyer, *Savoring
Disgust: The Foul and the Fair in Aesthetics* (Oxford: Oxford University Press,
2011), 46.
14 Edmund Wilson, "Tales of the Marvellous and Ridiculous," *Classics and
Commercials: A Literary Chronicle of the Forties* (London: Allen, 1951), 288.
15 Daniel Harms, *The Cthulhu Mythos Encyclopedia*, 3rd ed. (Oakland, MI: Elder
Signs Press, 2008).
16 See Victoria Nelson, *Gothicka: Heroes, Human Gods and the New Supernatural*
(New Haven, CT: Harvard University Press, 2012).
17 See Samuel R. Delany, "The Politics of Paraliterary Criticism," *Shorter Views:
Queer Thoughts and the Politics of the Paraliterary* (Middletown, CT: Wesleyan
University Press, 1999): 218–70.
18 M. John Harrison, "New Weird Discussions: The Creation of a Term," in Ann
Vandermeer and Jeff Vandermeer, eds., *The New Weird* (San Francisco, CA:
Tachyon, 2008): 317–31 (317).

19 See Gary Wolfe, *Evaporating Genres: Essays on Fantastic Literature* (Middletown, CT: Wesleyan University Press, 2011).

20 All quotes from China Miéville, "Long Live the New Weird," *The Third Alternative* 35 (2003), 3.

21 Miéville, "Introduction" to *At The Mountains of Madness* (New York: Modern Library, 2005): xi–xxv (xviii).

22 Miéville, "Long Live the New Weird," 3. See also Mark Fisher, *Capitalist Realism: Is There No Alternative?* (Winchester: Zero Books, 2009).

23 See Graham Harman, "On the Horror of Phenomenology: Lovecraft and Husserl," *Collapse* 4 (2008): 333–64. Harman's sustained readings of Lovecraft are collected in *Weird Realism: Lovecraft and Philosophy* (Winchester: Zero Books, 2012).

24 Eugene Thacker, *After Life* (Chicago, IL: University of Chicago Press, 2010), 23.

25 China Miéville, "Afterweird: The Efficacy of a Worm-Eaten Dictionary," in Ann Vandermeer and Jeff Vandermeer, eds., *The Weird: A Compendium of Strange and Dark Stories* (London: Corvus, 2011): 1113–16 (1115).

26 On the generic "re-mark," see Jacques Derrida, "The Law of Genre," trans. A. Ronell, *Critical Inquiry* 7 (1981): 55–81.

27 See Lief Sorensen, "A Weird Modernist Archive: Pulp Fiction, Pseudobiblia, H. P. Lovecraft," *Modernism/Modernity* 17.3 (2010): 501–22.

28 The notion of the "skin-ego" was coined by psychoanalyst Didier Anzieu; see for instance *A Skin for Thought: Interviews with Gilbert Tarrab*, trans. D. N. Briggs (London: Karnac, 1990).

29 See Mark Blacklock, "'On the Eve of the Fourth Dimension': Utopian Higher Space," in Rosalyn Gregory and Benjamin Kohlman, eds., *Utopian Spaces of Modernism: Literature and Culture 1885–1945* (Basingstoke: Palgrave, 2011): 35–51.

30 I am using the distinction between genre and mode made by Istvan Csicsery-Ronay Jr. about contemporary SF: "that we no longer treat sf as purely a genre-engine producing formulaic effects, but rather as a kind of awareness we might call ... a mode of response that frames and tests experiences." *The Seven Beauties of Science Fiction* (Middletown, CT: Wesleyan University Press, 2008), 2.

31 For discussion, see for instance Deborah Cartmell et al., eds., *Trash Aesthetics: Popular Culture and Its Audience* (London: Pluto, 1997).

32 Arthur Symons, "The Decadent Movement in Literature" (1893), in Sally Ledger and Roger Luckhurst, eds., *The Fin-de-Siècle: A Reader in Cultural History c. 1880–1900* (Oxford: Oxford University Press, 2000), 104–11 (105–6).

15

REBEKAH C. SHELDON

After America

There will be no more stupidity.
There will be no more mistakes.
It's a new day.
God help you all.[1]

Panem. The Republic of Gilead. The Christian Church of America. US-Ident.
The American Phoenix. The American Restoration Authority. Massive
Dynamics. Shorn Associates.[2] From deregulation farces and sprawling globalization picaresques to postapocalyptic wastescapes, contemporary visions
of the future reflect increasingly commonplace skepticism about the viability
of the nation-state in general and of the American project in particular. As
newly ascendant President-for-Life Edmund has it in the failed-state comedy
Masked and Anonymous, "It's a new day. God help you all." This formula-
tion may be satiric, but it is also precise. In the place of the expected universal, the second-person pronoun transforms the appeal to divine power
from a statement of nationalistic pride – God Bless America – to an unveiled
threat. For it is precisely the fiction that state power should or does act in
the interest of collective well-being, construed as national belonging, that
these narratives expose.

There has been, after all, no pandemic disease decimating the East Coast
as in Colson Whitehead's zombie novel *Zone One*, no mysterious ecological
devastation such as we witness in Cormac McCarthy's *The Road*, no home
front war beyond the shock of 9/11 and its representational reverberations.[3]
On the other hand, what unequivocally *has* been the case is the slow violence of four decades of neoliberal economic policies.[4] Since the 1970s, the
economic stability of the majority of Americans has become more precarious as more surplus value has gone to smaller portions of the population.
While the numbers are well known, they bear repeating. From 1979 to 2009
top earners' wages rose 275 percent.[5] The average CEO compensation in
2012 was 273 times greater than that of the average worker, who was likely

to make around $27,000 a year.[6] Accompanying this massive transfer of wealth was a surge of incarceration as policies like mandatory sentencing and three strikes laws took hold. In 1971 there were fewer than 200,000 people in state and federal prisons; today The Sentencing Project pegs prison population at 2.2 million.[7]

These brute and brutal facts engender the conditions of possibility for the world-ending disasters our fictions record. Over the past four decades, American neoliberalism has corroded the institutional infrastructures of the common good while bolstering state power to coerce, compel, and confine. It is tempting, then, to interpret after-the-end narratives of the sort we've been tracking as warnings of the end-points of these policies – and, thus, to see these narratives as encouraging changed actions in the present. And, indeed, many critics have done so. In her anatomy of the postapocalypse, for example, Claire Curtis explains that postapocalyptic settings "point out the caution zones we should realize now."[8] Placed in the economic context I have just been relating, however, these fictions begin to lose their connection to a projected future and to look more like our everyday reality. As Fredric Jameson argues, the future frame is a "strategy of indirection" that allows us to glimpse the "unmediated, unfiltered experience of the daily life of capitalism."[9]

But neither is it the case, I contend, that these fictions are about the present. In an NPR interview concerning his novel *On Such a Full Sea*, Chang Rae Lee relates that he had originally set out to write a realist novel about factory workers in China. Instead, he found himself at work on a dystopian science fiction inspired by the sprawl between Baltimore and Washington, DC. "I passed Baltimore as I always do and always have in my adult life," Lee says, "And I saw it again, after, you know, another 35 years of seeing it."[10] American fiction, film, and television repeatedly envision collapse, I am arguing, as a form of "seeing it again" in an obsessive retracing that tells the story of *what has been*. These near-future fantasies, in other words, are more accurately understood as historical fictions in a period, as Lauren Berlant explains, when the collapse of the norms of collective life induce a herky-jerk subjectivity intent on "catching up to what is already happening."[11] By allowing readers to "see it again," these fictions reveal the structural centrality of the apparently anomalous and the institutionalization of crisis-forms as the new ordinary.

In what follows, I look at three exemplary texts that trace the causes whose effects are pervasive in what Berlant calls "the historical present" and that are also occluded as anomalous: private property and resource depletion in Paolo Bacigalupi's short story "The Tamarisk Hunter," the cruel optimism of aspirational debt in Suzanne Collins's novel *The Hunger*

Games, and right neoliberalism in Octavia Butler's *Parable of the Sower*.[12] All three of these texts gain their exemplarity by virtue of being paradigmatic. By bringing them together, however, this chapter argues that neither these science fictional depictions nor the brute facts are themselves sufficient to apprehend and map the pasts at work in the present. Together, however, they generate an intuition of the vanishing point of the past forty years of neoliberal policy: not the unequal distribution of wealth nor the waning of affective investment in national power, but the abandonment of the social as such.

Neoliberalism and Private Property: "The Tamarisk Hunter"

"The Tamarisk Hunter" begins with numbers: 73,000, the amount of water in gallons that a single mature tamarisk tree sucks from the ground in a year; $2.88, the amount Lolo gets paid per day to poison and rip tamarisks.[13] One of the last homesteaders in a near-future Arizona decimated by ten years of "the Big Daddy Drought," Lolo draws water bounty and the right to occupy his "patch" from the Interior Department in exchange for his work uprooting trees. Both numbers mark small dramas of survival and resilience.[14] Through their capacity to hoard water, the trees thrive in the parched Southwest. Lolo and his wife Annie survive by exterminating them. But Lolo recognizes that the trees' resilience is crucial to his own, and so he maintains a secret, illegal grove of tamarisks that he carefully replants to look uncultivated and then rips and documents to make his living. While the majority of the tamarisk hunters fail and leave for more water-rich environments where they will work as migrant laborers, Lolo's reseeding has given him "insurance" against the very success of the tamarisk removal project for which he putatively labors.[15]

It is tempting to imagine that Lolo, by maintaining the rogue tamarisk stand, contributes to the perpetuation of the drought. This can only be the case, however, if Arizona actually had a water problem. But it doesn't. The Colorado River runs fresh and full behind the house Annie and Lolo share. What the drought dried up wasn't the river but the rights to take from it. "Rotten water rights," Lolo calls them, as if the rights themselves were natural objects subject to changes in the weather.[16] As Lolo relates, "the problem wasn't lack of water or an excess of heat, not really. The problem was that 4.4 million acre-feet of water were supposed to go down the river to California."[17] The number 4.4 million keys us to the longer history of this near-future, and particularly to the history of water disputes in the Southwest. Four point four million is the amount of water that the Colorado River Compact mandated to California in 1929. An initiative of President

Herbert Hoover, the Compact regulated water use between upper and lower Southwest states in the name of regional unity and to clear the way for the construction of the Hoover Dam. In ringing modernist strains, Hoover was said to have called the Dam's construction an increase in "human happiness... beyond computation."[18] By setting standard water distributions for the area, the Federal Resource Conservation and Allowable Use Guidelines set a framework for imagining the common good then concretized by the Dam.

Yet the mechanism that produced that collectivity was private property rights, a mechanism tethered to enforcement of individual over collective well-being. In *A Brief History of Neoliberalism*, David Harvey details the several ways private property rights forge a lasting coherence between neoliberalism's sometimes internally contradictory demands for small government at home, military strength abroad, and liberal individualism for some. He explains that making private property paramount acts as a check on governmental power and thus protects individual freedom, opens assets to corporate investments, and justifies police violence against the public as the enforcement of rule of law.[19] In this way, neoliberalism repudiates the benevolent paternalism of both liberalism and Fordism. Yet neoliberal abhorrence of state action does not extend to the state's monopoly of violence when it is used to protect private property interests. The resulting state form is inherently unstable, Harvey argues, as "the freedom of the masses" become increasingly circumscribed by the commitment to the property rights of the few.[20]

The full force of neoliberal privatization was for a long while, however, kept in check by the Cold War and its exceptionalist nationalism. Donald Pease describes the doctrine of American Exceptionalism as a "state fantasy" that couples government and citizen through the notion of a shared national history.[21] That shared national history designated a pure America as the culmination of preceding state forms and the yardstick against which other nations are judged. In turn, maintaining the ideals of America as a land of opportunity required investment in the public sphere. In opposition to the fantasied conformity of communism, the post-WWII period touted the "American" values of fairness, patriotism, and prosperity, embodied in representational democracy, personal liberty, and the expectation of privacy, all of course heavily circumscribed by class, race, sex, and gender positionalities.

Indeed, the post–World War II period was especially prolific in imaginations of disaster mapped around the axis of social control and liberal individualism. Works like Madeline L'Engle's *A Wrinkle in Time* (1962), Robert Silverberg's *The World Inside* (1971), and Pamela Sargent's *Earthseed* (1981) argue that human nature is so inalterably fixed that attempts to change it will result either in civil unrest or dystopian brainwashing.[22] In Kurt Vonnegut's short story "Harrison Bergeron," the desirable end of social equality is achieved through weights, masks, and other grotesque encumbrances intended to bring everyone to the same level.[23] The novels of Philip K. Dick reveal this pattern through their relentless exposure of the illusory nature of the ostensible choice itself. Consumerist conformists and angsty revolutionaries, shady government operators of all stripes, collapse into each other or prove to have been the same person all along. Palmer Eldritch, of Dick's *Three Stigmata of Palmer Eldritch* (1965), is capitalist and drug dealer, deity and demon, his name a potent reminder of the eldritch power of the commodity fetish.[24] The novel ends by suggesting that Eldritch has inhabited the body of Barney Mayerson, as bathetic a hero as ever has been penned, a sad sack businessman who carries his mechanical psychiatrist around in a suitcase.

Dick's novels, and their paranoiac certainty that things are never quite what they seem but are nevertheless always overseen by some malign power, remind us that with the establishment of the National Security State in late 1940s, the Cold War provided the opportunity to institute Carl Schmidt's "state of exception" as normative politics. This precedent was hardly undone by the end of the Cold War.[25] Instead the sovereign exception became increasingly trained on the American public, a trajectory culminating in the PATRIOT Act with its withdrawal of habeas corpus rights and its redefinition of the rules of warfare. In swapping out social harmony for preemptive surveillance and enshrining property as the ground of security, the law no longer even nods to the other constitutional protections, like right of assembly, that carved out the space for civil society.

In fact, though, the law no longer even nods to private property: combined with the logic of the preemptive state security, private property alone no longer safeguards right to life and limb. Instead, private property rights rise up as the fetishized legal justification after-the-fact. When "The Tamarisk Hunter" opens, Annie and Lolo are riding the whiplash end of the long tail from the California Compact, trying to protect a tiny bit of property from the massive federal anti-riot machines that decimated Annie's parents' town – one of hundreds that were forcibly evacuated after the drought's effects became apparent to make way for the pipeline they evocatively call the Straw.

So though it is no surprise to Lolo when he returns from the illegal tamarisk grove to find BuRec officers with machine guns outside his patch, it should be. Throughout Lolo has been anxious about his illegal grove. When the officers come – former friends of his, in fact – he recognizes that he is caught and begins to confess. But they don't want to hear it; they aren't there for his replanted trees, but to relocate him. "California's ending the water bounty," they tell Lolo. "They've got enough Straw sections built up now that they don't need the program.... I'm supposed to tell you that your headgate won't get opened next year."[26] In the figure of the BuRec, then, Bacigalupi's story shows us the bones of crony capitalism jutting out from the recession of state liberalism. In the face of that intent to dispossess, even the state recognizes the pathos of Lolo's crime. Lolo's world is bare, denuded of all pretense of collective well-being, an internalization of America's long-standing willingness to lend military support to the dispossession of other nations in the service of corporate interest.

For many people, however, the experience of dispossession does not come at the end of a police baton but through the mail. I turn, in the next section, to thinking about a formation I call "debt-optimism" through a reading of Suzanne Collins' Young Adult dystopia *Hunger Games*.[27]

Cruel Optimism and Aspirational Debt: *The Hunger Games*

"A relation of cruel optimism exists when something you desire is actually an obstacle to your flourishing." So begins Lauren Berlant's timely monograph *Cruel Optimism*. "It might involve food," she continues, "or a kind of love; it might be a fantasy of the good life, or a political project."[28] Whatever it is, the object is unimportant. What counts is the structure. Like reproductive futurism's malign cousin, cruel optimism justifies expenditure now in the hope that the odds this time will be in your favor. But the coin of the future can't compensate for the toll of the present's one last-one more attempt. It isn't even issued in the same specie. The debt acquired in the pursuit, however – *that* promise is more tenacious. Debt has its own futural attachments, untethered to the success or failure of the attempt. And in this age of credit, there's always someone willing to extend a helping hand. After all, the promise still stands – the promise of promising youth, the promise made in youth, the promise on which you spent your youth – that some day the promise would be redeemed. As the Levi's commercial urges: "You're gonna be great. You're gonna be great. You're gonna be great. You're gonna be great.... You're the next living leader of the world.... Go forth."[29]

The rhetoric of futurity here stands in metonymically for the action the commercial compels for the present: purchasing of course, specifically purchasing a pair of Levi's jeans. "Go forth" not only ends the copy of the 2013 ad, it also titles the whole series of post-2008 Levi's commercials.[30] In this one, the ad copy designates curing diseases and singing solo at Carnegie Hall as the endpoint of "going forth" and advocates wearing Levi's jeans as the first step in that direction. But we should not be surprised to find another kind of purchase in the background of these dreams: the shadowy presence of education and, more specifically, the debt it takes to acquire that education. This is especially poignant because the period of the "Go Forth" ads is also the period of the student debt crisis. From the late '70s to the present, state funding for colleges and universities has followed the pattern of disinvestment we have seen in state funding more generally. According to the American Council on Education, in the year 2011 state funding for higher education was down 40.2 percent from 1980.[31] Rising student liability for education sets the stage for current student debt levels hovering around $1 trillion. The rise to that inconceivably high number is also responsive to the cultural logic of the dream embedded in the "Go Forth" commercials and their collapse of the good life – career, security, happiness – into the "great" life of world-historical success.[32]

But just what is so cruel about this cruel optimism? Striving (or striding) for success is, after all, as American as Ragged Dick, and if its outcome isn't quite the expected rise in the world at least something has been gained: knowledge, a degree, self-confidence. What these commercials and other formations of this type cover over, however, is the compulsion that galvanizes desire, the compulsion generated by the incipient realization that there is no safety net, no place of refuge between the great life and destitution. *Hunger Games* strikingly uncovers that aporia.

Yet even this intuition is hard to substantiate, for Berlant's definition ties cruel optimism to a specific history, that of '90s neoliberalism in America and its disordering of the expectations associated with state-liberalism.[33] By contrast, the world of Panem is not capitalist in any meaningful sense. In the prehistory of the novel, America broke apart in civil war and was reconstituted as the police state Panem: twelve formerly rebellious districts, who now produce single products for direct expropriation by the luxury-soaked Capitol. Every year since the war, the Capitol exacts two children from each district as tributes for the eponymous games. Despite the fact that the Games are made to be aired on national television, they never go to commercial break or hear a word from the show's sponsors. Indeed, "sponsor" takes on a very different meaning.

For all of these reasons, Mark Fisher observes that Panem might be better described as "cyber-feudal."[34] Citing an interview with Collins, Fisher notes that the name Panem derives from the Latin phrase for "Bread and Circuses," which chimes with the Roman names of the residents of the Capitol. While that designation might apply to the Capitol and its enormous extravagances – with the proviso that the Capitol is less Petrarch's Rome than it is Mel Brooks' – the districts embody diverse periods and places.

Hard scrabble coal-mining District 12, from which our hero, Katniss, hails, resembles nothing so much as present-day filmic depictions of Appalachia. The train that takes them from District 12 to the Capitol manages to combine European-style high-speed rail with steampunk neo-Dickensianism. The training center and the arena, where the tributes are taken to fight to the death, both derive their generic protocol from other science fiction media. Finally, the novel self-consciously mirrors and thematizes the mediated hyper-visibility of reality television competitions through Katniss's negotiation of her own suffering as a consumable story.

The space of Panem, in other words, is not genuinely Roman or Feudal or any one thing at all. Rather, *Hunger Games* is a pastiche of styles, which makes it fundamentally of a piece with the postmodern context from which it derives and, more specifically, with the media icons that saturate contemporary youth culture. It doesn't need to incorporate the visible signs of consumerism because of the vital centrality of consumerism to the whole logic of its composition. All of which, perhaps, amounts to saying that *Hunger Games* is a Young Adult novel – written for and about contemporary youth readers. Thought about in this light, the novel returns us to the "Go Forth" commercials with which we started and their brilliantly lit enthusiasm for superbright futures. Like the confidently striding twenty somethings of the Levi's commercials, Katniss, Peta, and the other tributes leave their familiar homes, go to the city center where they meet other young people, learn new skills from trainers, and at the end of the training are put to the test. In this sense, *Hunger Games* is an *Erziehungsroman*, a college novel, that ends with the quest for employment.

Consider the preparations that precede Katniss' entrance into the arena: she is trained; along with her peers, she is tested and scored; she is scrubbed clean, shaven, and taught how to walk in high heels; her trainer mock interviews her and together they attempt to imagine what her audience would most like to hear; she dons new clothes, anxiously waits her turn, and performs her interview. Her very antagonism to these forms makes her a willing participant. She must gain sponsorship if she hopes to survive and the only way to win sponsors is the belief in the possibility of winning. Even her rebellion aligns her with the game-maker's aims, as the arrow she shoots through the apple in the mouth of their roast pig earns her the highest possible marks. That *she* is the roast pig is perfectly apparent, to her and to everyone else. But such is the cruelty of cruel optimism: get dressed to die, smile bright while they applaud, pretend it isn't a matter of life and death because the only way to beat it is to be it, and the only thing to aspire to is life. For the great life, as *Hunger Games* shows us, is any life at all.

Right Neoliberalism and the Collapse
of the Social: *Parable of the Sower*

In the foregoing reading, I have been arguing that *Hunger Games* helps us to see again the way that the promise of the great life chains us to an optimism to which we are bound less by desire than by the fatal effects of prior optimism. In this sense, the debt-optimism relationship of higher education fulfills Harvey's sense that neoliberalism is a "political project to re-establish the conditions for capital accumulation and to restore the power of economic elites."[35] Like the roast pig on whose fat the game-makers sup, the tributes and the generation of the indebted and underemployed for whom they stand in produce wealth and well-being for others from their ambition. In this section, I argue that this figurative and literal consumption of the nation's young is the benignant face of America-after-America. Insofar as the production of wealth maintains the fiction of a shared future, this form of debt-optimism is the lesser horror: it is the left neoliberalism of Bill Clinton and Michael Bloomberg, of Business Improvement Districts and, indeed, of Federal Student Loan Aid. I turn now to Octavia Butler's 1994 novel *Parable of the Sower* to sketch the contours of right neoliberalism, or the intentional despoliation of the social.[36]

Butler's *Parable* depicts a United States after climate change. In an eerie anticipation of the present, these transformed conditions are matched by the withdrawal, privatization, and monetization of the basic functions of government. Police and fire services are costly, slow, and often corrupt, and the state has abandoned both its traditional monopoly on violence and its biopolitical interest in population-level health and safety. Bereft of the formal equivalence of the rule of law and its abstract universals, the only safety is to be found in the realpolitik of direct relations. When *Parable* opens, Lauren and her family live on a cul-de-sac surrounded by a makeshift wall. But this is no gated burbcave; the township of Robeldo was never truly wealthy to begin with. What the wall protects isn't money but the possibility of society: garden, schoolhouse, church. Robeldo is one of uncountable numbers of micro-collectivities that California has become. The walled communities, online universities, and company towns have no state-fantasy holding them together anymore. Their authority is their own. On the road, those micro-collectivities bump up against each other as thieves, refugees, zealots, addicts, and declassed former landowners swarm northward in clan-like bands. By the middle of the novel, Lauren's family is scattered or dead, the wall breached, the tiny community burned, and Lauren herself set down the road.

Of the many people and circumstances that Lauren and her growing band encounter in their progress north, I'd like to focus on one group.

The picture of them is still clear in my mind. Kids the age of my brothers –
twelve, thirteen, maybe fourteen years old, three boys and a girl. The girl was
pregnant, and so huge it was obvious she would be giving birth any day. We
rounded a bend in a dry stream bed, and there these kids were, roasting a
severed human leg, maneuvering it where it lay in the middle of their fire atop
the burning wood by twisting its foot. As we watched, the girl pulled a sliver
of charred flesh from the thigh and stuffed it into her mouth.[37]

This passage is meant to shock. It is not at all clear, for example, whether the
foursome intend to raise the child or to slaughter it, especially coming soon
after the group spotted a wild dog gnawing on a child's forearm. Lauren
herself is still a teenager and the comparison between the two young women
is unmistakable. In light of these moments, the patriarchal confinement of
Lauren's family's compound – or indeed her own soon-to-be built utopian
community Earthseed – appear as the only sane alternatives.

The recent history of state-level disinvestment, however, suggests a different reading. Examples of such disinvestment have been widespread since
the Tea Party elections of 2010 and target a variety of traditional public services. But no service has been as affected by market-based reform movements
as primary and secondary education. Indiana, for example, has embarked
on one of the country's most radical transformations in public education.
While many states have voucher systems, Indiana also has a robust charter
school movement and a not-insignificant portion of those charter schools
are virtual. Some virtual schools are locally run but many, like Indiana
Connections Academy, hire local certified teachers to implement curricula
designed elsewhere and purchased wholesale by the state. At the same time,
voters in Indiana passed a referendum that changed the state constitution to
limit the local property tax rate to 1 percent for residential properties. In the
township of Muncie the tax cap generates a budget shortfall of $3.3 million.
A ballot measure to raise taxes failed and, in its wake, the school board was
forced to shut down one of its two local high schools.[38]

The Indiana example demonstrates how the disinvestment in the public
good aligns with the opening up of the public trust to the private profit-
seeking of third-party corporations in just the way predicted by Harvey's
analysis of neoliberalism. But the revolt against taxes also serves another
purpose: the elimination of state revenue streams means that the state can
easily justify the dereliction of spaces of public gathering. In consequence,
the zone of shared space – space understood as belonging to Americans by
virtue of their citizenship – collapses into the sphere of micro-communities.
Like Butler's two sets of children warily observing each other over the fire,
the sort of right neoliberalism we have seen here generates a refugee generation restricted to homogenous enclaves or cast out with no expectation of

shared hospitality. Pointedly, these decisions are not (just) the operations of shadowy cabals seeking to produce profit on the backs of the immiserated; rather, these are local political choices intended to roll back the past thirty years of social movements. Without the public sphere, there is no choice but to take refuge in the walled compound of hearth and home.

Conclusion: The Age of No Miracles

The rotation of the Earth started to slow on a sunny Saturday, the 6th of October, in a 1970s-era cul-de-sac in southern California. In Karen Thompson Walker's Young Adult disaster novel, *The Age of Miracles*, time has become unhinged: each day exceeds itself, growing in stutter-stop increments.[39] From the novel's opening in the household of eleven-year-old Julia to its conclusion, the slowing remains unexplained. Julia's story follows the usual YA conventions – she gains and loses friends, reckons with the death of a grandparent, discovers her father's illicit romance, and acquires a young love of her own. But these wheels turn in the background, and end abruptly and in tragedy. Her father's love interest moves away; her own dies young. What takes the place of the dramatic interest of these plots is what would have otherwise been the background in any other moment: the setting. The slowing kills the birds first, then the whales, as the changed gravity affects echolocation. Ultimately, the stretches of daylight become unbearable as the day grows to encompass weeks. The boyfriend dies of exposure from illicitly meeting Julia in the sunlight. By the end of the book, Julia's family has retreated to their home now covered in "thick steel sheeting ... to keep out the radiation.[40] Like the micro-collectivities of *Parable*, Julia's family takes the only available course of action and bars themselves in their domestic circle where they will remain until the oil runs dry or they die of exposure.

Of the works we have examined, two featured young adult protagonists, and one was explicitly marketed as YA fiction. The third, " The Tamarisk Hunter," was written by an author of several YA novels. The presence of children's literature in this argument is no accident. It is through the perspective of the teenager that we navigate the "seeing-it-again" history whose terms were both present from the start and inapprehensible in themselves. Through the figure of the teenager, we narrate a beginning that is also at the end of beginnings in order to see, from the perspective of the present and its diminished expectations, what we are now as a species as well as a people. For Julia, the amazing thing is "how little we really knew."

> We had rockets and satellites and nanotechnology.... We could manufacture skin, clone sheep.... And yet, the unknown still outweighed the known.

We never determined the cause of the slowing. The source of our suffering remained forever mysterious.[41]

NOTES

1 *Masked and Anonymous*, dir. Larry Charles, perf. Bob Dylan, Jeff Bridges, Penelope Cruz, John Goodman (Sony Pictures Classic, 2003), DVD.

2 These names are drawn from *The Hunger Games, The Handmaid's Tale, Parable of the Sower, Southland Tales, Zone One, Super Sad True Love Story, Fringe,* and *Market Forces*.

3 Colson Whitehead, *Zone One* (New York: Anchor Books, 2011); Cormac McCarthy, *The Road* (New York: Vintage, 2006).

4 Rob Nixon's monograph *Slow Violence and the Environmentalism of the Poor* (Boston, MA: Harvard University Press, 2013).

5 Congressional Budget Office, http://cbo.gov/publication/42729.

6 According to a Reuters report, "First Look at US Pay Data; It's Awful" by David Cay Johnstone. http://blogs.reuters.com/david-cay-johnston/2011/10/19/first-look-at-us-pay-data-its-awful/.

7 See The Sentencing Project at sentencingproject.org.

8 Claire Curtis, *Postapocalyptic Fiction and the Social Contract: We'll Not Go Home Again* (Plymouth, UK: Lexington Books, 2010), 17.

9 Fredric Jameson, *Archaeologies of the Future: The Desire for Utopia and Other Science Fictions* (London: Verso, 2007), 287.

10 Chang-Rae Lee, "*On Such a Full Sea*: A Fable from a Fractured Future." http://www.npr.org/2014/01/05/259400880/on-such-a-full-sea-a-fable-from-a-fractured-future.

11 Lauren Berlant, *Cruel Optimism* (Durham, NC: Duke University Press, 2011), 54.

12 Ibid.

13 Paolo Bacigalupi, "The Tamarisk Hunter," *Pump Six and Other Stories* (San Francisco, CA: Night Shade Books, 2008), 123.

14 Bacigalupi, "The Tamarisk Hunter," 126, 129.

15 Ibid., 124.

16 Ibid., 129.

17 Ibid., 125.

18 http://www.usbr.gov/lc/hooverdam/History/articles/hhoover.html

19 David Harvey, *A Brief History of Neoliberalism* (Oxford, UK: Oxford University Press, 2005), 64–5.

20 Ibid., 70.

21 Donald Pease, *The New American Exceptionalism* (Minneapolis: University of Minnesota Press, 2009), 4.

22 Madeline L'Engle, *A Wrinkle in Time* (New York: Farrar, Straus and Giroux, 1962); Robert Silverberg, *The World Inside* (New York: Doubleday, 1971); Pamela Sargent, *Earthseed* (New York: Harper and Row, 1983).

23 Kurt Vonnegut, *Welcome to the Monkey House* (New York: Dial Press, 1998).

24 Philip K. Dick, *The Three Stigmata of Palmer Eldritch* (New York: Doubleday, 1965).

25 Giorgio Agamben, *States of Exception* (Trans. Kevin Attell. Chicago, IL: University of Chicago Press, 2005), 1. Citing Carl Schmidt, Giorgio Agamben defines the state of exception as "the relation that binds and, at the same time, abandons the living to the law."

26 Bacigalupi, "The Tamarisk Hunter," 134.

27 Suzanne Collins, *The Hunger Games* (New York: Scholastic, 2008).

28 Berlant, *Cruel Optimism*, 1.

29 http://www.youtube.com/watch?v=F_AVMJFUq7I

30 http://www.wk.com/office/portland/client/levis

31 Thomas G. Mortensen, "State Funding: A Race to the Bottom," *American Council on Education* (http://acenet.edu/the-presidency/columns-and-features/Pages/state-funding-a-race-to-the-bottom.aspx).

32 Maggie Severns, "The Student Loan Debt Crisis in 9 Charts," *Mother Jones* (http://www.motherjones.com/politics/2013/06/student-loan-debt-charts).

33 Berlant, *Cruel Optimism*, 7–8.

34 Mark Fisher, "Precarious Dystopias: *The Hunger Games, in Time*, and *Never Let me Go*." (*Film Quarterly*. 65:4 [Summer 2012]): 28.

35 David Harvey, *The New Imperialism* (Oxford, UK: Oxford University Press, 2005), 19.

36 Octavia E. Butler, *Parable of the Sower* (New York: Griot, 1993).

37 Ibid., 250.

38 indianapublicmedia.org/stateimpact/tag/property-tax-cap/

39 Karen Thompson Walker, *The Age of Miracles* (New York: Random House, 2012).

40 Ibid., 268.

41 Ibid., 266.

FURTHER READING

Journals

Extrapolation (1959+)
Locus (1968+)
Foundation (1972+)
Science Fiction Studies (1973+)
The New York Review of Science Fiction (1988+)
Journal of the Fantastic in the Arts (1990+)
Paradoxa (1995+)
Femspec (1999+)
Science Fiction Film and Television (2008+)

General Reference Works

Ash, Brian, ed. *The Visual Encyclopedia of Science Fiction*. London: Pan Books, 1977.

Barron, Neil, ed. *Anatomy of Wonder: A Critical Guide to Science Fiction*. Fifth edition. Englewood, CO: Libraries Unlimited, 2004.

Bleiler, Everett F. *The Checklist of Science-Fiction and Supernatural Fiction*. Glen Rock, NJ: Firebell, 1978.

    Science-Fiction: The Early Years. Kent, OH: Kent State University Press, 1990.

    Science-Fiction: The Gernsback Years. Kent, OH: Kent State University Press, 1998.

    Ed. *Science Fiction Writers: Critical Studies of the Major Authors from the Early Nineteenth Century to the Present Day*. New York: Scribner's, 1982.

Booker, M. Keith, and Anne-Marie Thomas. *The Science Fiction Handbook*. West Sussex, UK: Wiley-Blackwell, 2009.

Clareson, Thomas D. *Science Fiction in America, 1870s–1930s: An Annotated Bibliography of Primary Sources*. Westport, CT: Greenwood Press, 1984.

Clute, John, and Peter Nicholls, eds. *The Encyclopedia of Science Fiction*. Second edition. London: Orbit, 1993. [Note: a third edition is currently in progress and is accessible as a fully online resource.]

Currey, Lloyd W., ed. *Science Fiction and Fantasy Authors: A Bibliography of First Printings of Their Fiction and Selected Nonfiction*. Boston, MA: G. K. Hall, 1979.

Day, Donald B. *Index to the Science Fiction Magazines, 1926–1950.* Revised edition. Boston, MA: G. K. Hall, 1982.

Fischer, Dennis. *Science Fiction Film Directors 1895–1998.* New York: McFarland, 2000.

Garber, Eric, and Lyn Paleo. *Uranian Worlds: A Guide to Alternative Sexuality in Science Fiction, Fantasy and Horror.* Second edition. Boston, MA: G. K. Hall, 1990.

Gunn, James, ed. *The New Encyclopedia of Science Fiction.* New York: Viking, 1988.

Hardy, Phil, ed. *The Overlook Film Encyclopedia: Science Fiction.* Second edition. New York: Overlook, 1995.

Magill, Frank N., ed. *Survey of Science Fiction Literature.* Five volumes. Englewood Cliffs, NJ: Salem, 1979.

Mann, George, ed. *The Mammoth Encyclopedia of Science Fiction.* New York: Carroll & Graf, 2001.

Nicholls, Peter. *The Encyclopedia of Science Fiction.* London: Granada, 1979.

Pederson, Jay P., ed. *St. James Guide to Science Fiction Writers.* Detroit, MI: St. James Press, 1995.

Prucher, Jeff, ed. *Brave New Words: The Oxford Dictionary of Science Fiction.* Oxford: Oxford University Press, 2007.

Stableford, Brian. *Historical Dictionary of Science Fiction Literature.* Lanham, MD: Scarecrow, 2004.

Science Fact and Science Fiction. New York: Routledge, 2006.

Tuck, Donald H., ed. *The Encyclopedia of Science Fiction and Fantasy.* Three volumes. Chicago, IL: Advent, 1974, 1978, and 1982.

Tymn, Marshall B., and Mike Ashley, eds. *Science Fiction, Fantasy, and Weird Magazines.* Westport, CT: Greenwood Press, 1985.

Warren, Bill. *Keep Watching the Skies! American Science Fiction Movies of the Fifties.* Jefferson, MO: McFarland, 1997.

Watson, Noelle, and Paul E. Schellinger, eds. *Twentieth-Century Science-Fiction Writers.* Third edition. Chicago, IL: St James, 1991.

Westfahl, Gary. *The Greenwood Encyclopedia of Science Fiction and Fantasy: Themes, Works, and Wonders.* Three volumes. Westport, CT: Greenwood Press, 2005.

Wolfe, Gary K. *Critical Terms for Science Fiction and Fantasy: A Glossary and Guide to Scholarship.* Westport, CT: Greenwood Press, 1986.

Histories and General Studies

Aldiss, Brian W., and David Wingrove. *Trillion Year Spree: The History of Science Fiction.* London: Gollancz, 1986.

Alkon, Paul K. *Science Fiction before 1900: Imagination Discovers Technology.* Boston, MA: Twayne, 1994.

Amis, Kingsley. *New Maps of Hell: A Survey of Science Fiction.* London: Gollancz, 1960.

Armytage, W. G. H. *Yesterday's Tomorrows: A Historical Survey of Future Societies.* London: Routledge & Kegan Paul, 1968.

Ashley, Mike. *The History of the Science Fiction Magazines*. Four volumes. London: New English Library, 1974–8.

The Time Machines: The Story of Science-Fiction Pulp Magazines from the Beginning to 1950. Liverpool: Liverpool University Press, 2000.

Atheling, William, Jr. [James Blish]. *The Issue at Hand: Studies in Contemporary Magazine Science Fiction*. Chicago, IL: Advent, 1973.

Berger, Albert. *The Magic That Works: John W. Campbell and the American Response to Technology*. San Bernardino, CA: Borgo, 1993.

Bould, Mark, ed. *The Routledge Companion to Science Fiction*. New York: Routledge, 2009.

Bretnor, Reginald, ed. *Modern Science Fiction: Its Meaning and Its Future*. New York: Coward McCann, 1953.

Carter, Paul A. *The Creation of Tomorrow: Fifty Years of Magazine Science Fiction*. New York: Columbia University Press, 1977.

Clareson, Thomas D, ed. *Many Futures, Many Worlds: Theme and Form in Science Fiction*. Kent, OH: Kent State University Press, 1977.

Some Kind of Paradise: The Emergence of American Science Fiction. Westport, CT: Greenwood Press, 1986.

Understanding American Science Fiction: The Formative Period, 1926–1970. Columbia: University of South Carolina Press, 1990.

Csicsery-Ronay, Istvan. *The Seven Beauties of Science Fiction*. Middletown, CT: Wesleyan Press, 2008.

Delany, Samuel R. *The Jewel-Hinged Jaw: Notes on the Language of Science Fiction*. Revised edition. Middletown, CT: Wesleyan Press, 2009.

Starboard Wine: More Notes on the Language of Science Fiction. Pleasantville, NY: Dragon Press, 1984.

Del Rey, Lester. *The World of Science Fiction: The History of a Subculture*. New York: Del Rey, 1977.

Disch, Thomas M. *The Dreams Our Stuff Is Made Of: How Science Fiction Conquered the World*. New York: Free Press, 1998.

Gunn, James. *Alternate Worlds: The Illustrated History of Science Fiction*. Englewood Cliffs, NJ: Prentice-Hall, 1975.

Hartwell, David G. *Age of Wonders: Exploring the World of Science Fiction*. Second edition. New York: Tor, 1996.

James, Edward. *Science Fiction in the Twentieth Century*. Oxford: Oxford University Press, 1994.

James, Edward, and Farah Mendlesohn, eds. *The Cambridge Companion to Science Fiction*. Cambridge: Cambridge University Press, 2003.

Knight, Damon. *In Search of Wonder*. Second edition. Chicago, IL: Advent, 1967.

The Futurians: The Story of the Science Fiction "Family" of the '30s That Produced Today's Top SF Writers and Editors. New York: John Day, 1977.

Kuhn, Annette, ed. *Alien Zone: Cultural Theory and Contemporary Science Fiction Cinema*. London: Verso, 1990.

Landon, Brooks. *Science Fiction after 1900: From the Steam Man to the Stars*. New York: Twayne, 1997.

Latham, Rob, ed. *The Oxford Handbook of Science Fiction*. New York: Oxford, 2014.

Lem, Stanislaw. *Microworlds: Writings on Science Fiction and Fantasy*. New York: Harcourt, 1985.

Luckhurst, Roger. *Science Fiction*. London: Polity, 2005.

Malzberg, Barry. *The Engines of the Night: Science Fiction in the Eighties*. Garden City, NY: Doubleday, 1982.

Manlove, Colin. *Science Fiction: Ten Explorations*. Kent, OH: Kent State University Press, 1986.

Moskowitz, Sam. *Strange Horizons: The Spectrum of Science Fiction*. New York: Scribner, 1976.

Panshin, Alexei, and Cory Panshin. *The World beyond the Hill: Science Fiction and the Quest for Transcendence*. Los Angeles, CA: Jeremy P. Tarcher, 1989.

Penley, Constance, et al., eds. *Close Encounters: Film, Feminism and Science Fiction*. Minneapolis: University of Minnesota Press, 1991.

Pohl, Frederik. *The Way the Future Was: A Memoir*. New York: Ballantine, 1978.

Rickman, Gregg, ed. *The Science Fiction Film Reader*. New York: Limelight Editions, 2004.

Roberts, Adam. *The History of Science Fiction*. New York: Palgrave MacMillan, 2007.

Science Fiction. Second edition. London: Routledge, 2006.

Sawyer, Andy, and Peter Wright, eds. *Teaching Science Fiction*. New York: Palgrave, 2011.

Seed, David. *Science Fiction: A Very Short Introduction*. Oxford: Oxford University Press, 2011.

Sobchak, Vivian. *Screening Space: The American Science Fiction Film*. New York: Ungar, 1987.

Stableford, Brian M. *The Sociology of Science Fiction*. San Bernardino, CA: Borgo, 1987.

Telotte, J. P. *A Distant Technology: Science Fiction Film and the Machine Age*. Middletown, CT: Wesleyan Press, 1999.

Science Fiction Film. Cambridge: Cambridge University Press, 2001.

Vint, Sherryl. *Science Fiction: A Guide for the Perplexed*. London: Bloomsbury, 2014.

Warner, Harry, Jr. *All Our Yesterdays: An Informal History of Science Fiction Fandom in the Forties*. Chicago, IL: Advent, 1969.

A Wealth of Fable: The History of Science Fiction Fandom in the 1950s. New York: Fanhistorica, 1976.

Wesfahl, Gary. *The Mechanics of Wonder: The Creation of the Idea of Science Fiction*. Liverpool: Liverpool University Press, 1998.

Critical Studies

Allen, Kathryn. *Disability in Science Fiction: Representations of Technology as Cure*. New York: Palgrave Macmillan, 2013.

Armitt, Lucie, ed. *Where No Man Has Gone Before: Women and Science Fiction*. London: Routledge, 1991.

Attebery, Brian. *Decoding Gender in Science Fiction*. London and New York: Routledge, 2002.

Attebery, Brian and Veronica Hollinger. *Parabolas of Science Fiction.* Middletown, CT: Wesleyan University Press, 2013.

Bacon-Smith, Camille. *Science Fiction Culture.* Philadelphia: University of Pennsylvania Press, 2000.

Balsamo, Anne. *Technologies of the Gendered Body: Reading Cyborg Women.* Durham, NC: Duke University Press, 1996.

Barr, Marleen S. *Alien to Femininity: Speculative Fiction and Feminist Theory.* Westport, CT: Greenwood Press, 1987.

Feminist Fabulation: Space/Postmodern Fiction. Iowa City: Iowa University Press, 1992.

ed. *Future Females: A Critical Anthology.* Popular Press, 1981.

ed. *Future Females, The Next Generation: New Voices and Velocities in Feminist Science Fiction Criticism.* Boulder, CO: Rowman and Littlefield, 2000.

Ben-Tov, Sharona. *The Artificial Paradise: Science Fiction and American Reality.* Ann Arbor: University of Michigan Press, 1995.

Booker, Keith. *Monsters, Mushroom Clouds, and the Cold War: American Science Fiction and the Roots of Postmodernism, 1946–1964.* Westport, CT: Greenwood, 2001.

Bould, Mark, and China Miéville, eds. *Red Planets: Marxism and Science Fiction.* Middletown, CT: Wesleyan University Press, 2009.

Broderick, Damien. *Reading by Starlight: Postmodern Science Fiction.* London: Routledge, 1995.

Bukatman, Scott. *Terminal Identity: The Virtual Subject in Postmodern Science Fiction.* Durham, NC: Duke University Press, 1993.

Burwell, Jennifer. *Notes on Nowhere: Feminism, Utopian Logic, and Social Transformation.* Minneapolis: University of Minnesota Press, 1997.

Butler, Andrew M. *Cyberpunk.* Harpenden: Pocket Essentials, 2000.

Canavan, Gerry, and Kim Stanley Robinson, eds. *Green Planets: Ecology and Science Fiction.* Middletown, CT: Wesleyan University Press, 2014.

Cheng, John. *Astounding Wonder: Imagining Science and Science Fiction in Interwar America.* Philadelphia: University of Pennsylvania Press, 2012.

Chu, Seo-Young. *Do Metaphors Dream of Literal Sleep? A Science-Fictional Theory of Representation.* Cambridge, MA: Harvard University Press, 2011.

Cioffi, Frank. *Formula Fiction? An Anatomy of American Science Fiction, 1930–1940.* Westport, CT: Greenwood Press, 1982.

Clark, Stephen R. L. *How to Live Forever: Science Fiction and Philosophy.* London: Routledge, 1995.

Clute, John. *Pardon This Intrusion: Fantastika in the World Storm.* Harold Wood, UK: Beccon Publications, 2011.

Costello, Matthew. *Comic Books and the Unmasking of Cold War America.* New York: Bloomsbury Academic, 2009.

Donawerth, Jane L. *Frankenstein's Daughters: Women Writing Science Fiction.* Syracuse, NY: Syracuse University Press, 1997.

Donawerth, Jane L., and Carol A. Kolmerten, eds. *Utopian and Science Fiction by Women: Worlds of Difference.* Syracuse, NY: Syracuse University Press, 1994.

Dunn, Thomas P., and Richard D. Erlich, eds. *The Mechanical God: Machines in Science Fiction.* Westport, CT: Greenwood Press, 1982.

Ferns, Chris. *Narrating Utopia: Ideology, Gender, Form in Utopian Literature.* Liverpool: Liverpool University Press, 1999.

Franklin, H. Bruce. *Robert A. Heinlein. America as Science Fiction.* New York: Oxford University Press, 1980.

War Stars: The Superweapon and the American Imagination. New York: Oxford University Press, 1988.

Freedman, Carl. *Critical Theory and Science Fiction.* Middletown, CT: Wesleyan University Press, 2000.

Gunn, James, ed. *Speculations on Speculation: Theories of Science Fiction.* Lanham, MD: Scarecrow Press, 2005.

Guthke, Karl S. *The Last Frontier: Imagining Other Worlds from the Copernican Revolution to Modern Science Fiction.* Ithaca, NY: Cornell University Press, 1990.

Haraway, Donna. *Simians, Cyborgs, and Women: The Reinvention of Nature.* New York: Routledge, 1990.

Hassler, Donald M. *Comic Tones in Science Fiction: The Art of Compromise with Nature.* Westport, CT: Greenwood Press, 1982.

Hassler, Donald M., and Clyde Wilcox, eds. *Political Science Fiction.* Columbia: University of South Carolina Press, 1997.

Hassler-Forest, Dan. *Capitalist Superheroes: Caped Crusaders in the Neoliberal Age.* Washington: Zero Books: 2012.

Hellekson, Karen. *The Alternate History: Refiguring Historical Time.* Kent, OH: Kent State University Press, 2001.

Hoagland, Ericka, and Reema Sarwal. *Science Fiction, Imperialism and the Third World: Essays on Postcolonial Literature and Film.* Jefferson, NC: MacFarland, 2010.

Hollinger, Veronica, and Joan Gordon, eds. *Edging into the Future: Science Fiction and Contemporary Cultural Transformation.* Philadelphia: University of Pennsylvania Press, 2002.

Jackson, Sandra, and Julie E. Moody-Freeman, eds. *The Black Imagination: Science Fiction, Futurism, and the Speculative.* New York: Peter Lang, 2011.

Jameson, Fredric. *Archaeologies of the Future: The Desire Called Utopia and other Science Fictions.* New York: Verso, 2005.

Jones, Gywneth. *Deconstructing the Starships.* Liverpool: Liverpool University Press, 1999.

Kerslake, Patricia. *Science Fiction and Empire.* Liverpool: Liverpool University Press, 2007.

Ketterer, David. *New Worlds for Old: The Apocalyptic Imagination, Science Fiction, and American Literature.* Bloomington: Indiana University Press, 1974.

Kilgore, De Witt Douglas. *Astrofuturism: Science, Race, and Visions of Utopia in Space.* Philadelphia: University of Pennsylvania Press, 2003.

King, Betty. *Women of the Future: The Female Main Character in Science Fiction.* Metuchen: Scarecrow Press, 1984.

Kirkup, Gill, et al., eds. *The Gendered Cyborg: A Reader.* London: Routledge, 2000.

Landon, Brooks. *Aesthetics of Ambivalence: Rethinking Science Fiction Film in the Age of Electronic (Re)production.* Westport, CT: Greenwood Press, 1992.

Langer, Jessica. *Postcolonialism and Science Fiction.* New York: Palgrave MacMillan, 2012.

Larbalestier, Justine. *The Battle of the Sexes in Science Fiction*. Middletown, CT: Wesleyan University Press, 2002.

Lavender, Isiah III. *Race in American Science Fiction*. Bloomington: Indiana University Press, 2011.

Lawler, Donald L. *Approaches to Science Fiction*. Boston, MA: Houghton Mifflin, 1978.

LeFanu, Sarah. *In the Chinks of the World Machine: Feminism and Science Fiction*. London: The Women's Press, 1988.

LeGuin, Ursula K. *The Language of the Night: Essays on Fantasy and Science Fiction*. Revised edition. New York: HarperCollins, 1992.

Leonard, Elizabeth Anne, ed. *Into Darkness Peering: Race and Color in the Fantastic*. Westport, CT: Greenwood Press, 1997.

Lerner, Frederick A. *Modern Science Fiction and the American Literary Community*. Metuchen: Scarecrow, 1985.

Lundwall, Sam J. *Science Fiction: What It's All About*. New York: Ace, 1971.

Malmgren, Carl. *Worlds Apart: Narratology of Science Fiction*. Bloomington: Indiana University Press, 1991.

McGrath, James F., ed. *Religion and Science Fiction*. Eugene: Pickwick, 2011.

Meyers, Walter E. *Aliens and Linguistics: Language Study and Science Fiction*. Athens: University of Georgia Press, 1980.

Miller, Fred D. Jr., and Nicholas D. Smith, eds. *Thought Probes: Philosophy through Science Fiction*. Englewood Cliffs, NJ: Prentice-Hall, 1981.

Mogen, David. *Wilderness Visions: The Western Theme in Science Fiction Literature*. Second edition. San Bernardino, CA: Borgo Press, 1993.

Moylan, Tom. *Demand the Impossible: Science Fiction and the Utopian Imagination*. London: Methuen, 1986.

Scraps of the Untainted Sky. Science Fiction, Utopia, Dystopia. Boulder, CO: Westview Press, 2000.

Moylan, Tom, and Raffaella Baccolini, eds. *Dark Horizons: Science Fiction and the Utopian Imagination*. London: Routledge, 2003.

Murphy, Graham J., and Sherryl Vint. *Beyond Cyberpunk: New Critical Perspectives*. New York: Routledge, 2010.

Otto, Eric C. *Green Speculations: Science Fiction and Transformative Environmentalism*. Columbus: Ohio State University Press, 2012.

Paik, Peter Y. *From Utopia to Apocalypse: Science Fiction and the Politics of Catastrophe*. Minneapolis: University of Minnesota Press, 2010.

Palumbo, Donald, ed. *Erotic Universe: Sexuality and Fantastic Literature*. Westport, CT: Greenwood Press, 1986.

Parrinder, Patrick, ed. *Learning from Other Worlds: Estrangement, Cognition, and the Politics of Science Fiction*. Durham, NC: Duke University Press, 2001.

Science Fiction. New York: Routledge, 1980.

Pierce, John J. *Foundations of Science Fiction: A Study in Imagination and Evolution*. Westport, CT: Greenwood, 1994.

Porush, David. *The Soft Machine: Cybernetic Fiction*. New York: Methuen, 1985.

Reilly, Robert, ed. *The Transcendent Adventure: Studies of Religion in Science Fiction/Fantasy*. Westport, CT: Greenwood Press, 1985.

Rieder, John. *Colonialism and the Emergence of Science Fiction*. Wesleyan, CT: Wesleyan University Press, 2008.

Roberts, Robin. *A New Species: Gender and Science in Science Fiction.* Urbana: Illinois University Press, 1993.

Rose, Mark. *Alien Encounters: Anatomy of Science Fiction.* Cambridge, MA: Harvard University Press, 1981.

ed. *Science Fiction: A Collection of Critical Essays.* Englewood Cliffs, NJ: Prentice Hall, 1976.

Russ, Joanna. *To Write Like a Woman: Essays in Feminism and Science Fiction.* Bloomington: Indiana University Press, 1995.

Sandison, Alan, and Robert Dingley, eds. *Histories of the Future: Studies in Fact, Fantasy, and Science Fiction.* New York: Palgrave, 2001.

Sawyer, Andy, and David Seed, eds. *Speaking Science Fiction: Dialogues and Interpretations.* Liverpool: Liverpool University Press, 2000.

Sayer, Karen, and John Moore, eds. *Science Fiction, Critical Frontiers.* New York: St. Martin's Press, 2000.

Schneider, Susan, ed. *Science Fiction and Philosophy: From Time Travel to Superintelligence.* Malden, MA: Wiley-Blackwell, 2009.

Scholes, Robert. *Structural Fabulation: An Essay on Fiction of the Future.* Notre Dame, IN: Notre Dame University Press, 1975.

Scholes, Robert, and Eric Rabkin. *Science Fiction: History, Science, Vision.* New York: Oxford University Press, 1977.

Seed, David. *American Science Fiction and the Cold War: Literature and Film.* London: Fitzroy Dearborn, 1999.

ed. *Imagining Apocalypse: Studies in Cultural Crisis.* London: Macmillan, 2000.

Shaviro, Steven. *Connected, or What It Means to Live in a Network Society.* Minneapolis: University of Minnesota Press, 2003.

Post-Cinematic Affect. Washington: Zero Books, 2010.

Shaw, Debra Benita. *Women, Science and Fiction: The Frankenstein Inheritance.* New York: Palgrave, 2001.

Shippey, Tom, ed. *Fictional Space: Essays on Contemporary Science Fiction.* Oxford: Blackwell, 1991.

Slusser, George, and Eric Rabkin, eds. *Aliens: The Anthropology of Science Fiction.* Carbondale: Southern Illinois University Press, 1987.

eds. *Hard Science Fiction.* Carbondale: Southern Illinois University Press, 1986.

Slusser, George, and Tom Shippey, eds. *Fiction 2000: Cyberpunk and the Future of Narrative.* Athens: University of Georgia Press, 1992.

Smith, Nicholas D., ed. *Philosophers Look at Science Fiction.* Chicago, IL: Nelson Hall, 1982.

Stockwell, Peter. *The Poetics of Science Fiction.* London: Longman, 2000.

Suvin, Darko. *Metamorphoses of Science Fiction: On the Poetics and History of a Literary Genre.* New Haven, CT: Yale University Press, 1979.

Vint, Sherryl. *Bodies of Tomorrow: Technology, Subjectivity, Science Fiction.* Toronto: University of Toronto Press, 2007.

Wagar, W. Warren. *Terminal Visions: The Literature of Last Things.* Bloomington: Indiana University Press, 1982.

Warrick, Patricia S. *The Cybernetic Imagination in Science Fiction.* Cambridge, MA: MIT Press, 1980.

Westfahl, Gary. *Cosmic Engineers: A Study of Hard Science Fiction.* Westport, CT: Greenwood Press, 1996.

Westfahl, Gary, and George Slusser, eds. *Science Fiction, Canonization, Marginalization, and the Academy.* Westport, CT: Greenwood Press, 2002.

Westfahl, Gary, and George Slusser and David Leiby, eds. *Worlds Enough the Time: Explorations of Time in Science Fiction and Fantasy.* Westport, CT: Greenwood Press, 2002.

David Leiby, ed. *Space and Beyond: The Frontier Theme in Science Fiction.* Westport, CT: Greenwood Press, 2000.

Williams, Evan Calder. *Combined and Uneven Apocalypse.* Hants, UK: Zero Books, 2010.

Wittenberg, David. *Time Travel: The Popular Philosophy of Narrative.* New York: Fordham University Press, 2013.

Wolfe, Gary K., *The Known and the Unknown: The Iconography of Science Fiction.* Kent, OH: Kent State University Press, 1979.

Wollheim, Donald A. *The Universe Makers: Science Fiction Today.* New York: Harper, 1971.

Wolmark, Jenny. *Aliens and Others: Science Fiction, Feminism and Postmodernism.* Iowa City: University of Iowa Press, 1994.

ed. *Cybersexualities: A Reader on Feminist Theory, Cyborgs and Cyberspace.* Edinburgh: Edinburgh University Press, 1999.

Womack, Ytasha L. *Afrofuturism: The World of Black Sci-Fi and Fantasy Culture.* Chicago, IL: Chicago Review Press, 2013.

Yoke, Carl B. *Phoenix from the Ashes: The Literature of the Remade World.* Westport, CT: Greenwood Press, 1987.

Yoke, Carl B., and Donald M. Hassler, eds. *Death and the Serpent: Immortality in Science Fiction and Fantasy.* Westport, CT: Greenwood Press, 1985.

Young, Elizabeth. *Black Frankenstein: The Making of an American Metaphor.* New York: New York University Press, 2008.

INDEX

Vinton, Arthur Dudley, 7
Visenor, Gerald, 55
Vividcon, 158
Vizenor, Gerald, 177
Vonnegut, Kurt
  mainstream success of, 100
  manufactured social equality in, 210
  postmodernist techniques of, 36
  WORKS:
    "Harrison Bergeron" (1961), 210
    Cat's Cradle (1963), 36, 100
    God Bless You, Mr. Rosewater
      (1965), 36
    Slaughterhouse-Five (1969), 36, 100
    Galápagos (1985), 36
    Timequake (1997), 36
  Voyage of the Space Beagle, The (van Vogt,
    1950), 182
  Voyage to the Moon, A (Tucker, 1827), 6
VR-5 (television, 1995), 122

Wachowski, Lana and Andy, 53
Waid, Mark, 130, 136
Waking Mars (mobile digital game,
  2012), 146
Walk to the End of the World (Chamas,
  1974), 74
Walker, Karen Thompson, 216
Walking Dead, The (film series, 2010-),
  46, 47
Wall of the Sky, the Wall of the Eye, The
  (Lethem, 1996), 105
Wanderground, The (Gearhart, 1979), 72,
  95n13
Wandrei, Donald, 198
"War" (London, 1911), 8
War of the Worlds (film, 2005), 46, 48
War of the Worlds, The (Wells, 1899), 1, 3,
  143, 172, 174
WarGames (film, Badham 1983), 119, 150
Warner, Harry, Jr., 156
wars and violence. See also Cold War;
  imperialism/colonialism; military
  science fiction
  Afrofuturist military technology, 61, 62
  Afrofuturist race war, 62, 64, 89, 95n17
  bloodless violence in magazines, 31
  bombings of Hiroshima and Nagasaki,
    172, 179
  critique of military-industrial-complex, 35
  Edisonade narratives and, 7
  frontier wilderness and, 174
  male aggression themes, 39

New Wave antiwar fiction, 35, 36
  in New Wave SF, 33
  planetary destruction and, 182
  post-9/11 military intervention, 45
  in post-9/11 SF, 11
  in post-apocalyptic zombie fiction, 10
  private military contractors, 56
  "Star Wars" space-based U.S.
    militarization, 40
  superweapon technology and, 172
  World War II revisionings, 37, 41
Wasp Woman, The (film, Corman and Hill
  1959), 115
Watchmen (comic book), 126, 133
"Water Devil, The" (Stockton, 1871), 8
Watson, James, 189
Way Station (Simak, 1963), 34
"We Also Walk Dogs" (Heinlein, 1941), 170
Weinbaum, Stanley G., 23, 60
Weird Tales (pulp magazine, 1923-),
  153, 194
weird, the
  as American genre, 196, 201, 202, 203
  as canonical genre, 200
  colonialism and, 203
  invented books in, 200
  literary precursors, 201
  Lovecraft concept of, 12, 195, 197, 199
  New Weird science fiction, 93, 199
  object-oriented philosophy and, 200
  trash aesthetics in, 203
Weisinger, Mort, 126, 137n14
Wells, H.G,
  DNA cloning and, 186
  influence in digital games, 141
  influence on SF, 8
  as pulp favorite, 194, 195
  as realist writer, 31
  scientific romance genre in, 99
  in SF survey courses, 3
  as transnational vs. national writer, 1, 3
  WORKS:
    The Time Machine (1895), 142
    The Island of Doctor Moreau (1896),
      142, 186
    The War of the Worlds (1899), 1, 3,
      143, 172, 174
"Wendigo, The" (Blackwood, 1910), 201
Westfahl, Gary, 4, 5
Westworld (film, Crichton 1973), 117
Whedon, Joss, 126, 135, 173
Wheeler, David H., 87
Wheeler, Joseph III, 63

Cambridge Companions to...

AUTHORS

TOPICS